FRENCH AND FRANCOPHONE STUDIES

Memories of May '68

Memories of May '68

France's Convenient Consensus

Chris Reynolds

UNIVERSITY OF WALES PRESS
CARDIFF
2011

British Library Cataloguing-in-Publication Data
A catalogue record for this book is available from the British Library.

ISBN   978-0-7083-2415-8 (hardback)
          978-0-7083-2416-5 (paperback)
e-ISBN 978-0-7083-2417-2

Typeset by Mark Heslington Ltd, Scarborough, North Yorkshire
Printed by CPI Antony Rowe, Chippenham, Wiltshire

Contents

Series Editors' Preface

This series showcases the work of new and established scholars working within the fields of French and francophone studies. It publishes introductory texts aimed at a student readership, as well as research-orientated monographs at the cutting edge of their discipline area. The series aims to highlight shifting patterns of research in French and francophone studies, to re-evaluate traditional representations of French and francophone identities and to encourage the exchange of ideas and perspectives across a wide range of discipline areas. The emphasis throughout the series will be on the ways in which French and francophone communities across the world are evolving into the twenty-first century.

Hanna Diamond and Claire Gorrara

*This book is dedicated to my mother, my daughter Aoife,
my partner Val and to the memory of my late father.*

Acknowledgements

I would like to thank the many people who have helped to complete this study, including all those involved with the distribution of the questionnaire, those who offered their time for interview and the library staff at the University of Ulster, the *Bibliothèque Nationale de France,* the *Institut National de l'Audiovisuel,* the *Bibliothèque Documentaire Internationale Contemporaine* and the British Library. I would specifically like to thank Paddy McCollam for his help in the compilation of the questionnaire, Richard York for his detailed comments and advice, and, above all, my supervisor Graham Gargett, without whom this work quite simply would not have been possible, and whose guidance, dedication and entertaining comments have guaranteed my eternal gratitude. My thanks also to the Nuffield Foundation, all those involved at the University of Wales Press and my indexer Nick James.

On a more personal level I would like to thank my friends and family in France, England and Ireland for having put up with my highs and lows along the way. Special mention to my brothers David, Joseph and Paul, my sister Regina, ma belle-mère Marie-Jo, the boys from 36, my good friend Hanna Diamond and Vincent, Steph and Bruno for their warm Parisian welcomes.

Introduction

And so we are told. . .

On 3 May 1968, in the courtyard of the Sorbonne, following a meeting held by a group of *gauchiste* students, the police were called amid rumours of impending violence. The students involved in the gathering were from the Nanterre faculty on the outskirts of Paris where, over the course of the previous year, tensions had been building between militant students and university authorities. Matters had taken a turn for the worse when, on 22 March 1968, radical elements occupied the administrative tower of the Nanterre faculty in protest over the arrest of a number of comrades during an anti-Vietnam protest earlier in the week. This occupation led to the creation of the *mouvement du 22 mars* which brought together the diverse *groupuscules* active on the suburban campus and included figures such as Daniel Cohn-Bendit. From this moment on, students increased their militant activity, eventually forcing the doyen to close the faculty on 2 May. This closure explains why the Nanterre students found themselves at the heart of the French university system on 3 May.

When the police moved in, the first riot of *mai 68* ensued. Clashes between the forces of order and the surprisingly determined and highly mobile students set the trend for the coming week. Between 3 and 10 May – in the absence of the Prime Minister Georges Pompidou (on a state visit to Afghanistan) and amid the silence of President de Gaulle – the protest movement gathered momentum as students formulated their demands. Initially, they were outraged by the treatment doled out during and as a consequence of the 3 May riot. The imprisonment of a number of students, the occupation by the police of the Sorbonne and their omnipresence in the student Latin Quarter provided enough ammunition for what had started as a minority to gradually attract support from the wider student population. The number of participants on demonstrations grew, the level of violence was cranked up with every passing day and the movement began to see widening support from the largest student union (*Union nationale des étudiants de France* (UNEF)), a university teachers' union (*Syndicat national de l'enseignement supérieur* (SNESup)), a movement of *lycée* students (*Comités d'action lycéen* (CAL)), as well as increasing sympathy from the general public. Such conditions paved the way for the pivotal 'Night of the barricades'.

On 10 May, a huge demonstration made its way through the capital before finishing at the Latin Quarter where a decision was made to occupy the area. In order to do so, a series of barricades was built. The forces of order simply stood back and observed the construction of these defences, awaiting the order from above to move in and clear the area. In the interim period efforts were made to bring the two sides together in negotiations. The protracted talks eventually failed and the police and in particular the CRS (*Compagnies Républicaines de Sécurité*) were given the order to put an end to the occupation. There then ensued a terrible night of violence as students and riot police clashed until 6am. The fact that the entire evening's events were covered live by a number of radio stations meant that around the country, the general population had listened with horror to the scenes of violence. The next morning, the country awoke bleary eyed and incredulous at what had happened the night before. The perceived heavy-handed actions of the police would prove to be a significant turning point.

In protest against the events of 10 May, all the major trade unions called for a one-day strike and nationwide demonstrations for 13 May. As preparations were under way, the prime minister, upon his return, decided to concede to the demands of the students by freeing those who were imprisoned as well as pulling the police out of the Sorbonne and the Latin Quarter. If such measures were intended to blunt the impact of the planned protest, they were a failure. On 13 May (the tenth anniversary of the process that brought de Gaulle's return to power) huge demonstrations took place across the nation. Students, *lycéens*, workers, farmers, politicians; all sectors of French society came out in protest at what had happened, with a reported one million marchers on the streets of Paris. The impact however, would not be limited to 13 May. From a student perspective, the day ended with their occupation of the Sorbonne. For the working class, the one-day stoppage was but the beginning of a general strike.

General de Gaulle's decision to go ahead with a pre-planned state visit to Romania on 14 May quickly appeared to be an erroneous one, as that day saw the beginning of a series of strike movements that would confirm that this crisis was not to be limited to students. The *Nantais* factory *Sud-Aviation* was the first to call for a general strike and occupation. Other, bigger and more significant factories, including the bastion of the working class – the Renault factory at Boulogne-Billancourt – soon followed suit. By 19 May, up to two million people were on strike and de Gaulle, having cut short his state visit, was clearly perturbed with the state of affairs declaring, 'la réforme oui, la chienlit non'. His attitude did little to stem the spread of the strike. If the sheer numbers were unprecedented, the nature of the strike and its magnitude were equally significant. They were characterized in particular by occupations. Many factories were taken over by the workers during which time they set about discussing the possibilities of a different future. General assemblies were held and commissions were set up as factories became hotbeds of discussion and debate. The workplace was transformed so that the cogs in the machine became the masters, but also a place of enjoyment as all forms of entertainment were organized to fill the long hours of occupation.

The forms of action and organization within the factories replicated to some extent what was happening in the university milieu. Following 13 May, students occupied faculties all around the country where they would spend the next few weeks *à refaire le monde*. They continued to march and demonstrate in the streets and violence remained a factor. This was particularly the case when on 21 May the government decided to ban Cohn-Bendit from re-entering the country following an excursion to Germany. However, if the students had certainly been some sort of inspiration, any aspirations they had of extending their movement to the working class were thwarted by the strict policy of the leading trade union, the CGT (*Confédération Générale du Travail*), to prevent any direct contact between workers and students. While the strikers may have been enthusing about a complete overhaul of the system, the reality was that any formal demands were strictly limited to material issues.

The joyous freedom and desire to talk was not limited to the factories and faculties. The strike movement took hold in all manner of industries and professions as the country was soon gripped by the sentiment that something very special was taking place. The lack of petrol, cash and basic supplies caused some degree of panic. However, such circumstances only served to heighten the exceptional nature of what was happening and to add to the camaraderie symbolized by the spontaneous conversations happening between perfect strangers. Life during May 1968, it appears, was not so bad. The weather was nice, people were enthused by the freedom and verbosity that so characterized the moment and a holiday feeling hung in the air.

Despite this positive atmosphere, the strike continued to gain momentum and the state was increasingly at a loss as to what could be done. On 24 May, de Gaulle decided to use his most potent weapon – the radio address – to shake the population from its momentary folly. His proposed referendum fell on deaf ears and the rejection of his way out only served to heighten the feeling that something significant was on the horizon. That evening saw one of the most extreme nights of violence in Paris, with many casualties on both sides of the barricades. Pompidou, who seemed to have a more conciliatory attitude, then stepped up to the plate with the Grenelle negotiations. Bringing together the major trade unions, the *patronat* and the government for a 36-hour marathon meeting initially appeared to have found a way out of the impasse. However, the Grenelle protocol was sensationally rejected on 27 May by the Renault workers at Boulogne-Billancourt. On the same day, students and those figures considered to provide the best possible political translation of the May movement (and, in particular, Pierre Mendès-France) gathered in their thousands at the Charléty stadium on the outskirts of Paris. By this stage, the police forces were exhausted and frustrated, there was genuine talk of calling in the army to restore order, both the prime minister and president had tried and failed to find a solution and left-wing political forces were beginning to position themselves as a possible alternative. It was the culmination of these factors that would lead to the third and final phase of the events.

On 28 May, the political pressure was increased with François Mitterrand's television appearance during which he declared his candidacy for what he considered as inevitable presidential elections. Despite later being heavily criticized for such an opportunistic manoeuvre, his proposed alliance with Pierre Mendès-France briefly suggested that a viable political alternative to Gaullism was possible. The next day would demonstrate that any left-wing political force needed to include the PCF (*Parti Communiste Français*). Hitherto distanced from the movement, the Communist Party – keen not to allow a golden opportunity pass it by – decided to make it known that any political alternative would be impossible without its involvement. On 29 May the PCF organized (and controlled) a huge demonstration in Paris. The calm and order that characterized this march sent out a message to all concerned of the importance and strength of the Communist Party. De Gaulle and Pompidou's failed attempts to bring the revolt to an end, the jostling for positioning on the left and the show of communist strength provided the grounds for the general's mysterious disappearance that further underscored the growing sense of tension.

Having earlier suspended a planned ministerial meeting for the morning of 29 May, the president was to fly back to his residence *Colombey-les-deux-Eglises* in order to rest and consider his options. However, it soon transpired that he did not go there, and for a period of time, no one was quite sure where he was. Not until that evening did it become clear that he had in fact visited a French military camp in the German border town of Baden-Baden where he consulted with an old army acquaintance General Massu. The disappearance may well have been brief but given the context, the level of panic in the capital was considerable. Nevertheless, once back, de Gaulle contacted Pompidou to let him know of his intention to fight on, beginning with an address to the nation on 30 May. This pivotal day began with a head-to-head meeting between the president and prime minister, following which de Gaulle made a defiant speech to the nation that demonstrated his determination to stand strong. He dissolved the National Assembly and called for a general election. Almost immediately, the 'silent majority' poured out on to the streets in support of the general. The situation had been turned on its head.

Petrol pumps were miraculously reopened as Parisians left the capital in their droves to take advantage of the Whitsun weekend. The Cabinet was reshuffled and following the renegotiation of the concessions offered at Grenelle, the workers began the slow return to work. Over the course of June 1968, extreme elements tried to resist the end of the revolt, leading to some violent clashes and the first deaths directly related to the events. However, by mid-June, the population's attention was firmly fixed on the upcoming elections. When they finally went to the polls on 23 and 30 June, the result was a crushing victory for the Gaullist party with a huge 294 out of 488 seats in the National Assembly. Even before this final denouement, for many, the focus had shifted towards trying to make sense of what had happened. No one then could have imagined the sheer diversity and longevity of the revolt's influence and impact. Equally difficult to foresee would have been the extent to which it has become a subject of intense scrutiny and fascination that has secured the very words *mai 68* a significant place in the French national psyche.

For over forty years now, the events of 1968 around the world have been the focus of much attention. The French upheaval has been of particular interest both within France and without. As the years have passed, a certain common narrative has become increasingly prominent. While 1968 is certainly seen as an important turning point and a watershed in the development of French society, it is at the same time considered in an increasingly reductive light. In fact – and as demonstrated in the brief account above – it is less and less portrayed as the very serious nationwide crisis and largest strike in French history but more as a *bon-enfant* tantrum led principally by a spoilt generation of Parisian students intent on wreaking havoc during a period of much required – and today much longed-for – political and economic stability. The fortieth anniversary saw a continuation in the decennial commemorations that, as will be demonstrated, have been fundamental in shaping the doxa and has provided a reminder of the exceptional place these events occupy. Furthermore, it furnished an excellent opportunity to evaluate to what extent its portrayal has continued in the trend that has been emerging or whether 2008 marked a turning point in how these events are represented and thus perceived.

The aims of this study are to examine just how the common narrative has come to dominate representations of the events, to gauge the influence on how they are perceived by today's youth and finally to measure to what extent this interpretation falls short of painting the entire picture of what happened. In order to achieve these objectives an interdisciplinary methodological approach is used which includes archival research, a literature and media review as well as oral interviews and a survey of current attitudes. The insistence on diversity will be a common thread running through the study in order to emphasize the shortcomings of the dominant portrayal in reflecting the heterogeneous nature of the 1968 movement and revolt. While it will be argued that the history and memory of 1968 appear to be set in stone, the aim is to open new perspectives on these events. Instead of offering an opportunity to confirm the conventional representation, it is argued that the increased interest brought about by the anniversary commemorations should be used to force a major reappraisal that could ultimately lead to a truer understanding of these exceptional and crucially important events.

This book will focus on three principal arguments. First, it will be demonstrated that a great paradox exists between the level of attention afforded to the 1968 events in the forty years since and the scope of conventional representations. Despite periodic reassessments and the persistence of 1968 as a popular topic for debate, so narrow has the portrayal become that many of the elements that made 1968 exceptional are absent in how it is portrayed. Second, the nature of the events' coverage has seen them assume a very particular place in the hearts and minds of the French despite very obvious lacunae in their understanding. An assessment of current attitudes will reveal the scant recognition of the true diversity of 1968 yet confirm the continued recognition of its prominence. The final argument is one based on the complicated relationship between history and memory. In many respects, 1968 provides an exceptional case study of this much discussed relationship. Enough time has now passed since 1968 to allow the events to be considered in historical terms and, as Jan Asmann argues, the passing of forty years is a significant milestone in the development of the memory of such an event.[1] Consequently some important questions can be addressed. For example and in particular, how has the history of 1968 influenced memories of it and vice versa? Additionally, the fact that 1968 has been the focus of periodic reassessments that have unquestionably played a part in the construction of a dominant narrative permits an examination of the role of the increasingly prominent commemoration in influencing memories of past events. These and other elements will lead to the suggestion that the memory of 1968 has been shaped and cultivated in such a way that undermines the history of 1968. Why this is the case, to whose benefit the construction of such a limited perspective would be and to what extent the history of 1968 is retrievable are all questions to be examined.

In order to reflect and confirm the nationwide diversity of the events this study will de-centre its analysis by going to the geographical, historical and cultural peripheries. Unlike the majority of writings to date, the focus will be very much on the nationwide nature of the revolt as well as Paris. Interviews with provincial protagonists and analyses of regional dimensions will provide a new, broader angle and do much to underline the need to see beyond those ideas that have come to dominate the portrayal of the events. Throughout, first-hand accounts of those involved in regional movements and those who experienced the events in the system of higher education will be used to counterbalance current attitudes and the common narrative. Chapter one provides an overview of the manner in which the history of 1968 developed between 1968 and 1998. The focus on this thirty-year period stems from the need to set up just how the events of 1968 were framed for those who will be the focus of the survey, which was conducted in the 2002–2003 period and which will be covered in chapter three. Drawing on the leading theorists, it is argued that the 1968 events and their trajectory provide a particularly pertinent example through which to examine the complex debate on the relationship between history and memory and in particular the notion of 'collective memory'. A focus on the commemorative aspect and how that feeds into the construction of a particular history will permit a discussion on how such practices are influential in framing collective memory. Using the decennial anniversary reappraisals of 1978, 1988 and 1998 as reference points, particular attention will be afforded to academic analyses, intellectual debate, coverage in school history textbooks, television and press coverage, as well as an examination of filmic representations. It will chart how these vectors of memory have contributed to general perceptions and argue that despite being the subject of diverse studies and interpretations, the history of 1968 remains dominated by a limited representation. To explain why this particular representation of 1968 has emerged it will be argued that the role of the media and the modern-day preference for compact, easy-to-manage information, ripe for quick consumption, has inevitably seen the spectacular, romantic elements of 1968 take precedence over those requiring more careful consideration. Furthermore, the idea that the emergence of this image – dominated by the spectacular – has been facilitated and encouraged by the unlikely 'tango' of former *gauchistes* and the state will be discussed. No study of current attitudes to 1968 nor the French collective memory of it would be possible without making sense of the journey of the events' history – this opening chapter sets out to lay the grounds for such a study.

Chapter two examines specific areas of the events' portrayal so as to help explain two significant elements of the French collective memory of 1968. First, how is it that, despite the phenomenal amount of focus, important areas of what happened remain devoid of consensus? Second, it will be argued that, as a result of such attention, enough agreement exists in a sufficient number of areas to allow a certain general understanding of the events. The aim of this chapter is to demonstrate how both the areas of consensus and of disagreement have helped shape current perceptions. Such a comparison between these categories demonstrates how, on the one hand, debate is perpetuated through a lack of consensus, while on the other, how this debate has only served to strengthen the influence of the narrow dominant history. For example, it will be argued that instead of underlining the great diversity of the 1968 events, the vast array of interpretations has facilitated the emergence of a dominant narrative. So wide-ranging have the interpretations been that general perceptions have focused understandably on the reading that dominates quantitatively, i.e., the spectacular. The failings of the historical analyses have thus created a paradoxical situation that, while guaranteeing continued debate and attention, has confirmed the dominance of this narrow perspective in the minds of the French. To what extent such a process is indicative of a contrived effort to paint 1968 in a particular fashion or whether it is simply another example of the events' *insaisissable* nature will be addressed.

Chapter three assesses the impact of the events' portrayal on current attitudes towards them. It presents the results of a survey carried out amongst more than 500 French university students during the period October 2002–June 2003 regarding their understanding of the 1968 crisis. Students were chosen as the target audience for the questionnaire for several reasons. First, sufficient time has passed for the current student generation to be far away enough from the events to avoid any direct personal experience of them from affecting their responses. Although it is true that certain young people may be more aware of the events than others (as a result of their parents' involvement, for example), on the whole, the generation of students analysed can hardly be considered as children of May '68 since most of them were born in and around the early 1980s. Second, due to the obvious importance of the university system and students during the events of 1968, it is interesting to chart how those in the very same institutions as the *enragés* consider the crisis some thirty-five years later. Finally, as French society's future intellectuals, the way today's students perceive and consequently portray the events will have an important influence on how the history of May–June 1968 is passed on to the next generation. By no means claiming to represent the French population as a whole, the results nonetheless provide an interesting snapshot of how perceptions of this important sector have been moulded. Divided into five sections, each of which examines a specific hypothesis relating to assumptions on how the events are viewed, this study will contribute to testing the general idea that young French people are unaware of the true magnitude of the events and their consequences. It therefore provides compelling evidence of the impact of a narrow historical perspective on the collective memory of such a significant event.

Chapter four begins with an overview of how the university movement of 1968 has been presented across a number of key texts focusing on 1968. It reveals how representations of the events in relation to the university sector are centred on the notion that students provided the spark from which the revolt emerged. Whilst this is undoubtedly the case, the prevailing narrative posits the student input as emanating principally from a *gauchiste* element that, once having achieved its mission of translating their revolt to an all-out social crisis, by 13 May disappears firmly into the background. One is left with the impression that from this point on, nothing of any true significance took place in the occupied faculties around the country. In order to challenge this approach, this chapter provides a more concentrated analysis of the conditions that led up to 1968 within the university system and provided the grounds for the student world to serve as the starting point of this revolt. Furthermore, it highlights the role of the reformist element – so often pushed to the background – in continuing the revolt through the work carried out in *commission paritaires* around the country in occupied faculties over the course of May–June 1968. It will be argued that these elements, much more so than the extremists – who were in effect only a minority of the student population – are more representative of the 1968 revolt. By examining the compilation and implementation of the Faure reform that followed the events as well as gauging how current-day academics perceive the legacy of *mai 68,* it will be argued that the reformist elements were those that had the most significant impact in the university domain. Their absence from the dominant narrative is yet another example of how the spectacular elements are preferred to those that reflect more accurately the spirit of 1968. It could be argued that by focusing on the student milieu in 1968, this study risks contributing to the over-emphasis on the university revolt to the detriment of other important sectors (such as the general strike). However, the fact that it highlights the lack of coverage afforded to the reformist element will emphasize the reductive role of the dominant narrative that all too often focuses principally on the spectacular actions of minority *gauchiste* elements. This chapter juxtaposes the results of interviews and archival research with current day attitudes and the dominant narrative to highlight surprising lacunas in the level of understanding of a domain that is very commonly and logically associated with the 1968 events. It is argued that such differences are an example of how the stereotypical image has permeated even those areas where one would expect a sound grasp to be forthcoming. As such, it is an interesting example of how the history of 1968 has guaranteed a certain level of understanding; but one that remains limited, underlining the paradoxical influence of the events' coverage on the French collective memory of them.

The final chapter further highlights the impact of the shortcomings of the dominant narrative. By providing a case study of the events in the cities of Brest and Strasbourg, it highlights negative consequences brought about by the increasingly narrow perspective. The absence of concerted analysis of events beyond the capital is demonstrated through an overview of how this area has been covered (or not) in conventional representations. It is subsequently argued that such a reductive lens has occulted the heterogeneous nature of this nationwide crisis as well as ignoring the contribution of regional movements in rendering 1968 exceptional. The telescopic focus on Paris has left little or no room for an exploration of regional diversities in how the 1968 events were played out. Furthermore, and arguably as a result, the reductive focus has been translated into how the regional consequences of the events are recounted and therefore perceived. 1968 was a watershed moment throughout French society and across the nation. For example, it provided an opportunity for certain regional movements to turn the page on past errors and would prove pivotal in the reinvigoration of regional cultures and identities.[2] The absence of thorough analyses of the significant, yet divergent impact of *mai 68* on regional cultures, movements and identities is a further symptom of the dominant narrative. In both Brest and Strasbourg the university movements confirm the conclusions of chapter four that the role of reformists was more significant than that of extremist elements. Furthermore, the cultural and historical specificities of these two cities provided the grounds for events that do not conform to the dominant narrative. Through archival research and interviews with protagonists in each of the regional movements, this chapter reveals the shortcomings of the over-emphasis on the events in the Latin Quarter of Paris. The gaps between current attitudes and those of participants together with differences between regional and Paris-centred narratives provide the grounds for a thorough examination of how conventional representations have affected the collective memory of the 1968 events.

The conclusion, drawing together the ideas from the different chapters, argues that the very special manner in which the events of 1968 have been analysed, portrayed and interpreted over the years has seen them carve out a particularly interesting place in French collective memory. The survey reveals that 1968 is relatively well understood by young people today. However, and as highlighted by insights into the literature, media and scholastic coverage and filmic portrayals to date, it is argued that such a level of understanding is drawn from a progressively narrow depiction of the crisis. Therefore, 1968 presents a very interesting, two-pronged study of the relationship between history and memory. First, it suggests that an increasingly narrow portrayal of such an event imposes a specific dominant history which, in turn, permeates the memory of it. The impact is the negation of significant areas, such as, for example, the absence of regional studies. Second, as a subject that, despite an unprecedented level of attention, is still open to interpretations, 1968 continues to be the focus of considerable coverage and thus forever present. This paves the way for the surprisingly high degree of understanding present amongst today's youth. However, and as will be demonstrated via an overview of the outpouring of fortieth-anniversary material, it is the need for more understanding, further debate and investigations to fill existing lacunas that, to a certain extent, explains why 1968 keeps coming back. As an extremely intriguing moment in recent French history, 1968 is consequently and under-standably of obvious interest to French people, young and old. It will be argued that, in addition, it is the focus of a self-perpetuating debate that promises to preserve their special place in French collective memory. Finally, just how and why this specific image has come to dominate the history of 1968 will be discussed in relation to the idea that a convenient consensus exists for both the state and those who have appropriated, monopolized and dominated representations. On the one hand, *gauchiste* elements are given a certain sense of credibility as the source of what has become an iconic set of events. On the other, the state has managed – by emphasizing the role of one minor element of the 1968 revolt – to conceal the very serious nature of the mass and varied movement and as such perpetuated its image as an irresponsible utopian revolt, inspired by a spoilt generation that in reality posed no real threat thus discouraging any possibility of another such insurrection.

Chapter One
The emergence of a convenient consensus

Introduction

Over the last two decades, memory studies have become extremely popular, spawning an impressive research output that some have described as a 'memory industry'.[1] There are a number of explanations for such a phenomenon. For example, Geoffrey Cubitt highlights societal, historical, cultural and epistemological shifts towards an emphasis on the past that can help explain this so-called 'turn to memory'.[2] Kendall R. Phillips points to an increasing mistrust of 'official history' as one of many potential explanations.[3] A certain obsession with history, heritage and commemorations has inevitably focused attentions on the issue of remembering. However, a heightened interest in the past cannot entirely account for the wide-ranging debates on memory. The ambiguity, malleability and 'elasticity' of the term itself are important considerations.[4] Also, there are many different categories of memory (social, cultural, popular, individual, collective, etc.) that are each subject to varying interpretations which further complicate major areas of debate. For this study, the focus will be on collective memory, which – as the subject of debate itself[5] – is defined here as the dominant perspective of how a group (in this case, French society) collectively considers a past event. Before outlining why the events of May–June 1968 provide a particularly revealing and appropriate optic through which to examine the intricacies of the memory question, it is important to highlight a particular area that can be described as underpinning debates surrounding memory thus far.

The issue of the relationship between memory and history is complex and has consequently led to much debate.[6] The lack of consensus can be explained by the inherent intertwining of the two elements. History (which is itself the focus of diverse interpretations)[7] can be defined as the story of the past as told through a variety of vehicles and activities that draws on concrete evidence as the source of its validity. Therefore, for example, the history of the Second World War is multifaceted and can be found in a number of mediums including books, films, photographs, oral testimonies and so on. Over time, the collective memory of the Second World War has been shaped by its history and vice versa. The material chosen, the dominant perspectives and the nature of representations that shape its history are unavoidably influenced by memory. The stories told, the interpretations and explanations of documents, and the subsequent choices made have all at some stage been influenced by issues of recollection and remembering. As such, certain memories are passed on and inevitably permeate historical representations. The history then in turn exerts its influence on the collective memory.[8] Such portrayals form the basis of how successive generations are introduced and exposed to the past.[9] The memories that help mould the historical perspective of a past event determine how later groups will collectively recall it. The ideas that memory and history can be considered independently from each other or that they ought to be separated (with the former acting in opposition to the latter as 'antihistorical discourse')[10] have not been without their proponents.[11] However, and what the rest of this chapter will demonstrate (through the example of the 1968 events) is that, in order to begin an appreciation of the complexities surrounding the notions of memory and history, one must emphasize and examine their symbiotic relationship, the tensions therewithin and the resulting impact on how the past is perceived.

When one considers the extent of the coverage dedicated to the French 1968 events over the last forty years, it becomes clear that the *prise de parole*[12] so prevalent during the crisis has been mirrored in its subsequent analysis. Even before the conclusion of the events and in their immediate aftermath (1968–72), the level of attention was unprecedented as participants, observers and experts engaged in what has been described as a 'rush to bear witness, to recount, to prophesise'.[13] Interest eventually dissipated before re-emerging on the occasion of the tenth anniversary. This marked the beginning of a trend that would see the May/June 1968 events undergo repeated reassessments in 1988 and 1998 in what has been described as a 'May industry'.[14] Nevertheless, in spite of the production line of material that has accompanied these periodic surges in interest, the events of 1968 remain '*insaisissables*'[15] or, as Bousquet describes, 'One of the most indeterminate set of events [. . .] maybe one of the least understood historical moments.'[16] The incomprehension surrounding the crisis is reflected in the lack of consensus concerning its interpretation and legacy, a fact exacerbated by the wide-ranging ideas outlined in the plethora of material produced[17] – the quality of which has not been without its critics.[18]

Nevertheless – and arguably as a result of the confusion[19] – a certain 'official history' has come to dominate representations.[20] The manner in which the events have been portrayed – particularly around the tenth, twentieth and thirtieth anniversaries[21] – has been progressively reductive.[22] For example, despite the nationwide impact of the events and the involvement of almost every sector of French society '[t]hree words have come to represent '68: May, Paris, Student'.[23] Any violence is described as the purely symbolic actions of a handful of utopian extremists based in the Parisian Latin Quarter and whose attitudes are often characterized by the now legendary slogans, such as *sous les pavés la plage* or *Il est interdit d'interdire*.[24] Furthermore, any consequences attributed to the events are limited to specific areas such as feminism, ecology, morals and, in particular, cultural advances.[25] Whilst Parisian students were unquestionably important at the beginning of the crisis and the areas mentioned as having been influenced are beyond debate, their predominance has led to what has been described as a 'May '68 [. . .] persistently diluted, mutilated, distorted, reconstructed and mythologized without any possibility of a more general historical perspective rectifying or shifting the focus of this work of memory.'[26] In order to understand how we have come to this point, one is able – using the decennial commemorations as plotting points – to chart the evolution of the events' portrayal and, in so doing, delineate and explain the emergence of the dominant narrative.

1968–72 – The immediate aftermath

Whilst the influx of material produced as the events were petering out and in their immediate aftermath provide valuable insights by capturing the feelings of the participants, objectivity is at a minimum and the required distance for a balanced analysis absent.[27] Nevertheless, two texts in particular rose to promin-ence during this period that very much characterize the essence of the debate concerning the crisis at the time.[28] Raymond Aron's *La Révolution introuvable* and Alain Tourraine's *Le Mouvement de mai ou le communisme utopique* both underscore the early desire to make sense of the tumultuous events of the previous spring.[29] Whilst both authors accept the importance of what happened, they are equally keen – for different reasons – to play down the revolutionary aspect attached to the crisis. Instead, they attribute the magni-tude of the upheaval to a culmination of separate problems mishandled by authorities that were seized upon by an irrational, illogical movement. Both appear as wishing to represent the voice of reason during a period when imagination threatened to seize power. Their minimizing of the revolutionary potential of 1968 would set a trend – aided by developments in the years following – in steering understanding of the crisis away from the extreme views so prominent during the events and in their aftermath. Other important memory vectors reflect such sentiments.

In terms of filmic representations produced at this time, one only has to consider two examples to get a sense of the emerging consensus. Jean-Pierre Mocky's 1969 film *Solo* recounts the story of the violent fallout of the events.[30] The lead character Vincent Chabral (played by Mocky himself), a renowned international musician and diamond smuggler, returns to Paris in the after-math of the events only to find his younger brother caught up in a terrorist organization. Made up of disaffected youths, this militant body is clearly frus-trated by the failure of 1968 to bring about real change. In a bid to help his brother, Vincent unintentionally becomes embroiled in his troubles before eventually paying the ultimate price. Set in a sombre atmosphere, no better represented than by the repetitive, haunting score,[31] the portrayal of the 1968 'spirit' is dominated by the violent, irrational, irresponsible and ultimately fatalistic objectives of the student militants. The film is punctuated with refer-ences to what would become stereotypical clichés; sexual promiscuity and irresponsibility; utopian idealism, wanton violence; Paris and its Latin Quarter. That such groups existed in the post-'68 period is not in question. However, the choice to focus on this minor facet of the overall upheaval is indicative of early moves to portray *mai 68* as an irresponsible, pointlessly utopian and ultimately failed revolt. The utopianism that characterizes the objectives of the student militants in *Solo* is equally discernable in *L'An 01*.[32]

This adaptation of Gébé's comic strip of the same name tells the story of how an entire society decides to put an end to the status quo at a specific time and date with a view to considering an alternative way of life. This *An 01* or year dot (starting from scratch) moment is a clear reference to the events of 1968, evidenced by the range of *clin d'oeils* to the now (already) accepted symbols of what occurred. For example, the *L'An 01* movement is depicted as acting without any real consideration for what it was trying to achieve. It takes place in a festive, joyous atmosphere where people suddenly find their voice and find themselves free to converse with those they have never spoken to before. Furthermore, the ideas and actions are extreme with property abolished, consumerism rejected and a new, more open approach to life. Older generations are depicted as struggling while young people revel. And, in what becomes an international movement, France is the country that goes the furthest. This film could be perceived as a manifestation of the frustration felt by those who believed that the 1968 events were a missed opportunity to introduce real changes. However, once again, it is the more extreme, unrealistic and utopian elements that are pushed to the fore. Such a portrayal can only lend weight to the emerging trend at this time that appeared to be striving to depict the events as somewhat of a psychodrama.

Such a trend is evident in the 1969 documentary *Mai–Juin 1968*.[33] This short UDR (*Union pour la défense de la République*) propaganda account of the crisis, with commentary by Michel Droit, unsurprisingly paints it in a very negative light. It is highly critical of the movement and pays particular attention to the most negative aspects of the events and in particular scenes of reckless violence. Describing those that led the movements as simply interested in creating anarchy, the overall message is that the only achievement of the revolt was to seriously undermine a country and regime that had hitherto been doing so well. Overall – and despite the immediacy of the events – one can, through a number of vectors, discern the early signs of a common, emergent core narrative. By the time of the tenth anniversary, such a discourse would not only be firmly in place, it was further consolidated.

1978 – *Les Années Orphelines*

By May 1978, France was in a difficult place. Under Giscard's presidency, the country was beginning to experience serious economic problems (in particular, unemployment) triggered by the oil crisis of 1973. In spite of such difficulties, the mainstream Left had failed to capitalize and found itself with its own set of problems. For the extreme Left, a series of international developments and revelations (in particular, the publication of *L'Archipel du Goulag* by Alexandre Soljenitsyne in 1973) in the years leading up to 1978 had rocked the ideological foundations of the so-called *soixantehuitards*. This led to much disenchantment amongst *gauchistes*, many of whom would become involved in *les Nouveaux Philosophes*. The failure of the mainstream left in the March 1978 legislative elections to build on the initial success and enthusiasm surrounding the Common Programme of 1972 further compounded the sense of negativity. Such circumstances are important when considering the dominant character-istics of this first decennial anniversary, of which two texts in particular exemplify the tone.[34]

In *Les Années orphelines*, Jean-Claude Guillebaud paints a very depressing picture of the motivations behind the 1968 movement by highlighting the difficulties that those who immersed themselves in the revolt have had to endure as a result of the vast changes experienced in the intervening period.[35] For Guillebaud, the motivations that drove the 1968 revolt are no longer present or relevant and the senselessness of the exuberance of the *soixantehui-tards* has become so evident that the time has come to accept the mistakes of the past and move on.[36] Regis Debray's *Modeste contribution aux discours et cérémo-nies officielles du dixième anniversaire* is further confirmation of the gloom at this juncture. Whilst there is an acceptance of the fact that 1968 has led to some positive consequences, in a scathing criticism of the movement, what it stood for and what it has produced, Debray refuses to accept the events as a revolu-tionary movement.[37] Describing it as divisive, not interested in challenging the authorities and lacking direction, he considers the 1968 movement to have resulted in the complete opposite of what it promised to achieve. Instead, it aided the dominance of capitalism by forcing the state to modernize many of its institutions, the principal beneficiaries of which have been the bourgeoisie. Like Guillebaud, Debray insists on the need to face up to the reality of the fail-ures of the revolt.[38] Pessimism is the term that best describes his feelings regarding the events in 1978. No longer in any way considered revolutionary, the portrayal of the crisis is increasingly limited to a Parisian revolt by an irre-sponsible, directionless minority that has aided the modernization of capitalist France and led to fringe benefits concerning moral issues. Such a perspective is once again evident when one considers just how other vectors framed 1968 on its tenth anniversary.

The 1978 Gérard Oury film *La Carapate*, starring Pierre Richard, provides a valuable glimpse into the direction portrayals of 1968 were taking.[39] Set during the events, the film tells the story of a barrister (Jean-Philippe Duroc, played by Richard) who, when visiting his client (Martial Gaulard, played by Victor Lanoux) in a Lyon prison – where the two men were to discuss the possibility of a presidential pardon for Gaulard who is facing the death penalty – is caught up in a breakout engendered by the crisis. The remainder of the film is taken up with the two protagonists' journey from Lyon to Paris where Duroc manages to secure the pardon as a result of a chance meeting with de Gaulle just as he is leaving for Baden-Baden. If the film bucks the trend by featuring the existence of upheaval beyond the capital, it nevertheless firmly underscores the domin-ant discourse through the use of numerous clichés. Opening with an overview of Paris, with the now stereotypical slogans, posters and general *chienlit* that by this stage had come to represent the 1968 events, the film goes on to reduce the main players in the revolt to students and inevitably the CRS. Clashes between the two sides are characterized by a certain *bon-enfant*, jovial atmosphere with at one stage the students being described as 'these little idiots and their barricades'.[40] There is very little reference to the strike movement except for when this 'idiotic strike'[41] provides some degree of hindrance to our protagonists' progress. The stereotypical notion of *la bourgeoisie en fuite* from the revolution is featured in the very comic depiction of the attempt of the middle-class couple (Jacques and Gisèle Pavinaux, played by Jean-Pierre Darras and Yvonne Gaudeau) to flee the country in a Rolls Royce filled with gold bullion.

Whilst such characteristics are indicative of an emerging framework from which the events were to be increasingly portrayed, the very fact that a film of this genre could be made so soon after speaks volumes for the popular image of the crisis. Only ten years on, and as a result of the changes experienced since, together with the predominant framing, the 1968 events had already been stripped of their importance and considered ripe to provide the backdrop for such a film. As such, one can understand the negativity and pessimism so evident in the works outlined above. Instead of providing the grounds for a veritable *remise en question* of French society, 'May '68' had been emptied of its gravity, widespread nature and could be (as Oury himself declared) considered as 'drôle'.[42] Such developments will have confirmed the sense of frustration, failure and disappointment experienced by those who had invested so much of themselves at the time; sentiments prevalent in Romain Goupil's *Mourir à trente ans*.[43] Inspired by the death of fellow militants – and in particular the suicide of his best friend Michel Recanati in 1978 – Goupil charts the spectacular rise and even more spectacular demise of the 1968 generation. One cannot help but sense the underlying thread that was the immense difficulty that those who genuinely believed 1968 to have marked a significant turning point experienced in coming to terms with the ensuing failure. In many respects, Goupil's chilling documentary captures the sentiments of *les années orphelines* that characterized the period in and around 1978.

A further example of this emerging representation can be found in the 1978 television documentary *Histoire de Mai*.[44] Whilst this four-part film provides quite a comprehensive account of the events, it does little to break out of the increasingly omnipresent and narrow framework and in many respects could be perceived as adhering to the negativity so prevalent at this time. For example, as well as being predominantly focused on Paris, it describes any violence as symbolic with the movement at one stage even described as non-violent. The gravity of the situation is frequently explained not as a result of a fundamental malaise across French society but rather as a consequence of a series of errors on behalf of the government. In what would become a recurrent theme in years to come, the student movement is represented by media-chosen personalities such as Alain Geismar and Daniel Cohn-Bendit; with the latter at one stage describing the motivations of the 'Night of the Barricades' as a desire to have the university opened so that they could throw a party. Throughout, there are discussions on the tensions between the trade unions and students, represented in particular by what would become the iconic images of the students being turned away from the gates of the Renault factory at Boulogne Billancourt, so as to drive home the lack of student–worker osmosis. The role of the PCF – described as working hand in hand with the government in opposition to the movement – is continually flagged up so as to downplay any revolutionary potential. Finally, whilst the month of June is given some extensive coverage, its depiction is characterized by Raymond Marcellin's negative and self-congratulatory perspective on the evacuation of the Sorbonne and the Odéon, his success in breaking the strike and how he managed to ensure the peaceful election of later that month. All in all, whilst this documentary depicts the events as significant, the overwhelming impression is best summed up the concluding phrase: 'They did not demand the impossible but rather hoped for the unlikely.'[45] The prevalence of this narrow representation was given even greater credence with the 1978 airing of William Klein's *Grands soirs et petits matins*.[46] Focusing exclusively on the Parisian student quarter, this documentary will only have helped further reduce the significance of the involvement of those beyond Paris and the university milieu. Together with other television documentaries,[47] the telescopic focus of journalists added yet another layer to the narrowing perception.[48]

It was equally around this stage that the events began to find their place in school history texts. Jo McCormack's recent study of the Algerian conflict underlines the significance of this vector as 'a crucial way that collective memory is transmitted in France across generations'.[49] An overview of the portrayal of *mai 68* is revelatory through its confirmation of emerging trends. By 1979, the very short period of time that had elapsed did not prevent the events being given some degree of coverage. However, in most cases, it is minimal and, when developed, quite limited.[50] Nevertheless, even at this early stage one can delineate the emergence of features that will shape the dominant discourse. It is however in 1983 (despite some texts affording little attention to the events)[51] that a clear trend began to emerge in the nature of coverage in school textbooks, and one that is characterized by contrasting tensions. On the one hand, it is clear that the 1968 events are considered to have some importance. The degree of coverage is significant and portrays their diversity and widespread nature. For example in Hatier's edition, a two-page dossier accompanies the standard chronological overview.[52] In it, as well as describing the events as 'La crise de mai–*juin* 1968', it focuses on some of the more complex areas of debate. The tensions between revolutionaries and reformers are covered, there is recognition that the strike was not simply based around quantitative demands and there is an insight into the serious clashes between workers and the CRS at Flins. The Bordas edition of the same year, in a section entitled *'La Révolution Manquée?'*, sheds some light on the nationwide impact of the general strike.[53] It also discusses the difficulties faced by the authorities in trying to break the strike in June at Montebeliard and Flins as well as highlighting the complexity of interpreting the events. The difficulty in pinning down an understanding of the crisis is equally present in Nathan's edition.[54] As well as highlighting the interpretative debate – particularly with reference to Bénéton and Touchard's text[55] – there is also significant detail on the month of June, including the deaths of 1968. Finally, Delagrave's edition touches on the spread of the crisis beyond the capital and in particular to Lyon where two workers are killed in clashes with the forces of order. Equally notable is the inclusion of photographs of the events elsewhere than the Parisian Latin Quarter with images of a student demonstration, a workers' march and heavy CRS presence in Toulouse.[56]

Whilst these examples unquestionably demonstrate how by this early stage the events were afforded considerable attention, allowing for a reasonably thorough appreciation of their magnitude, one is nonetheless able to identify the creeping dominance of a discourse that will become commonplace and play a significant role in shaping perceptions. For example, in terms of framing how the events are presented, the tendency of splitting them into three distinct phases is prevalent.[57] Another notable trend is the virtual dominance of Paris and in particular the Parisian Latin Quarter. This is particularly the case in the diverse documents (photos, etc.) that accompany the accounts.[58] Consequently, a small number of elements such as posters, slogans or graffiti are pushed to the foreground.[59] Such a telescopic focus lends even greater credibility to a specific image, dominated by *gauchiste* elements.[60] Particular attention is also paid to the lack of working-class–student osmosis with the crisis described as being made up of two separate movements with very little in common. Finally, the issue of consequences is, some fifteen years later, difficult to analyse. However, as one text describes, the impact is not exactly perceived as significant, having left 'little trace'.[61] The combination of these factors continued and consolidated the discourse that had been evident in the early aftermath and helped pave the way for the next significant staging post in the emergence of the dominant narrative.

1988 – *Génération*

A number of converging factors are important to consider before outlining the tendencies of the dominant discourse on the twentieth anniversary of the events. The presidential elections that were to take place in May 1988 had a definite impact on the nature of the commemoration, turning the spotlight away from 1968. This was particularly true as the election would bring to an end a very tense period of *cohabitation* and one where both sides (Mitterrand and Chirac) were keen to avoid any allusion to *mai 68*. The events were pushed even further down the pecking order by the upcoming (and in some degrees already launched) bicentenary of the French Revolution. It has been argued that the twentieth anniversary experienced some sort of premature ejaculation brought about by the 1986 Devaquet protests.[62] During this revolt, much was made of the influence and impact of *mai 68* as well as the comparability of the '68/'86 generations. Nevertheless, the twentieth anniversary of the events showed another marked increase in the number of texts and reveals a significant development in how the events were being discussed, with the lapse of twenty years facilitating the emergence of complete and balanced accounts[63] as well as the beginning of interpretative debates.[64] However, three specific texts produced to coincide with the 1988 commemoration are vital in understanding the moulding of perceptions.[65]

The two *Génération*[66] texts by Hervé Hamon and Patrick Rotman are amongst the most lauded of all those concerning the events of 1968, marking a significant point in the development of the events' history.[67] Focusing on politically motivated Parisian students, *Générations* chart the thirteen-year period 1962–1975 through the experiences of a select band of *soixantehuitards* to describe the special characteristics of this particular generation.[68] Jacques Capdevielle and René Mouriaux's *Mai 68 – L'Entre-deux de la modernité* moves the debate to another level.[69] Despite the devaluation of the ideals that were so inspirational to much of the 1968 movement, the authors continue to consider 1968 as amongst the most significant moments in French history. The meagre concessions afforded as a result of the crisis – in comparison to its magnitude – explain the sense of disappointment and negativity surrounding it. The authors attempt to dispel such gloom by describing the events as a necessary pause in the modernization of France that rendered her institutions more flexible and allowed the process of modernization to continue.[70] The two *Génération* texts and *L'Entre-deux de la modernité* reveal a further limiting of the magnitude of the crisis and demonstrate the positive slant increasingly attached to the consequences that characterized attitudes on the twentieth anniversary. They illustrate the growing consensus that had been emerging for some time; the events are portrayed as a Parisian revolt, led by militant extremists who formed a generation apart that consequently facilitated the modernization of France and inspired a renaissance in the feminist, cultural and ecology movements. What happened in the provinces is ignored, the strike glossed over and the political chaos forgotten. Whilst the significance of the Rotman and Hamon texts in focusing the debate on the idea of 'generation' was given added impetus through the series of television documentaries that were released to coincide with the publication of the two books, the emerging consensus is identifiable in other mediums.[71]

Perhaps one of the most famous films that uses 1968 as its backdrop is Louis Malle's 1990 *Milou en mai*.[72] It tells the story of how an extended bourgeois family copes with the death of the head of the family during the events of 1968. Following an elderly mother's passing, her entire family descends on its provincial residence in order to organize the funeral, but more importantly to discuss the issue of inheritance. The paralysis brought about by the events prevents the funeral procedure taking its normal course and, instead, the family is forced to wait in order to make the arrangements. As news of the events pour in, the family is whipped up into a panic that sees them flee the residence, fearing an imminent attack from revolutionaries. During this brief escapade, the protagonists are consumed by a momentary folly that sees them engage in all sorts of irrational behaviour before returning rapidly to the house, to reality and to the business at hand – but not without consequences and much questioning of one another. One is able to yet again delineate a continuation in the way that the events of 1968 have been portrayed. For example, news of the revolt is relayed via the radio. However, what is being broadcast is very much Paris-centred. The idea that provincial movements were only ever really acting in reaction to events in the capital is reinforced here, negating the possibility that local issues may have been at play. Beyond the fragments from the radio, the only sense we get of what is going on beyond the residence comes when a younger member of the family – a Parisian student – arrives. Over dinner he tells tales of the Sorbonne; its utopian atmosphere and sexual liberation to the fore. As the plot unfolds, the characters become consumed by the spirit of the time, leading to a degeneration in their behaviour as they embark on a communitarian approach to life with utopian ideals and a large helping of irresponsible behaviour. More broadly, the film could be interpreted as an analogy of the 1968 events. The family (representing French society) becomes intoxicated by and dragged into a Parisian, student-led movement whose objectives were more than questionable before being snapped from their folly and swiftly returned to normality. With such an analogy in mind, it is interesting to note the translation of the film's title for distribution in the US – *May Fools*. The idea that the 1968 events were to some extent foolish might well help explain one very prominent television programme that went out to coincide with the twentieth anniversary.

Procès de Mai, as the title suggests, very much places the 1968 events in the dock, accused of engendering a major crisis at a time when France was doing so well.[73] The programme is set up in the manner of a court case with a jury made up of 20-year-olds who listen to a series of arguments from special guests. For the defence we have Bernard Kouchener (who attempts to explain the root causes of the events by insisting on the idea of *Une France bloquée*), Henri Weber (who points to the positive impact on French society by describing the revolt as a *désordre créatif*) and Laurent Joffrin (who examines (without much success) the possibility of a link between the generations of 1968 and 1986). For the prosecution, Dominique Jamet highlights *Les excès de mai*, describing the events as a waste of time and a psychodrama that created all sorts of problems for French society and its institutions. Michel Albert is even more critical in his analysis of *Le prix du changement* in which he argues that the events have held back the French economy by up to ten years by preventing the installation of important changes. The ensuing debate amongst the 'jury' reveals the difficulty that this generation has in any comparison with that of 1968. One can sense a certain tension or even envy amongst the young people assembled towards the generation of 1968. That the events are the focus of a *procès* is indicative of how the narrow portrayal has started to impinge on common perceptions. Furthermore, this programme does little to challenge or force a rethink of the dominant portrayal, particularly as the events' defendants are what are quickly becoming the 'usual suspects' trotting out the same old discourse. If anything, this programme highlights the emergence of a new pattern that would consolidate the stereotypical representation and go on to gain some momentum; i.e. the idea that the 1968 events are to blame for a whole raft of contemporary socio-economic ills in France. It is worth noting that not all the media focus in 1988 was centred on the chosen few who were beginning to monopolize how the events were represented.

However, as the example of *Que sont nos vingt ans devenus? 1968–1988* demonstrates, when we do see beyond the conventional representation, the picture is not very positive.[74] This television documentary visits three people/couples who were implicated in the Parisian events of 1968 in various guises and who subsequently decided to drop everything for a new start in rural France. It would be incorrect to describe any of those people featured as completely satisfied with their choices and trajectory since the events. The first couple (former students) are divided over the issue, with the woman openly regretful of their move and wishing she had done things differently. The second couple (former *ouvriers*) are clearly more content with how things have panned out for them but are visibly embarrassed or ashamed of their behaviour and actions during the events. The final case is that of a single male who describes himself as having been active violently during the events. He declares how he has firmly turned his back on those years and in particular the violence. He seems unsure as to whether or not he made the right decision to move from Paris and is even contemplating a return. His post-'68 trajectory and his general attitude come across as unstable and uncertain. He declares his surprise at the lack of understanding amongst the general population of the true nature of the events – particularly regarding the issue of violence. Overall, this documentary is an interesting departure from the norm. However, what is perhaps most striking is the overwhelming sense of regret or shame that permeates the demeanour and accounts of those questioned – a sense that, despite some attempts to portray the 1968 events in a more positive light,[75] certainly fits the dominant discourse on this twentieth anniversary.

The wave of history school textbooks that is most appropriate at this juncture is that which appeared in 1989. In the first of two Bordas editions, one is able to make out a shift in the nature and level of coverage.[76] In a two-page section entitled *La Crise de Mai et le départ du Général*, there is a clear narrowing of the perspective from ten years previously. Despite some mention of working-class involvement and allusions to the subtleties of the CFDT/CGT positions, one can see the beginning of the consolidation of a narrative that was emerging in 1978 but would firmly take root in 1988. This discourse is dominated by a focus on May, on Paris and on *gauchiste* elements. Little detail of the strike is forthcoming and any worker/student alliance is depicted as impossible. The dramatic denouement and crushing Gaullist election victory are underscored to weaken any gravity of the crisis in what is steadily emerging as a youth-led tantrum. The accompanying documents are indicative of the slide towards the narrow perspective, with the majority (despite the inclusion of a photograph of a workers' demonstration) of them focused on the capital, the role of *gauchistes* and the significance of the Gaullist victory. In the second of the Bordas editions, there is a five-page dossier entitled *La Crise de Mai 68* that centres on de Gaulle's 30 May speech.[77] Despite providing quite an extensive degree of coverage including recognition of the international dimension of the revolt and a chronology that attempts to go beyond May 1968, the major emphasis remains in keeping with the familiar line. The events are built around the increasingly common phases; the student phase is dominated by *gauchistes*, the strike is glossed over and there is little mention of what happened in June. De Gaulle's miraculous speech is analysed as the major turning point. There is recognition of a lack of *recul* and the need for more time to digest the complete impact of the crisis. Nevertheless, one cannot help but identify an emerging consensus. This trend is discernible in the 1989 Hachette edition where once again there remain elements of an extensive analysis but a genuine reductive depiction of the magnitude of the crisis.[78] In the main chronological overview, the *étrange révolution* is given scant attention and remains very much focused on Paris. However, there then follows a two-page dossier entitled *Les Soixantehuitards* where the 1988 buzzword 'Generation' is very prominent. Beginning with the inclusion of an excerpt from Ory and Sirinelli entitled *Une Génération Intellectuelle*, this dossier discusses the plethora of material produced on the events and how the twenty years since 'seem to have further obscured [the debate]'.[79] It is in the second section of the dossier that it falls into line with the dominant discourse. In response to the question *Qui etaient-ils?* (i.e. those who were protesting) the list of groups provided is predominantly made up of *gauchistes*. As for *Que voulaient-ils?* (i.e. what were they demanding?), we are presented with a list of the classic and clichéd slogans of the revolt. In terms of what legacy the events left behind, a section from Rotman and Hamon's *Génération* on how the 1968 generation forced a re-composition of the French political landscape that they now occupy is provided and in so doing fits the dominant narrative so prevalent on the twentieth anniversary. Also included is M. Humbert-Jean's 1988 *Le Monde* article that consolidates the idea that the events were in fact a boost for the *patronat* rather than the working class as they forced the former to modernize and improve.[80] This text is an example of how whilst the depiction of the events is narrowed it is nonetheless being shaped by those ideas prominent around the anniversary commemorations. However, it is worth pointing out that such notions would remain, as can be confirmed by the fact that the same content is regurgitated in the 1992 Hachette edition. In terms of the transition from one edition to the next, the 1989 Hatier text provides a revealing example of a narrowing perspective. There is very little change from the 1983 edition with the usual build-up and the account of the events focusing on the three phases. The only differences can be found in the use of the same dossier entitled *La Crise de mai–juin 1968*. Whilst mirroring the strengths and weaknesses of the earlier edition, one cannot help but note the omission of two particular documents. The first is an excerpt from Georges Marchais' 3 May 1968 *Humanité* article[81] and the second is a section of Pompidou's *Pour établir une vérité*.[82] The exclusion of these two documents can be interpreted as symbolizing the progressively reductive nature of the coverage as time elapses. The complexities of the student/PCF relationship and the intricacies of the Grenelle negotiations, as initially covered by both texts, do little to contribute to the consolidation of the dominant narrative and as such are easily left aside in the later edition. The Istra and Gammaprim *Histoire Terminales* texts of this time can be cited to confirm that the dominant line at the period was one that focused on the clichés.[83] Paris is prevalent and the regions are absent; *mai* is to the fore and *juin* forgotten; students dominate and the strike is airbrushed. All of these features are prominent in the conventional account of the events that is increasingly discernible across numerous school history textbooks (regardless of the publishers) as well as other important vectors and which was not to be without influence ten years later.

1998 – The May 1968 industry

By May 1998, France was again in the throes of *cohabitation*. A miscalculated Chirac gamble in calling a snap general election in 1997 led to a surprise Socialist victory and the nomination of their leader Lionel Jospin as prime minister. Despite the continuing problem of unemployment and economic constraints forced on France as she attempted to meet requirements for European monetary union, the first year or so of Jospin's government was relatively successful and popular. The intervening period did throw up some upheaval that reflected opinions in relation to the 1968 events. In 1995, the then prime minister Alain Juppé attempted to push through austerity reforms only to be met with the most significant wave of protest and strikes since (and therefore led to inevitable comparisons with) 1968. However, despite such attempts to find similarities, many pointed to the fact that in 1968 protestors wanted to overturn the system in place whereas in 1995 they were fighting to hold on to their situation within it. By 1998, the events of 1968 were very much in the past and the general consensus was that there was little sense in comparing current conditions with those of this (now accepted) exceptional period. The thirtieth anniversary of the events saw the most significant resurgence in literature to date. However, many of the texts released were re-editions of previous accounts of the crisis as the commemorative 'industry' took hold.[84] Other re-publications highlight the stagnant nature of the debate on the 1968 events, with ten-year-old analyses remaining amongst the most prominent.[85] Whilst some new publications did little to further the debate,[86] two texts in particular do allow an appreciation of the direction the history of May/June 1968 had taken.[87]

In *Mai 68, la Révolution fiction,* Jacques Tarnero places much emphasis on the importance of young people in the events, their frustration with the authoritarian regime of the time and the mounting dominance of the consumer society and opposition to it amongst this baby-boom generation.[88] The influence of international developments is given particular attention in defining this generation's characteristics on both a cultural and political level. Paris is the main focus of attention, there is a limited assessment of the strike and one notes the virtual absence of any description or analysis of the events of June 1968. A party-like, fictional revolution, played out principally by young people in opposition to the consumer society without any real leadership or direction, the events are described as having aided the system they were rebelling against with any successes attributed to the revolt remaining limited.[89]

Jean-Pierre le Goff's *Mai 68, l'héritage impossible,* concentrating on extreme left-wing students, examines the prelude to the crisis, the events themselves and their aftermath as well as their significance in the evolution of French society. By focusing its analysis strictly on the role played by *gauchiste* militants, it reinforces the growing limitations of the way the events are portrayed. Particular attention is paid to the rise in ecology movements, feminism and a changing attitude to education as the most tangible influences of the 1968 events.[90] The ambivalent importance of 1968 in the evolution of France is underlined together with its positive impact. Emphasizing the jovial, fraternal and party-like nature of the events, le Goff details the paradox between the utopian ideals expressed by *soixantehuitards* and the conformism, liberalism and individualism it has helped introduce in France in the years since.[91] By 1998 the mould had been set, and these two texts are pertinent examples of this trend. Little attention is paid to the strike or involvement of the working class. The limited consequences and the argument that the crisis somehow boosted the system it was fighting are reiterated. The thirtieth anniversary marked a consolidation of the historical view of 1968 that had been begun in its immediate aftermath and is reflected in the TV coverage, filmic representations and its treatment in school textbooks at this time.

Romain Goupil's 1998 film *A Mort la Mort,* which tells the story of a forty-something editor Thomas (played by Goupil) and the lives and deaths of his band of friends and acquaintances, fits the thirtieth-anniversary trend.[92] The one common denominator that binds together the diverse group of characters in this film is the fact that they all experienced the 1968 events. As well as portraying the eventful relationships that Thomas has with his friends, the major theme – as the title suggests – is death. The opening scenes in the cemetery set the tone as the film goes on to be punctuated with a number of funerals. Furthermore, suicide is more often than not the common cause of death and there are several failed suicide attempts. In what is at times a bizarre dramatic comedy, one is able to identify clear traits that reflect the mood of the time vis-à-vis the 1968 events and in so doing consolidate the dominant narrative. One of the most prevalent notions that comes through is that surrounding the idea of a generation and in particular how that of 1968 continues to struggle with remaining loyal to their past ideas. Given the number of deaths and suicide attempts it is clear that this is proving more than difficult. The stereotypical depiction of the 1968 generation as irresponsible is by no means challenged as the major protagonists show scant regard for fidelity, sexual liberation remains a core principle and their general attitude to life is one that remains out of sync with the rest of society. It is also noteworthy that in addition to the idea of a specific generation of 1968, the people that represent it are carefully chosen to portray a certain idea of the type of people it was composed of. Not only are they those that by this stage have come to dominate perceptions, they are also those that have been at the forefront of perpetuating the narrow portrayal. This is strikingly evident in the opening scenes when the 1968 generation gathered at the funeral includes people such as Daniel Cohn-Bendit, Henri Weber, André Glucksmann and Daniel Bensaid.

The idea of a generation incapable of coming to terms with its past is equally prominent in Philippe Garrel's 1999 *La Vent de la nuit*.[93] In this film, a young art student (Paul) who is having an affair with an older woman (Helène, played by Catherine Deneuve) meets a successful architect (Serge). As Serge and Paul get to know each other during their interminable road trips, the former reveals his substantial involvement in the 1968 events and, despite his obvious success since, is clearly having difficulty equating his past with current day society. Paul is intrigued by Serge's past – particularly the drugs and violence he associates with 1968 – while Serge is clearly more concerned about how this era is looked upon by younger generations. Despite finally meeting and sharing an evening with Helène which for both characters provides some grounds for happiness at last, the film ends – inevitably – with Serge's suicide. Throughout, Serge, who could be interpreted as representing the 1968 generation, is morose, down-beat, regretful and clearly mentally insecure – all traits that further underscore the emerging dominant discourse surrounding the events.

The thirtieth anniversary unsurprisingly saw a spate of television documentaries and programmes that contributed to the emerging consensus surrounding the events. For example, France 2's *Débat Mai 68: D'une Génération à l'autre*, which brings together a number of 'usual suspects' and their children, examines the idea of how young people perceive the generation of 1968.[94] France 3's *La Preuve par Trois. Mai 68 a 30 ans, et alors?* questions the real impact of the events, highlighting the vast differences that separate 1998 from 1968.[95] However, most notable is the omnipresence of Daniel Cohn-Bendit, who, in view of his monopolization of media coverage, has, by 1998, clearly become the veritable face of *mai 68*. Not only does he appear as a guest in a wide range of shows and on the news; he even has an entire show dedicated to himself; *Dany dans tous ses états*.[96] Nevertheless, not everything produced simply perpetuated the dominant trend. For example, Patrick Rotman and Virginie Linhart's documentary *Mai 68. Dix semaines qui ébran-lèrent la France* is a very detailed and complete historical account that manages to avoid an over-emphasis on the stereotypical elements.[97] However, perhaps the most significant piece that very much goes against the grain at this time is Hervé le Roux's 1997 film *Reprise*.[98]

In this refreshingly novel approach to the events, le Roux sets out on a mission to track down a female worker who featured prominently in a short film *Reprise du travail aux usines Wonder* shot by IDHEC (*Institut des hautes études cinématographiques*) students at the exact moment in 1968 the workers at the Wonder factory ended their strike and returned to work. In his investigation, le Roux travels the country interviewing other people who featured in the short film and those who worked at the factory at the time in a bid to track down the young woman. Despite failing to find the elusive Jocelyne, *Reprise* provides a fascinating and novel insight into an all too often forgotten element of the 1968 events. Unlike the majority of coverage to date, it is not focused on a select band of Parisian, *gauchiste* students recounting the heady days of their youth. Instead, we are re-introduced to the anonymous side of 1968, the aspect that has over the course of thirty years been airbrushed from its history and memory. What *Reprise* reminds us is that 1968 existed beyond the Sorbonne and the Latin Quarter and that it had a profound impact on people other than the media celebrities that have appropriated its memory. *Reprise* certainly demonstrated that the thirty years' distance was perhaps beginning to force analysts to take a step back and see the broader picture of the 1968 events. However, the reality is that, given the plethora of material it was up against that continued to perpetuate, confirm and consolidate the narrow, limited and telescopic focus of the dominant narrative, it would require more than one film to reverse a trend that was seemingly increasingly rooted and would prove difficult to overcome. No more was such a trend evident than in press coverage on the thirtieth anniversary. Despite the veritable boom in coverage and the opportunity afforded by the opening of police archives, little emerged to match the fresh perspective of *Reprise*. Whilst special editions in *L'Express* and *Le Nouvel Observateur* promised much, they are in fact indicative of how the stereotypical view was generally bolstered by this medium.[99]

The thirtieth anniversary coincided with the publication of a new set of history textbooks that once again provide valuable insights into the direction of representations of the events. As a contrast between the Betrand Lacoste and Nathan editions shows, the extent and quality of coverage was not uniform.[100] In the former, which, like many editions, includes a separate dossier on the events, there is no major departure from the dominant narrative. Despite flagging up the interpretation debate and asking questions as to the legacy of the events, overall, one is struck by the dearth of detailed analysis and the use of dated material that only confirms the consensus. The Nathan edition does attempt to push the debate slightly further. However, its dossier, entitled *Mai 1968, Crise politique ou Crise culturelle*, whilst tentatively asking searching questions through the use of critical material, nevertheless focuses heavily on a limited chronology and a Paris-based perspective. When looking at other editions, it becomes evident – particularly when one considers the documents chosen to accompany 'the facts' – that a certain consensus exists on how the events are portrayed. Revelatory of this trend are the 1998 Hachette and Bordas editions.[101] Both texts, in their main chronological overview, do little to challenge the prevailing discourse on the events. The usual build-up focusing on the *usure du pouvoir* is followed by the surprise explosion that unfolds in the ever-prevalent three phases. Paris is the centre of attention with *gauchiste* students very much to the fore whilst the strike and the month of June are all but forgotten. It is, however, the selection of documents chosen in both editions for particular attention that is most indicative of the consolidation of the limited perspective.

In the Bordas edition, students are asked to carry out a *commentaire du photo*. The image chosen is that of a Parisian, student demonstration where one can pick out a range of banners with slogans such as *CRS-SS, France; Etat Policier* or *Vive Cohn-Bendit*. The image and the text within do not problematize the dominant perspective but instead consolidate it; the same can be said for *l'étude du document* in the Hachette edition. Here, students are given a transcription of de Gaulle's 7 June 1968 televised interview with Michel Droit. In it, the general gives his take on the crisis now that the worst seems to have passed. As a well-known admirer and supporter of de Gaulle, Droit does not exactly challenge the president. Instead, this interview could be described as little more than a party political broadcast for the UDR with the forthcoming election in mind. The general reduces the events to no more than a subversive movement that may have challenged him but ultimately against which he proved (once again) that he was up to the job. The choice of this interview together with the questions students are asked to respond to in relation to this document demonstrate a clear desire to highlight the role of de Gaulle and his great skill in overcoming the revolt and bringing it to a successful conclusion. This is a trend evident in other 1998 editions. For example, in Hatier's text, which provides a typically limited perspective focusing heavily on *gauchistes*, students are asked to respond to a set of questions related to a photograph of the 30 May, pro-Gaullist demonstration in Paris.[102] It is the importance of de Gaulle, his supporters' ideas and their dependence on him to save France from the events that is given most significance. There is little detail on the many other aspects of the events and, when there is, one is left with the impression that the country was faced with a violent, anti-France revolt. The impact on current attitudes cannot have been without significance and, as examples from two other editions demonstrate, such an impact was clearly a point for consideration. In the Belin and Bréal 1998 editions, the typical coverage no longer surprises.[103] The usual chronology, the focus on Paris, the lack of coverage of June and the strike (the Belin edition manages to pass directly from 13 to 27 May), the highlighting of clichéd posters, slogans and documents all drive home the consolidation of the dominant discourse. It is, however, the reference to current attitudes that is most revealing. If the Belin text asks the question whether or not the 1968 movement's 'aspirations remain relevant',[104] the Bréal edition provides the answer when describing how 'the youth of today look at it with a degree of astonishment'.[105] Given the telescopic focus on the spectacular elements of the events, one can frankly not be surprised.

It is possible therefore to see just how, in the thirty-year period between 1968 and 1998, the nature of the extensive coverage afforded to the events has been progressively narrowed. Through the range of vectors outlined above, the significance of the events, their widespread nature, as well as their extensive impact, have been reduced. The nationwide crisis that involved so many sectors of French society, young and old, that led to the largest strike in French history and threatened the regime in power has not been represented as such.

The collective memory

'Mai 68' is a particularly useful case study in memory debates for a number of reasons. The period since 1968 has coincided with the rise of the fascination with the past as discussed above. It therefore provides an example untainted with previous memories through which to examine the formation, emergence and development of the representation of an historical moment and the subsequent impact on the collective memory. Pierre Nora highlighted the modern-day obsession with commemorations as evidence of the heightened interest in the past and how in particular, 'May '68 [. . .] embodied the empire of the commemorative memory' in an 'Era of Commemoration'.[106] John Bodnar is one of many to also have discussed the significance of commemorative practices in memory studies.[107] As demonstrated in the overview above, the 1968 events are a perfect example of such a trend with the decennial anniversaries of 1978, 1988 and 1998 providing periodic opportunities for an assessment of the relationship between history and memory. In order to understand such a relationship, one must consider the interplay between history and memory as an ongoing process, the initial stages of which are fundamental.

Questions have been asked as to whether or not such immediate focus on an event can be considered as history as the required *recul* is absent for any objective assessment to emerge.[108] However, it is argued here that the so-called *histoire du temps présent* is critically important in relation to the collective memory of an historical moment or event. It is during this early period that living memory and historical framing come together and lay the foundations of the collective memory. The thirty years between 1968 and 1998 are therefore a perfect example of what can be described as the formative period of the collective memory of the 1968 events. Their potency as an example of such a process is strengthened when one considers the role that those directly involved have had during this period. The *soixantehuitards* have played a prominent part, particularly during the anniversary surges, in shaping, consolidating and developing a certain image of *mai 68*. Nevertheless, despite the early rooting of a certain general perspective, it would be inaccurate to claim that representations have remained unchanged. In fact, through the periodic reappraisals, one is able to delineate a certain trajectory in the events' history. In order to make sense of why such changes have occurred and how we are nevertheless left with a sense of continuity, it is useful to begin with a consideration of the ideas of one of the leading theorists on collective memory, Maurice Halbwachs.

In *Les Cadres Sociaux de la Mémoire* and *La Mémoire Collective* Maurice Halbwachs pioneered the notion of collective memory.[109] As well as identifying memory as a group construct, the most influential aspect of his theory concerns the relationship between past and present. For Halbwachs, collective memory is not set in stone but is instead, as described by Lewis A. Coser in the introduction of his translation of *La Mémoire Collective*, 'shaped by the concerns of the present'.[110] Such changes are determined by what he describes as social frameworks. These *cadres* can be viewed as the determining factors moulding the collective memory; a filter through which decisions over what is included and what is omitted are made. These parameters are, for Halbwachs, 'the instruments used by the collective memory to reconstruct an image of the past which is in accord, in each epoch, with the predominant thoughts of the society'.[111] Therefore, in order to understand the journey of a certain event's history and memory one must consider the contextual developments experienced over time, for, as James E. Young highlights: 'The motives of memory are never pure.'[112] Most analysts now accept the notion that the image of a historical event at any given time is not the result of pure coincidence or something that has remained static from an early stage but instead, as described by Robert Gildea, 'a construction of the past elaborated by a political community for its own ends'.[113] Therefore, in the example of the 1968 events, by using the three decennial anniversaries, one is able to discern shifts in the dominant discourse that can be linked to contextual circumstances. By 1978, the preceding collapse of ideologies that had underpinned *gauchisme* can help explain the negativity that so tempered the tenth anniversary. The 1988 presidential election campaign, dominated by two figures unlikely to over-emphasize the significance of 1968, and the focus of commemorative fervour on the upcoming bicentenary of the French Revolution, paved the way for the selective *génération soixantehuitarde* to consolidate its grasp during the twentieth anniversary. By 1998, a programme of austerity measures and privatizations under the Chirac–Jospin *cohabitation* had underscored the intangibility of 1968-style ideals. Such a consolidation of that era's exceptionalism saw the dominant narrative gain even greater credence at a time when the events themselves became a product in the emerging 1968 industry.

Whilst the Halbwachian notion of reconstruction of the past determined by the present is certainly applicable to the memory of 1968, it nevertheless could be interpreted as leaving it completely hostage to present day concerns. Taken by the letter, such a theory suggests the possibility of a complete sea change in the collective memory from one period to the next. This would imply the absence of a continuous thread over time. However, as the example of May 1968 demonstrates, despite the unquestionable developments in the events' history (and therefore memory), one can nevertheless see that from an early stage a core discourse has been consistently present regardless of contextual changes. Barry Schwartz and Jeffrey Olick have demonstrated the importance of such continuity through examples of commemorations of people and events in the US Capitol and the 1945 Commemorations in Federal Germany.[114] The basic premise centres on the idea that one commemorative period cannot exist in isolation from – or without being influenced by – those that have come before. Even when contextual shifts have led to a complete overhaul in a nation's relationship with the past, the nature of previous commemorations leaves an ineffaceable imprint. New elements can be introduced and emphasis shifted, but the core discourse remains. Therefore, and as described by Olick 'we must not treat these histories as successions of discrete moments, one present-to-past relation after another; images of the past depend not only on the present but also on the accumulation of previous such relationships and their ongoing constitution and reconstitution'.[115] In the case of the 1968 events, not only has this core representation remained, but the shifts brought about by contextual changes have further embedded the predominant over-arching interpretation and reading. The framework that has shaped representations of the 1968 events in France was, as demonstrated, established very early on. Since then, the majority of the events' history has been filtered through this paradigm. The wide-ranging vectors through which the history and memory of 1968 have been developing have not only remained within that framework but the contextual changes have both maintained it and in many respects reduced its scope. This explains the ever-narrowing perspective of the events' history with inevitable consequences for the collective memory. However, a certain specificity that sets the journey of the 1968 events' history and memory apart from the examples of Olick and Schwartz necessitates examination in order to fully understand how and why the French collective memory of 'May '68' has emerged as it has.

As Halbwachs and others have argued, the reconstruction of the past that inevitably impinges on collective memory is done so in order to suit the agenda of the powers that be.[116] From a French perspective, Gildea argues how, through the examples of Franco-US relations, the Franco-German axis and the issue of decolonization, 'policy goals have a decisive influence on how memory is constructed'.[117] One can understand how the dominant narrative of the 1968 events has suited consecutive governments over the years. In the immediate aftermath, the depiction of the events as an irrational 'psychodrama' led by extreme left-wing students intent on wreaking havoc before eventually being brought to heel by the president surely helped de Gaulle survive in the short term and arguably consolidated the institutions of the Fifth Republic. Since then it has not been in the interests of any president or government to challenge the dominant narrative. Airbrushing the full magnitude of the crisis from popular perception negates any potential influence as an example to be followed. Over the years, the state would not have been served by any exposure of the true magnitude, diversity and potency of the 1968 events. *Mai 68* is one episode in a long French tradition that places *la rue* as an important and not to be ignored arena in how the country is governed. However, the conventional representation as a Parisian, *gauchiste*-led student rebellion starkly reduces its potential influence. For example, the eradication of the general strike from the 1968 story has made it less of an inspiration for the working class and increasingly the preserve of the more elite social classes. Additionally, its portrayal as a momentary rush of blood to the head by a spoilt generation during a time of full employment and unprecedented growth has made it virtually impossible for subsequent generations to relate to what happened and see it as a source of inspiration. Therefore, instead of serving as an example of a mass revolt that brought people together on a nationwide scale and encompassed all sectors of French society, the events have become no more than a blip, an exceptional and unreasonable jolt, any repeat of which is impossible and even in some cases undesirable. However, unlike the examples drawn on by Olick and Schwartz, between 1968 and 1998, the state has not had any direct influence on how the commemorative periods have been characterized; there has been no official, state-sponsored commemoration of the 1968 events in France.

Instead, and as demonstrated, the anniversary celebrations have been dominated by a certain group of *soixantehuitards*; 'self-declared and elected by the media, they are held up as the spokespeople of the generation'.[118] Taking the example of a debate over an exhibition on Hiroshima and Nagasaki at the National Air and Space Museum (NASM) in Washington, James Wertsch reveals the power that actual participants have when determining how a certain event is remembered. He highlights how public opinion favoured the views of the Second World War veterans drawing on autobiographical memory over those of professional historians.[119] Such an example can be applied to the French collective memory of *mai 68*. The voices of those that have become widely recognized as the 'veterans' of the events have 'reverberated much more strongly' than any others. This lends weight to the argument that such 'experience often seems to give those that lived through the events a particular status in cultural and political debates'.[120] These 'usual suspects' have propagated a certain representation of the revolt that has gone unchallenged by the state. As the years have passed, the select band of Parisian-based former militants has been complicit, if not fundamental, in the progressive reduction of the events' portrayal. In order to understand how and why this has been the case, one has to consider the post-'68 trajectories of those that have become the faces of *mai 68*.

First, this exclusive group has become representative of an iconic revolt that many consider as the most significant historical moment of the post-war era. This has meant that (as well as the kudos of being held up as leaders of such a revolt that some of them clearly revel in) many of these figures have gone on to have successful careers as politicians, journalists or academics. Consequently, they have been much better placed to get across their version of the events than the anonymous *piétons*.[121] Cubitt explains how the shaping of the past is the result of tensions and contestations where:

> *understandings of the past that appear to be dominant in a given society at a given moment will be the product [. . .] of complex political interactions, in which different interests vie for ascendancy, influence and survival – and in which some interests will be more successful at asserting themselves than others.* '[122]

He goes on to highlight how '[a]ccess to the media through which transmission of information is effected, and motivations to use those media to influence the way the past can be viewed, are not evenly distributed within society'.[123] As Gedi and Elam argue: 'In reality [. . .] social dynamics is at work by which, often enough, certain individuals or a group of individuals, powerful and presumptuous enough, take over and assign themselves as the spokesmen of this so-called "society".'[124] In the case of 1968, that certain group has been made up of the former Paris-based *gauchistes*. Their dominance of the history and memory of *mai 68* is unsurprising. Not only is their access to the avenues through which to get their message across facilitated by their social standing, as argued by Patrick Demerin, their version of the events both suits the state and is consistently a source of attraction and fascination for the media:

> *The quest for advertising revenue encourages producers to invite the 'stars' rather than the 'foot soldiers'. Such choices have nevertheless also reflected precise social and political ideals. The 'commemorated stars' through their adherence to such principles serve to strengthen them.*[125]

A further telling element in explaining how the dominant discourse has prevailed concerns the role of the communist left in its emergence. As detailed in chapter two, it is widely accepted that the PCF/CGT duo was both a major obstacle to the expansion of the 1968 revolt and in many respects pivotal in bringing closure to it. Such a consensus finds it origins in the PCF interpretation during the events themselves. Seeing it as a *gauchiste*-inspired revolt that risked undermining long-term communist policy, the PCF held back any support. Over the course of the events there may have been a certain degree of softening in PCF/student relations but there is little or no real debate over the fact that the former largely opposed the latter. Whilst some have argued that the communist interpretation has changed from one of opposition to understanding, assimilation and in some respects a certain degree of *récupération*, it is important to note that in the early formative years, there was little or no real deviation from the 1968 line and this was not without consequence for conventional representation.[126] By virtually ruling out its own investment in the revolt, the PCF helped propagate a narrow image of the events. Given the strength of the PCF/CGT at the time, the portrayal of them in opposition to the *gauchistes* underscored and over-emphasized the role of this minority element whilst pushing the significance of the part played by any other participants (and significantly the working class) further and further into the background.

By simultaneously writing itself out of the narrative whilst overplaying the role of *gauchiste* students, the communist left paved the way for representatives of the latter to come along and monopolize how the story of 1968 would be told. They became the faces of *mai 68* and as demonstrated went on to be pivotal. As the years have unfolded, contextual changes have meant that the communist left has been able to afford more significance to the events of 1968.[127] However, by this stage their capacity to have any real impact on how they were portrayed was significantly curtailed for a number of reasons. First, it would be very difficult – given the widely held consensus surrounding how the PCF was a major obstacle for the movement of 1968 – for the communist left to credibly reverse its discourse. Second, given the enthusiasm with which former *gauchistes* have seized the initiative to ensure that they became the representatives of this movement, it would prove impossible for the communist left to undo the emerging consensus that it itself had been crucial in creating. In line with Olick and Schwartz's theory concerning the maintenance of a core discourse, the communist left, by allowing the 'usual suspects' to dominate, contributed to the creation and consolidation of a dominant perspective that has been a constant in the years since 1968. The difficulties of a U-turn on the communist line and the challenge of overcoming a narrative increasingly set in stone have been exacerbated by the inextricable demise of the PCF over the last thirty years. Such a decline has undermined the possibility of a revised communist interpretation impinging with any real conviction on the popular narrative.

Those that have been most pivotal in shaping the common image represent just one, very small element of the 1968 revolt that espoused very radical, *gauchiste*-inspired ideas. Quite soon after the events (and in particular by the time of the first decennial anniversary) the foundations of their ideologies had been undermined by international events and were devoid of any credibility. They nevertheless continued to be held up as representatives of the 1968 generation. Contextual changes forced a softening of their rhetoric that subsequently cleared the path for the emergence of the dominant discourse that they would be fundamental in consolidating. The very people considered as those that best represent the events have consistently been at the forefront of ensuring that future generations would not consider *mai 68* as a source of inspiration. In so doing *les soixantehuitards* have reduced the potential for a challenge to the system that they have clearly done so well in.

What has emerged then is an unlikely tango between the state and the *soixantehuitards* that has been driving the progressively narrow, stereotypical and limited perspective of the events. The dominant portrayal, propagated by the select (and unrepresentative) few, has not been challenged by the state as it has consistently suited its agenda as much as it has the former *gauchistes*. That there has been no official, state-sponsored commemoration of *mai 68* is not simply because it is something the state would not consider worthy of celebration. One must also take into consideration the fact that the nature of the events' portrayal in the 'unofficial' commemorations poses no difficulties. With the characteristics of the doxa becoming and remaining, in the words of Schwartz, 'convenient objects of consensus' there is no reason for the state to intervene.[128] The closest one can get to some sort of official discourse is that which can be found in school textbooks on the topic; 'the mode of social transmission of memory par excellence'.[129] However, as demonstrated, there is nothing therein that challenges the dominant narrative. In fact, if anything it follows it very closely and as such is a perfect example of how the ongoing and symbiotic relationship between the history and memory of the 1968 events has facilitated the construction of a convenient consensus.

Conclusion

The debate concerning the inadequate manner in which the events have been portrayed over the years is certainly nothing new. Indeed, since – in particular – the twentieth anniversary, many questions have been asked of the historical analyses of May/June 1968.

Ambiguity surrounding the portrayal of the events was a prominent feature in both literature and media representations in 1988. In a series of articles published in *Le Débat*, a reassessment of the events comes under the title *Le Mystère 68*[130] which, focusing on the difficulties associated with gaining a real understanding of the crisis, highlights the ambiguity of analyses of the events of which the history remains incomplete.[131] Antoine Prost, in *Quoi de neuf sur le Mai français?*, examines new material on 1968 that can shed some light on an area he considers to be devoid of quality analysis.[132] Luisa Passerini's *Peut-on donner de 1968 une histoire à la première personne?*, of the same year, is equally critical of the poor quality of literature produced in the fifteen years since the crisis, pointing in particular to the lack of objectivity to explain the difficulties involved in interpreting the events.[133] In *Mai 68 raconté aux enfants*, Jean-Franklin Narot questions the plethora of literature that has only managed to minimize the importance of 1968 and the diversity of the various movements.[134] He highlights the negative impact of those who have come to represent 1968, particularly during the mediatized commemorations. In *Un anniversaire interminable: 1968–1988*, Daniel Lindenberg describes the periodic assessments of the crisis as doing little to improve understanding and, like the events themselves, have become no more than a talk-shop.[135] Equally critical of the anniversary 'celebrations' is Patrick Demerin in *Mai 68–Mai 88. Choses tues* in which he describes the periodic misrepresentation of the crisis as a typically French trait of manipulating past events to suit their needs.[136]

Such negative appraisals of how the events have been portrayed have continued beyond the twentieth anniversary. Jean-Pierre Rioux's *A propos des célébrations décennales du mai français* depicts the manner in which the periodic celebrations of the events force us to assess them in a particular way, leading to a lack of genuine appreciation.[137] Gilles Bousquet's *Où en est-on de mai 68?* is revelatory of the frustration concerning the distinct lack of comprehension despite the advantages of time and the undeniably vast amounts of literature dedicated to assessing what happened in 1968.[138] Isabelle Sommier's *Mai 68, sous les pavés d'une page officielle* examines the construction of an 'official history' of 1968 devoid of analyses of some of the most significant factors.[139] However, since then and – as the above analysis shows – despite the huge influx of texts coinciding with the events' thirtieth anniversary, no significant change in direction as to how they are assessed has been undertaken. Instead, topical debates concerning 1968 have seen the crisis held responsible for the social ills of twenty-first-century French society.[140] Whilst this debate, amongst others, including the recent assessment of the influence of 1968 on left-wing ideology,[141] has revealed the continued relevance of, and interest in, 1968, such approaches have done little to address the problems outlined concerning the lack of complete analysis. They have as such perpetuated the dominance of the now generally accepted, stereotypical and narrow history of the 1968 events that underpins the convenient consensus.

As with all significant moments in history, 1968 has been the focus of intense debate. However, as the above analysis demonstrates, that surrounding *mai 68*, despite being characterized by a huge amount of interest bolstered by periodic reassessments and continued relevance, has led to the dominance of a specifically limited portrayal of what occurred, why and its consequences. When one considers the characteristics of the 'official' history of 1968 (Paris, students, bourgeois, etc. . . .) compared to the complete nature of the events that touched every region, every social class and so many of the nation's most important institutions, the shortcomings are clear. However, the now traditional periodic reassessments of the 1968 events offer continual opportunities for the reappraisal of their history. Such periodically recurrent windows of opportunity are just some of the many specificities of an event whose 'interpretative and analytical history [. . .] shows no signs of having said its last word'.[142] As the next chapter demonstrates, it is nevertheless this history and its incompleteness that has been crucial in shaping how young people perceive the events today.

Chapter Two
1968: consensus and disagreement

Introduction

The following chapter provides an assessment of areas of agreement and dis-agreement in analyses of the 1968 events and suggests how such factors have influenced current attitudes. One is struck by the fact that, in spite of the huge amount of work that has been produced, many areas still remain devoid of consensus. Whether one considers the events themselves, their consequences, interpretations or explanations, it is quite difficult, if not impossible, to find real consensus. As Joan Brandt observes: 'The many tracts, documentaries and analyses that have been published over the years serve only to underscore the complete lack of agreement among critics as to the ultimate meaning of those events.'[1]

When discussing the controversial issue of the 'devoir de memoire' concerning the deportation of Jews during the Second World War in France, Olivier Lalieu highlights how over the years 'debate remains as the history is written'.[2] A similar notion can be applied to the history of *mai 68*. As time has passed, opinions on the 1968 events, influenced by ideas and interpretations that have become accepted or taken for granted, have developed and evolved.[3] With such an abundance of texts, articles, film and television documentaries concerning 1968, the result has been that the actual history of May has become unclear. Areas of disagreement have emerged and it has therefore become quite difficult to come to any solid conclusions on certain areas. The result, as Ross indicates, has been paradoxical: '[I]n the case of '68, an enormous amount of narrative labor – and not a shroud of silence – has facilitated the active forgetting of the events in France.'[4] Whilst 1968 has proved to be a prolific source of debate spawning innumerable analyses, a certain mystery still appears to surround a complete understanding of it. Although the exist-ence of so many texts has served to heighten confusion and fuel debate, it has also had a positive impact. The periodic reassessment of the events and the fact that they remain a constant source for discussion has led to a proliferation of ideas. Consequently, there is no shortage of material permitting a broad understanding of what happened and why; as well as some appreciation of the legacy of 1968 for the many French institutions it has influenced. The exist-ence of such 'consensus' issues has been pivotal in shaping how 1968 is perceived today, particularly through the emergence of the dominant narrative.

Consensus issues

When examining 1968, there is little difficulty in pinpointing the various sources of anxiety, frustration and malaise that were influential in triggering the events. Such an exercise is common in most texts that analyse the crisis.[5] Politically, it is often argued that, in spite of the fact that France was experiencing a period of prolonged stability, discontent was mounting. The focus of frustrations was Charles de Gaulle who, having been in power for ten years, had become a source of tension amongst the population. It is claimed that the general feeling was that de Gaulle had done the job he had been asked to do, in other words solve the colonial problems and install some sort of political authority and stability, and that it was time for him to step aside in order to allow France to move with the times.[6] Prominent descriptions of the public mood in the late 1960s centre on the idea that his authoritarian style of leadership was dated and it was time for France to modernize, beginning with a less anachronistic style of governance where the population should have more of a say in the running of the nation. From an economic perspective, after an undoubted period of expansion, the French economy was beginning to experience difficulties that it had not known since the Second World War.[7] The threat of unemployment is described as an important source of this anxiety. Several large strikes had flared up and industrial action had been increasing in the period before 1968, highlighting the fact that the economy was beginning to take a turn for the worse. The difference between high wage earners and those at the lower end of the scale was growing, and this led to a feeling of injustice caused by the belief that not everyone was benefiting from the modernization that the French economy had undergone throughout the 1960s.[8] The concentration of such economic and political problems is represented as having been most prevalent amongst the younger sections of the population.

This social phenomenon is often attributed to vast differences between generations and can perhaps explain the prominence of the idea of a 'generation clash'. The youth of the 1960s had had such a different upbringing to that of their parents that it could only lead to discord.[9] Not having experienced the horror of war, young people are described as having found it difficult to understand the need for such an authoritarian form of leadership. Equally, born into a society in full economic expansion, young people were used to having what they wanted materially and therefore lacked the same appreciation of sacrifice and priorities as their parents.[10] That the youth of the 1960s was highly influenced by events in other countries is unquestionable. Television had become an important way for the population to see what was happening throughout the world. When problems began to arise with the system in which they lived (whether in terms of university problems, frustration with the stagnant political situation, opposition to capitalist dominance or a perceived threat of unemployment), those offering a political and economic alternative became increasingly popular. Highly romantic and inspirational figures such as Castro, Che and Ho Chi Minh gave young people the belief that there was an alternative, one that was much more attractive than the Gaullist regime of the 1960s they viewed as ill-adapted to the needs of modern society.[11] The situation in the education system is portrayed as having heightened the desire of young people to challenge the status quo. The post-war baby-boom brought about an explosion in the number of people entering third-level education in the late 1960s and the government (despite some efforts)[12] had simply not done enough to deal with this massive increase in university enrolments.[13] Faculties became chronically overcrowded and, as a result of poor teacher– student relations and the idea that a university education was an inadequate preparation for the challenge of modern day society, a perfect breeding ground for rebelliousness was created.[14] Whilst much is commonly made of protests demanding *libre circulation*,[15] the inability of the university system to absorb such an increase in students added to increasing anxiety amongst young people concerning future employment prospects and helps to explain why the faculties served as the spark for the crisis of 1968.

The general consensus is that the upheaval resulted from the convergence of the factors outlined above. However, such an approach has facilitated a certain normalization of what happened and in turn has helped the material-ization of a progressively constricted outlook. Reducing the revolt to something with identifiable causes dilutes its *insaisissable* nature that made it so difficult to control and such a focus of interest and controversy.[16] Furthermore, the heavy emphasis on the university as the origin has led to an inappropriate promi-nence of students, i.e. only one element of what was a society-wide revolt. In addition, placing the French revolt within the context of an international upheaval arguably undermines its originality and reduces it to none other than a typically Gallicized extension of a worldwide jolt – or, as Guillebaud claims, 'the French (metropolitan, and all told "Parisian") version of a strange tremor that swept the planet'.[17] Such a representation highlights a further frequent and critical characteristic of the dominant narrative that is indicative of its limitations.

France saw upheaval across the country with every region experiencing the events in its own way with varying motivations behind its diverse demands.[18] Whilst students from the Latin Quarter were instrumental in triggering the crisis, the subsequent wholesale revolt revealed the existence of a general social malaise. However, when examining the conditions that led to 1968 considerable emphasis is placed on Parisian experiences, with the capital seemingly seen as representative of the nation as a whole.[19] Consequently, little is known of the true magnitude of the nationwide insurrection, the driving forces behind provincial revolts and the ensuing impact of 1968 on regional issues.[20] The overriding depiction is one of a principally Parisian student move-ment that precipitated a general strike. Only when the focus moves to the widespread nature of the strike movement do regional divergences receive, admittedly limited, coverage.[21] The underlying characteristics of regional student and social movements are ignored and provincial events are repre-sented as evolving strictly in relation to the unfolding developments in the capital.[22] This approach has helped to mould the characteristics of the limited representation that prevails today. Such conclusions can equally be drawn from how the events themselves are analysed and recounted.

It is generally agreed that the events fell into three specific phases.[23] Phase one, which has become known as the 'student crisis', runs from 3 to 13 May. It includes the period beginning with the police intervention in the courtyard of the Sorbonne on 3 May, the escalating violence and rise in support for the student movement culminating in the infamous 'Night of the Barricades' on 10 May. It was as a result of this night of terrible violence and extreme police brutality that the one-day strike (supported by all the unions) and the massive demonstration of 13 May were organized.[24] The second phase, between 14 and 27 May, is known as the 'social crisis'. Throughout this stage, the one-day stoppage expanded to an all-out general strike in which France was brought to a complete standstill. It is characterized by the different attitudes of the two major unions, the CFDT (*Confédération française démocratique du travail*) and the CGT, and the inability of the communist-controlled union to stop the spreading of the strikes. The powerlessness of Pompidou and de Gaulle in dealing with the situation and the eventual rejection of the Grenelle agreements on 27 May gave the impression, briefly, that the state had exhausted all possible avenues to a resolution.[25] The events then moved into their shortest, yet most critical, phase. The political crisis, from 27 to 30 May, saw France on the brink of an overthrow of the Gaullist regime. This chapter is distinguished by the president's mysterious trip to Baden-Baden, the failure of the Left to find common ground, the general's eventual return, his defiant address to the nation and the subsequent massive demonstration in support of him. It is common for this rise of the 'silent majority' on 30 May in support of de Gaulle to be described as the moment that brought the curtain down on the events of 1968. Charting the amplification of the 1968 revolt using these three phases allows for an appreciation of the manner with which the upheaval spread so quickly across so many sectors of French society. However, by dividing the events into three separate crises, it is possible to glean the impression that there was no real convergence of participants and their ideas. The pre-eminent portrayal suggests that there was virtually no contact between workers, students and politicians. This notion has aided the concretization of the belief that the student 'movement', incapable of providing a viable political alternative, was hijacked by a working-class movement that was only really ever interested in material gains. The possibility of the 1968 revolt posing any significant threat to the political status quo of the time is consequently undermined. The effects of this quite rigid, chronological overview are not restricted to undermining any possible interaction between the diverse participants. Limitations can also be perceived through the virtual absence of coverage of what took place in June 1968.

As mentioned earlier, the majority of analyses regard the general's speech on 30 May as spelling the end of the crisis. What happened in the weeks that followed is little analysed. With such minimal coverage one could be forgiven for believing that what occurred in June was of no significance. This, of course, is not the case. The events leading up to the general election at the end of June could be considered as less exciting or romantic than what happened during May. However, this period was not without notable incident. After all, it was during June that 1968 saw its first fatalities that could be directly associated with the events. The police cranked up the violence to bring the strike to an end and to ensure the smooth running of the election campaign. The Sorbonne, the Théâtre de l'Odéon and other occupied buildings were cleared of demonstrators.[26] It was then that the government implemented some of the most oppressive measures.[27] Many left-wing groups were outlawed,[28] the sale of their newspapers was forbidden, demonstrations were banned and the government benefited from the help of groups like the CDR (*Compagnies de défense de la République*) and the SAC (*Service d'action civique*) to guarantee that there would no longer be any chance of the movement starting up again.[29] Yet, as Capdevielle and Mouriaux point out: 'Rare are those that speak of the events of May–June 1968.'[30] One can only speculate as to why this has become the case. It is arguably easier for all concerned to focus on the spectacular, romantic and positive elements of May as opposed to the more negative June 1968. In the light of the heightened degree of violence, the deaths and the realization that the revolt was coming to an end, it is no real surprise that June is increasingly absent from the focus of the 'May 1968 industry'. Whether calculated or not, the elimination of June 1968 does little to provide a complete picture of the events. The simple fact that what happened in this spring of 1968 is all too often described as the events of '*May* '68' and not often enough the events of '*May–June* 1968' only serves to underline the scant importance attached to a vital period of the overall crisis. Analysts appear to concur as to the structure of how the events should be presented. However, as with the causes, the increasing dominance of a certain method to analyzing the crisis has arguably facilitated the emanation of a stereotypical image of it that has progressively minimized its seriousness and significance. Such a reductionist consequence is equally apparent when considering the level of consensus surrounding the role of some of the major protagonists.

It is widely accepted that the French Communist Party and its trade union, over which it had supreme control, played an extremely important role in the events of 1968. The paradox is that the policy of the PCF, in name at least a revolutionary party, was one of the major reasons for the failure of the 1968 crisis becoming a revolution. From the beginning of the events, the PCF was strongly opposed to the movement. Their initial attitude regarding the student movement is often summed up by an article published in the Communist newspaper *L'Humanité* on 3 May 1968 by the future leader of the PCF, Georges Marchais, entitled 'False revolutionaries to be unmasked'.[31] During the 'student crisis' the PCF did all in its power to differentiate itself from what it considered as irresponsible left-wing elements and encouraged the working class not to become involved with them. When the events moved into the second phase, the PCF realized that they would not be able to stop the spread of the general strike. They subsequently ensured that students were kept at a distance and that the strike's aims were limited to purely material demands. Seeing the potential for significant gains, the PCF/CGT did not wish to undermine such an opportunity through fraternization with elements beyond their control.[32] It was not until 28 May that the PCF turned its attention to the possibility of overturning the Gaullist regime.[33] However, even then it was only half-hearted and they were partly responsible for the failure of the Left to provide a united front in a possible provisional government. The reasons for the controversial attitude of the PCF are commonly described as threefold in nature. First, for some time the PCF had been having difficulty with dissension within its ranks. This was particularly the case amongst student elements who had been expelled in 1966 as a result of their refusal to toe the party line.[34] It was therefore impossible for the PCF to agree to launching the working class into a movement that was not of its making and which disagreed with its ideological doctrine. Second, the PCF had been pursuing a softer approach to achieving the revolution and any involvement in the movement of 1968 would have run contrary to the long-term strategy that had been put in place and followed since 1963.[35] The final reason often given to explain the strategy of the PCF concerns its relationship with the Kremlin.[36] It has been argued that the authorities in Moscow favoured de Gaulle's foreign policy and, in particular, his opposition to American dominance. Fearing that a change in power might lead to a change in this stance, the Kremlin is said to have advised the PCF not to get involved in a movement that could bring down the Gaullist regime.[37] The fact that when, on 30 May, de Gaulle proposed a general election, the PCF was one of the first to accept the offer, thus ending any hope of a revolution, is often pinpointed to emphasize the PCF's approach to the events. In general, the role of the PCF and the reasons for its stance in 1968 are afforded considerable importance in analyses of the 1968 events. Much agreement exists over the role played by the Communist Party and the CGT. Furthermore, the various explanations for such a 'paradoxical' stance are widely accepted. The fact that the PCF was to prove one of the most formidable obstacles to a revolution in 1968 is no longer in question. However, the fact that so much attention is focused on pitting the communists against the students only serves to further strengthen the circumscribed image of the revolt. Excessive emphasis on the role of the PCF/CGT in rendering a revolutionary outcome of the crisis impossible anchors the impression that the majority of the 'movement' was made up of exclusively extreme left-wing elements intent on wreaking havoc with their utopian political agendas. The great diversity of participants, their ideas and motivations are ignored and subsumed into a certain image of what those involved were actually striving for, how they behaved and how their movements were organized. The fact that even the PCF was opposed has facilitated a further undermining of the credibility of the 'movement' – a term that in itself has its limitations.

Just as the chronology of the events has been simplified with significant implications for how they are seen today so too has there been a categorization of those who participated that has had a diminishing impact. When assessing 1968, many analyses allude to a 'movement'. This is particularly the case when describing the upheaval within the university world. One could consequently be forgiven for considering the revolt as having been orchestrated by a single organization with a common set of aims and objectives. Nothing could be further from the truth. The 'movement' was in fact an extremely diverse collection of groups and organizations with different ideologies and aims.[38] There were Trotskyites, Leninists, Stalinists, Maoists, Situationists, Communists and Anarchists all of whom, throughout the events, were continually in competition with each other.[39] Furthermore, while such groups have become increasingly considered as typifying the entire 1968 upheaval, the truth is that they formed only a minority of one section of an entire society in revolt. In fact, most of those involved were non-militant students, not at all politically motivated.[40] Many on the front line were simply protesting against the heavy-handed tactics of the police and the intransigence of the state. Cohn-Bendit, Sauvageot and Geismar are often considered as having been the leaders of the student movement. This, however, was not the case.[41] It would be a misjudgement to declare that any of these media-chosen personalities were the leaders of a movement that prided itself on a deliberate absence of direction – a characteristic that could be described as somewhat of a double-edged sword. On the one hand, it was undoubtedly one of its strengths as it made the students' upheaval extremely difficult to control. It was impossible for the authorities to negotiate a settlement with a student movement that had no real representatives.[42] On the other hand, this diversity and lack of organization that was, at the beginning of the events, undoubtedly one of the movement's strengths turned out to be one of its greatest weaknesses. The fact that the different groups were unable to come up with a common platform limited their potential success.[43] The lack of attention afforded to the heterogeneous nature of the student 'movement' and the over-emphasis of the role of such a minority is symptomatic of the increasingly blinkered view that has come to dominate the history of the events in general. Further contradictory implications of the events' history are evident in analyses of the part played by two other major figures.

From the beginning of the events, General de Gaulle is described as seeming to completely misunderstand the revolt or failing to consider what was happening as important. This attitude is seen to have increased the frustration of those involved and encouraged the public to support what had started as an exclusively student movement.[44] When considering his performance during the events of May 1968, many people refer to the address on 30 May in which he appeared magically to resolve one month's chaos in a four-minute speech. However, the reality is somewhat different and many point to his difficulty in coming to grips with the situation in 1968 as paving the way for his departure the following year.[45] There is a marked difference with the attitude of the prime minister, Georges Pompidou. Despite some initial errors, such as his own state visit to Afghanistan and his much-criticized decision to concede on initial student demands, the position taken by Pompidou was certainly much more pragmatic and realistic than that of the general. He worked tirelessly throughout the events with the chief of police, with de Gaulle, and at the Assembly to ensure that the crisis be brought to a successful conclusion. The content of the miraculous speech made by de Gaulle on 30 May was forced upon him by the prime minister. He persuaded the general that the best thing to do would be to dissolve the Assembly and call for a general election. This, of course, is exactly what de Gaulle did.[46] Of the two leaders in power during the events of 1968, it was undoubtedly Pompidou who emerged the stronger. De Gaulle's sacking[47] of his prime minister is regarded by all as an acceptance of the latter's qualities to become president. The general consensus is that the events were extremely detrimental for de Gaulle while at the same time Pompidou's performance confirmed his credentials as a capable successor to the general.[48] Much is made of de Gaulle's very negative approach, particularly in the opening weeks of the crisis. And while he was the focus of much opposition, portraying him as the source of most of the frustration is to further water down the diversity of the 1968 outburst. Grievances were numerous and varied across the nation and 1968 was much more than a simple desire to oust the president. Additionally, an over-emphasis on the individual errors of de Gaulle and Pompidou in some way obscures the precariousness of the situation. The escalation of the crisis could be perceived as much a result of clumsiness and miscalculation on the part of the president and his prime minister as it was of the existence of a determined movement striving for change. Finally, the real political impact of the general's departure is minimized as a result of two factors. First, the sweeping majority obtained by Gaullists in June 1968 general elections is seen as further proof of the inability of the 1968 'movement' to harness the outpouring of rebelliousness in order to threaten Gaullist hegemony, thus confirming the irresponsible image largely propagated today. And second, although de Gaulle was (eventually) forced to step down, it was not as a direct result of the 1968 upheaval. And, in any case, the man who replaced him was none other than his *dauphin*, his very own choice and in many ways a continuation of his ideas, morals and concept of the nation.

This first section has flagged up the advantages and disadvantages of the unprecedented level of attention afforded to the 1968 events. On the one hand, consensus in many areas has facilitated a certain degree of understanding of the main themes and issues of the crisis. Whether discussing the causes, what actually happened or the leading players, there certainly appears to be agreement amongst analysts and commentators. However, while such consensus areas can perhaps explain why – even amongst young people today – 1968 appears to be generally well understood, it has been suggested that their impact has not been all positive. In fact, it is argued that principal areas that are no longer the focus of any real debate have been crucial in anchoring a specific representation of the events, one that does not tell the full story. The conditions from which the crisis is described as having erupted, the manner in which its unfolding is structured and confined to a specific time span, the categorization of its protagonists and the telescopic focus on only certain elements are all factors that have been fundamental in shaping the narrow image so prevalent today. As the second section will demonstrate, the rise and predominance of the convenient consensus has been assisted and strengthened by the distinct lack of agreement in several other pivotal areas.

Areas of disagreement

The debate concerning how 1968 should be interpreted is one that has been present since the events' conclusion but upon which no real agreement has been reached. As well as describing the crisis as anything from a dress rehearsal for an imminent revolution[49] to carnival-like psychodrama,[50] early texts also saw it as the beginning of a new era of class struggle that would prove influential in the development of society.[51] Later, the crisis became shrouded in negativity as the inspirations that served as its driving force lost credibility. Contrary to the revolutionary aspirations expressed by some of the most prominent militants, 1968 has been described as furthering the dominance of capitalism in France by breaking down the barriers to modernization thus creating the exact opposite of what it aspired to.[52] The alleged individualism of the 1980s, reflected in the apathetic, egotistical indifference of the population at the time, is portrayed as having emerged from the 1968 movement.[53] The perceived march towards narcissistic individualism has been described as having been given a boost by the ideas expressed in the revolt of 1968.[54] Only one branch of an international revolt, the events have been described as a generational conflict characterized by misplaced revolutionary tendencies that has nonetheless succeeded in bringing about significant changes to French society, particularly in terms of cultural advances.[55] More recently, the events have come under criticism as an irresponsible moment that has created significant difficulties for French society.[56] As society develops, the legacy and heritage of the crisis is adapted to fit in with new circumstances; leading to a situation whereby, in the case of *mai 68*, examinations of how the events are interpreted have become as prevalent as interpretations themselves.

As early as 1970, the wide-ranging analyses concerning the events were the inspiration behind Ph. Bénéton and J. Touchard's 'Les interprétations de la crise de mai/juin 1968'.[57] In a bid to classify the spiralling number of interpretations, the authors of this article are able to propose eight categories that summarize the plethora of ideas expressed to date. Ranging from *Mai 68 comme complot* to *Mai comme une crise de civilisation*, their analysis demonstrates that whilst each has a case to be argued, no one thesis can completely explain the events. It is perhaps for this reason that they favour *Mai comme enchaînement de circonstances*, i.e., that which describes the events as an exceptional chain of circumstances. Claude Fohlen's *Mai 68, révolution ou psychodrame?* also addresses the growing problem of interpretation by highlighting the sheer diversity of possible explanations.[58] Summarizing the various interpretations under the heading *Révolution?, Soubresaut?, Tragi-comédie?*, he argues that theses centring on the notion of *crise de jeunesse/université* are insufficient and rejects those concerning a *complot*.[59] The fact that the others certainly have a case to be argued underlines the complication created by such diversity. The groundbreaking changes experienced around the world over the course of the 1970s, and, in particular, the demise of revolutionary aspirations, the economic crisis and the ever-growing dominance of the consumer society, had important implications for interpreting 1968. As some theses became obsolete, others changed and novel propositions emerged. The upshot was a further complication of the issue.

By 1986 the question of how to approach 1968 was such that it was the subject of a conference involving many of the principal commentators in this field. Published in a special edition of *Pouvoirs*,[60] the findings underline the continued problems with this area almost twenty years after the end of the events. Consensus was no closer, and as the introduction comments: 'If the months of work to produce it [the special edition of *Pouvoirs* dedicated to the conference] have confirmed anything, it would be the urgent need for another conference, another publication on the events of May 1968.'[61] By the time of the twentieth anniversary, some of the issues raised in the 1986 conference concerning interpretations were reiterated. This is particularly true of Henri Weber's *Que reste-t-il* and Luc Ferry and Alain Renaut's *La Pensée 68*. By analysing the invalidity of both his own early interpretation in *La Répétition générale* and that of Raymond Aron in *La Révolution introuvable*, Weber underlines the persistence of unanswered questions surrounding interpretations of the events in what he describes as 'la confusion générale'.[62] In *La Pensée 68*, Luc Ferry and Alain Renaut underline the difficulties of 1968 interpretations. By using the eight proposals of Bénéton and Touchard they classify the diverse theses into three categories; *le point de vue des acteurs, Mai comme pseudo-révolution ou: le changement dans la continuité* and finally *l'événement de mai*. The three categories are described as insufficient and only by integrating chosen elements of each will a more complete interpretation be acceptable. This *pluralisme interprétatif* is best found, according to Ferry and Renaut, in Raymond Aron's *La Révolution introuvable*.[63] The twentieth anniversary of the events marked the peak of discussions concerning the issue of interpretations. Since then, little or no attention has been paid to this inconclusive debate and no novel approaches have emerged. The thirtieth anniversary provided the opportunity for a further development of the debate. However, the majority of texts produced were concerned with other issues and in particular simple straightforward accounts of what happened as the events' commemoration became an industry in itself. Most indicative of the stagnant nature of the debate concerning inter-pretations is that the two of the most prominent texts in this domain ten years previously, *La Pensée 68* and *Que reste-t-il*, were re-released without any changes to their theses. Henri Weber reinforces this point in the preface to the 1998 edition of his text: 'To my knowledge, no new theory concerning the May revo-lution has emerged adding to the body of available interpretations. This is why this essay, to my mind, has lost nothing of its relevance.'[64]

The sustained and varied debate surrounding this issue of interpreting the events has done little other than to confirm the 'historical obscuring' mentioned by Kristin Ross.[65] As the question remains open to discussion, there appear to be no limitations to the labels that can be attached to this extraor-dinary set of events. The more time passes the more it appears to be difficult to truly pin down what happened, why and what the consequences have been. The overall inconclusiveness as regards the interpretation of 1968 has meant that those notions that dominate the stereotypical picture of the crisis (e.g., Parisian, bourgeois, student, utopian, etc.) are given increased credibility, mainly as a result of their prominence. Many factors can help explain just why

1968 is so immune to definition, including the lack of agreement over some important areas of debate.

The vast majority of texts indicate that the crisis was completely unforesee-able and that this in fact was one of its greatest strengths, often cited to explain the powerlessness of the state.[66] The relative political and economic stability of 1960s France made it extremely difficult for anyone to foresee the tumultuous events of 1968. However, there are many who point to the economic, political, social, international and educational conditions prior to May 1968 and draw the conclusion that the crisis was not only predictable but also inevitable. One of the most interesting accounts comes from the Dean of Nanterre at the time of the events, Pierre Grappin. In *L'Ile aux peupliers*, he describes clear signs (of which the government were aware) that things were beginning to get out of hand.[67] He recounts how his friend, Alain Peyrefitte, Minister for Education, called him as early as 1967 and pleaded with him to accept a post elsewhere so that he could avoid what he describes as 'terrible problems'.[68] He also talks of how an old army acquaintance came to see him at the faculty and after visiting it and talking with the students came back to Grappin advising him 'get out of here quickly'.[69] Grappin clearly is of the opinion that something could have and should have been done to prevent what for him was predictable. He describes his disappointment with the authorities who refused to heed his warnings and is particularly critical of Pompidou's failure to react to his pleas. Another example of what can be considered as a warning of what was to come is the now famous article *'La France s'ennuie'*, by the journalist Pierre Viansson-Ponté, published in *Le Monde* just weeks before the events exploded. Detailing how the population was bored, Viansson-Ponté describes a weary General de Gaulle faced with the static and insipid period in which France found itself. By drawing comparisons with the highly exciting and romantic events taking place elsewhere in the world, this article was not only prophetic but also accurate in pinpointing some of the factors that would go on to inspire the revolt.[70] Viansson-Ponté did not foresee what exactly was going to occur but with hindsight it is clear that this was in fact a very good analysis of the atmosphere within French society and a clear warning to the authorities that something had to be done to prevent things entering a stage of revolt.

Several other analyses detail a refusal to accept the events as unpredictable. For example, Kristin Ross argues that the events were not in fact a 'thunder-clap in the middle of a serene sky'. Instead '[I]t was an event with a long preparation, dating back to the mobilization against the Algerian War.'[71] The Algerian War politicized many universities, a factor that unquestionably continued to be influential in the late 1960s. It also showed how the student world was both able and willing to mobilize organized opposition. From an economic point of view, Jacques Kergoat – pointing to 'all the sporadic and violent local and sectional movements triggered just about everywhere'[72] as indicative of mounting working-class frustration – finds it hard to believe that the general strike itself was not predictable. It would have been impossible for anyone to predict exactly what was going to happen. In no way could anyone have foreseen the chaotic month of violence and uncertainty that was May

1968. However, what is clear is that there were indications of mounting tension that could have served as warning signs to possible future social unrest. The debate surrounding the predictability of the crisis is in keeping with the difficulties in coming to firm conclusions on important questions. The malleability of the history of 1968 is clear in this example. For those wishing to criticize the government of the time, certain areas can be pointed up in order to bemoan the state's inability to anticipate such obvious discontent. However, and as discussed earlier, highlighting such causes only serves to undermine the great surprise with which the events struck. On the one hand, the authorities can claim irresponsibility as a result of such unpredictable and exceptional circumstances. On the other, those wishing to lend credence to the extraordinariness are bound to be weary of concurring on the existence of quite normal reasons for such a revolt. Finally, for those who refuse to see the events as none other than a freak occurrence, they too can point to an unprecedented convergence of domestic and international factors as the main explanation for such an outlandish rebellion. In other words, whether or not the events can be considered as predictable or as a surprise is in fact dependant on one's appreciation of what 1968 means or meant in general. No consensus on interpretation leaves areas such as this, and discussions on the role of some of the important actors and turning points, open to discussion.

The role played by the police, and in particular the CRS, was of great importance. However, there seems to be a significant difference between analyses of this element of the crisis. On the one hand, we have what can be described as the official position which describes the behaviour of the police as commendable in the face of extreme provocation. Such analyses often point to the fact that the police were faced with a situation of immense difficulty in which they excelled due to the fact that there were very few deaths in relation to the level of violence. Maurice Grimaud puts forward an unsurprising explanation for the violence of his forces during the events: 'One understands better that when the opportunity to strike out presents itself, these men enter the mysterious realm of violence. The blows they deliver replace the life they have no right to take.'[73] It is true that the police were faced with the difficult task of trying to contain an exceptionally motivated, highly mobilized section of French society who benefited, particularly at the beginning of the events, from the fact that the general public was very much on their side. The police undoubtedly suffered from the unenviable position of being caught in the middle. It is subsequently unsurprising to find many who credit the forces of order for their 'cool heads'.[74] However, when one considers some of the images recorded from the clashes between the police and the protestors in 1968 or reads some of the first-hand accounts given by the victims, the impression is very different.[75] There were clearly examples of what can only be described as extreme brutality that call into question the idea that the behaviour of the police was exemplary.[76] The police fell victim to a calculated attempt on behalf of certain elements of the student 'movement' who deliberately aimed to provoke violent confrontations. Such tactics increased sympathy for the movement and effectively helped it spread from a strictly student revolt to an all-out general strike.[77] The police could therefore be held responsible, to a certain extent, for the spreading of the movement beyond the universities. Throughout the events and particularly towards the end, the police were used by the state as a tool to bring the crisis to an end. Beyond their responsibility of keeping order that led to a level of brutality that was – at times – extreme, the police were also used in June to help break the strike. This period of the events remains in fact the most controversial (and, as we have seen above, not exactly at the forefront of the 1968 folklore) since this was when three people died as a result of police action.[78]

The problem is clear; can the behaviour of the police be described as commendable, as many pro-government or official texts claim? Or, can we talk of excessive violence as some of the first-hand accounts and recorded images of the confrontations lead us to believe? That an assessment of the role played by arguably one of the most important elements of the revolt remains so inconclusive is yet another example of the difficulty in forming a complete picture of what happened. Due to the inconclusive nature of this debate, it would appear that those on each side of the barricades can interpret and recount what happened as they see fit. It is the adaptable manner of such pivotal issues that has prevented solid conclusions as well as encouraging varied and continued debate. Without any real agreement on this question, a genuine analysis of the role of the police and its impact has been airbrushed from the dominant discourse with more attention focused on those convenient areas of consensus. Other important turning points such as the rejection of the Grenelle agreements or General de Gaulle's trip to Baden-Baden also remain open to interpretation and as such contribute to the pliable nature of the overall interpretation of the crisis as well as adding further layers of mystery and intrigue.

Following an exhausting round of negotiations, led by the prime minister who had surrounded himself with a team of experienced politicians (interestingly without the Minister for the Economy, Michel Debré),[79] it seemed as though the government had finally managed to find a resolution to the crisis. When the negotiations were finished, the general feeling was that the major participants were satisfied with the results and the end of the strike seemed inevitable. Just after the negotiations, the leader of the CGT, Georges Séguy, declared: 'It is a fruitful agreement [. . .] we think that based on the estimations and information we will give them, the workers will be able to make a decision as soon as possible.'[80] What happened afterwards was surprising and has been a particularly divisive subject of debate. When Georges Séguy, immediately after the end of the negotiations, attended a meeting at the bastion of the working class at the Renault factory at Boulogne-Billancourt, in which he outlined the concessions gained, the workers rejected the agreement, causing a sensation.[81] This rejection saw the crisis move into its most critical phase and opened up the real possibility of an overthrow of the regime. However, whilst the significance of the rejection is undoubted, the reasons behind it are not so evident. On the one hand, it is argued that it was rejected quite simply because the workers found what was proposed inadequate. This explanation is quite difficult to accept as the greater part of what was proposed was later accepted and implemented. The concessions offered by the government were considerable and included certain elements that the major trade unions had been demanding for quite some time (in particular, the recognition of union activity in the workplace). It is also difficult to accept that the CGT, which until this point had been in complete control of its members and was clearly directing the strike movement to obtain material gains of this sort from the government and the employers, would have so gravely misunderstood the feelings of its troops. Critics of the CGT, however, have claimed that the fact that the workers rejected the agreements only served to show how out of touch the CGT was with the movement.[82] Another explanation given for the rejection is much less controversial but equally inadequate. It is claimed that the agreements were rejected because of a misunderstanding between two of the leaders of the trade union. The suggestion goes that before Séguy arrived at Billancourt the meeting had already begun and that the speaker who was charged with warming up the crowd, Aimé Albeher,[83] had not been aware of the results of the negotiations and called for the strike to continue. Therefore, when Séguy arrived, the workers had already made their decision and, regardless of what he had to offer, were agreed on continued action. There is no doubt that Séguy was not expecting a negative reaction and was forced to change his speech once he sensed the hostility coming from the crowd.[84] That an organization so capable of controlling the strike up to this point spectacularly failed due to a minor misunderstanding appears unlikely.[85]

Yet another important factor of the 1968 crisis appears clouded. Without agreement on explanations for such significant turning points in the crisis, complete understanding becomes very problematic. Furthermore, the rejection of the Grenelle accords becomes different things to different people. On the one hand it could be viewed as confirmation that the working class was much more concerned with qualitative rather than quantitative demands. On the other, it could be argued that it was confirmation that the working class were opportunistic and saw this as a chance to wrest as much material gain from the authorities as possible. Finally, the idea that the rejection was the result of a simple misunderstanding sits well with those who are intent on playing down the significance of this rejection. This chapter of the crisis, over forty years later, is left with numerous possible interpretations and, as we will see, is not the only one. It was in the atmosphere of the working-class rejection of Grenelle that one of the most intriguing episodes of *mai 68* would take place.

The sense of desperation at the failure of both Pompidou and de Gaulle to find a resolution as well as the tentative moves on the Left to provide a viable political outlet for the revolt was exacerbated by one of the most highly debatable moments of May 1968. On the morning of 29 May, de Gaulle announced that the scheduled ministerial meeting for that day was to be cancelled and that he was to return to his residence for a rest. However, this was not what he had in mind. Instead of going to *Colombey-les-Deux-Eglises* he, along with his wife and his son's family, went to visit the Commander of the French Army in

Germany, General Massu, at Baden-Baden. The fact that he did so in great secrecy, without informing anyone, even Pompidou, increased the sense of panic in Paris. For a number of hours the Republic was without its president and the situation seemed to be entering a new stage of gravity.[86] However, at 6pm de Gaulle was back in his residence and, in a bid to fight on, would once again address the nation the next day.

The mystery surrounding de Gaulle's disappearance on 29 May only lasted a matter of hours and there has never been any secret made of where he had been. The question however, remains: why did the general go to Baden-Baden? Analysts are very much divided, with three explanations in particular very common amongst those put forward. First, there is the suggestion that de Gaulle left for Baden-Baden because he genuinely felt that he had no option other than to stand down. Such a scenario seems improbable for de Gaulle, particularly when we consider the difficulties that he had endured throughout his long and illustrious career. However, this hypothesis is backed up by several factors; first of all, the fact that he asked his son to follow him along with his wife and children to Baden-Baden. Was the general seriously contemplating stepping down and therefore fearing for the safety of his immediate family? This is not impossible, and is reinforced by the account of that day given by the man in question, General Massu, who claims that de Gaulle arrived in a state of complete desperation.[87] Massu goes on to describe how he persuaded the general that this was not the time to abandon France and that he should return to Paris. The second explanation for de Gaulle's visit to Baden-Baden concerns the army. Many believe that the general went to see Massu because he feared a *coup d'état*.[88] If one considers that left-wing forces, and in particular the PCF, were beginning to realistically consider the possibility of seizing power, de Gaulle could be justified in fearing an imminent coup. Whether or not he really considered doing so, this visit might well have been enough to discourage the not so extremist elements on the Left. This 'calling the bluff' hypothesis ties neatly in with the third explanation. Certain experts believe that this visit to Baden-Baden by the general was none other than a perfectly executed *coup de théâtre*.[89] By disappearing as he did, the general hoped to create a sense of fear amongst his supporters who, up until this point, had remained silent. In his absence, even if it was only temporary, the general public would be forced to consider what would remain if he were really to leave. This hypothesis, however dramatic, would perhaps help explain why he informed nobody of his destination. In doing so, not only did he create a sense of panic that became widespread, he was also able to expose the opportunism of those wishing to take power.

With Massu's passing in 2002, his 'ultimate enigma' will perhaps never be resolved.[90] Although his own explanation remains dominant, others appear feasible. Just like the reasons explaining the rejection of Grenelle, the continued debate over the Baden-Baden episode allows for analysts and commentators to mould its significance in order to adapt it to their overall interpretation or view of the events. For example, those wishing to call into question the *sang-froid* of the authorities would endorse the idea that the president's visit to Massu was as a result of his inability to deal with what was happening. Intent on resigning or left with no other option than to call in the army, either way, it exemplifies the notion that he was out of his depth in 1968 and accentuates the precariousness of the situation. Conversely, it could be argued that de Gaulle was only right to verify that he had the backing of his army and that he knew exactly what he was doing in disappearing as he did. Finally, the idea that the president's brief absence was enough to bring the population back to reality lends weight to the notion that the revolt was far from being a serious, credible threat. As such, it becomes no more than a momentary blip, thus further undermining its significance. At the time, de Gaulle's disappearance served to heighten uncertainty and the feeling that something extraordinary was unfolding. As such, it is yet another feature that renders the events so special. Furthermore, the fact that this episode, some forty years later, remains unresolved is typical of the general elusive nature of the 1968 events and exemplifies the lack of consensus surrounding such crucial moments.

Conclusion

The continued debate surrounding the issue of interpreting the 1968 crisis reveals the sheer difficulty of getting to the bottom of a highly complex set of events. Such problems are further complicated by the lack of consensus on some critical features of the crisis. Were the events predictable? How should the attitude and behaviour of the police be assessed? What explanation can be given for the significant turning points that were the rejection of the Grenelle agreements and de Gaulle's trip to Baden-Baden? All these questions, despite the plethora of material available and the great advantage of hindsight and perspective, still remain open to discussion. The fact that such pivotal questions remain unanswered has meant that numerous interpretations of the events appear feasible. Furthermore, the fact that some of the most compelling episodes of the crisis are still to be resolved serves to heighten the intrigue surrounding it and thus adds to the general mystification.

The constant presence of 1968 in topical debates, together with the now traditional decennial commemorations, has ensured the iconic status of these events. However, despite such a positive impact of the history of 1968, this chapter has argued that its portrayal has not been without negative consequences. Characterized by consensus, limitations and disagreement, the sheer mass of coverage has given rise to a certain, restricted perception of the events. The possibility to shape and mould some important aspects has been crucial in the rise of the stereotypical and limited idea of *mai 68*. The popular history has been logically and increasingly based on those areas where consensus has been achieved. However, and as demonstrated in the first section, these do not exactly tell the whole story and, as a result, have facilitated the anchoring of the convenient consensus. Increasingly, the events are seen as no more than a tantrum by a spoilt generation that has gone on to create diverse problems for twenty-first-century France. That such a perception exists is due largely to how the events have been analysed and represented. The overall impact of the nature of 1968's history can therefore be described as two-dimensional. While unquestionably essential in the acquisition of such a special place in the collective memory of the French, the dominant representation is based on restrictive analyses. Such limitations stem from the fact that the portrayal from which perceptions are naturally formed stops short of presenting the complete picture; a fact that cannot be without consequence in shaping current-day perceptions.

Chapter Three
Current attitudes to the events of 1968

Introduction

The manner in which the events have been portrayed over the years and the advantages and disadvantages brought about by the unprecedented level of focus on them have been discussed in chapters one and two. This second section, comprising three chapters, aims to examine what identifiable impact there has been on attitudes and whether perceptions, like (and because of) the dominant narrative, also fall short of capturing the full picture. The first of the three provides, through the analysis of the results of a survey carried out amongst French university students during the period October 2002–June 2003, an examination of what young people think of the events and their impact, both on society and on their own lives.

From the outset, the aims of the questionnaire were clear; to ascertain as far as possible what young people thought of the events of 1968. Did they consider them important? Did they feel that the events had had an influence on their lives? Did they think that the events were a good or bad thing for France? Could it be concluded that young French people were aware of what actually happened in 1968 and why? A concerted effort was made to have a widespread geographical representation of young French people and the universities selected were carefully chosen so as not to concentrate solely on certain areas.[1] In order to present the regional variations logically it was necessary to introduce a simplification to the breakdown of the results. Geographically speaking, the spread of results was not uniform. As Table 3.1 shows, some regions had considerable returns whilst others had very few.

Regions were therefore grouped into six categories in order to simplify an appreciation of regional variations to the questions asked. Table 3.2 and Figure 3.1 outline how these have been organized.

The limitations of this survey are obvious. In no way can its results be considered as an overall picture of what young French people think of the events. However, due to the selection of the target audience, the choice of questions and the geographical distribution of the questionnaires, the results are a good reflection of what university students think of 1968, how they feel the events have had an influence on their lives and whether or not they fully understand what happened and why.

The results of the 505 questionnaires proved very extensive. The following chapter will focus on five hypotheses concerning general opinions on how

Table 3.1 Regional breakdown

Region	Frequency	Per cent
Nord-Pas-de-Calais	1	0.2
Haute-Normandie	2	0.4
Basse-Normandie	2	0.4
Picardie	1	0.2
Champagne-Ardenne	1	0.2
Lorraine	3	0.6
Alsace	54	10.7
Bretagne	55	10.9
Paris Ile-de-France	78	15.4
Franche-Comté	5	1.0
Bourgogne	7	1.4
Centre	99	19.6
Pays de la Loire	30	5.9
Poitou-Charentes	27	5.3
Limousin	1	0.2
Auvergne	1	0.2
Rhône-Alpes	10	2.0
Aquitaine	15	3.0
Midi-Pyrénées	9	1.8
Languedoc-Roussillon	5	1.0
Provence-Alpes-Côte d'Azur	35	6.9
Corse	49	9.7
Total	490	97
Missing	15	3.0
Total	505	100

Table 3.2 Regional groupings

North/ Northwest (N/NW)	South/Southwest (S/SW)	South/ Southeast (S/SE)
Bretagne	Poitou-Charentes	Languedoc-Roussillon
Basse-Normandie	Aquitaine	Provence-Alpes-Côte d'Azur
Haute-Normandie	Midi-Pyrénées	Corse
Pays de la Loire	Limousin	Rhône-Alpes
North/ Northeast (N/NE)	*Paris, Ile de France*	*Centre*
Franche-Comté		Centre
Alsace		Bourgogne
Lorraine		Auvergne
Champagne-Ardenne		
Picardie		
Nord-Pas-de-Calais		

young French people consider the events of 1968 and how such assumptions are reflected in the results. Examples from the 'any other comments section' will be used as a conclusion. Table 3.3 provides an overview of the results of each question and allows a general appreciation before the discussion goes on to the specific aims of the survey.

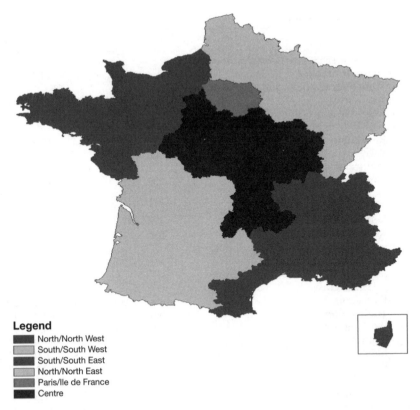

Legend
- ■ North/North West
- ▨ South/South West
- ■ South/South East
- ▨ North/North East
- ▨ Paris/Ile de France
- ■ Centre

Figure 3.1 Regional groupings

Analysis

As indicated in chapters one and two, the history of the 1968 events has been on a journey that has helped them secure a very particular place in the collective memory of the French. However, the overemphasis on the romantic, spectacular and media-friendly aspects – whilst areas such as the importance of the strike and the significance of the political crisis have progressively receded into the background – has meant that the image of a *mai 68 festif* has taken precedence.[2] This overriding perspective has been fundamental in scaling back the significance of what happened and as a result ensured that the events are viewed to a certain degree as having been somewhat innocuous. Such a dominant view has made it much easier to consider the events in a positive light.

In question 4 the respondents were asked their opinion on the statement: 'The events of 1968 have been a positive experience for France.' This question sought to test the extent to which the conventional representation had influenced popular perceptions. Are people weary of an upheaval that brought the country to a standstill, threatened the regime and was punctuated with violent

Table 3.3 Overview of results

	SA	D	N	A	SA
4. The events of 1968 have been a positive experience for France.	0.8	5.7	17.6	59.4	13.7
5. The French should be proud of 1968 as an historic event	1.2	9.5	29.7	46.9	10.3
6. The following expressions describe well the events of 1968 in France					
• Revolution	4.4	15	14.1	47.7	15
• Party	16.2	31.9	26.3	18	2.8
• Political demonstration	1.2	3.8	12.7	59	19.2
• Student unease	0.6	3	6.7	49.7	36.6
• Generational clash	1.2	5.3	15.2	48.3	24.6
• Enough of de Gaulle	2.2	12.1	47.9	26.9	6.3
• Left wing opportunism	4.2	13.1	52.9	21	3.6
• Rush of blood	2.4	7.9	25.5	48.1	11.9
7. The events of May 1968 brought about real changes to French society.	1	5.5	14.1	60	16.2
8. The following sectors were most affected by the 1968 events.					
• Education	0.4	2	6.1	59.2	29.3
• Trade unions	0.6	3.2	29.5	49.9	11.1
• Working conditions	0.2	8.9	33.1	43.4	7.9
• Politics	1	7.7	31.9	47.9	5.9
• Judicial system	4	27.1	55.8	6.9	0.4
• Regional movements	4	18.6	57.4	12.1	1.6
• The media	1.2	9.1	33.3	41.2	9.1
• The police	2	12.7	41.2	31.9	5.7
• Feminism	1	4.4	18.2	46.3	25.9
• Social mores	0.6	3.8	10.7	49.3	31.1
9. The events of May 1968 have had an influence on your life.	7.1	14.5	39.6	29.7	6.1
10. If yes, in what areas?					
• Education	0.6	1.1	7.7	66.3	21.5
• Working conditions	2.2	6.6	45.9	35.9	3.3
• Politics	1.1	9.9	43.6	33.7	6.1
• Family relations	2.2	7.7	25.4	45.9	12.7
• Regional identity	4.4	21	60.8	5.5	1.1
• Social mores	2.2	3.3	15.5	54.1	22.1
• Feminism	1.7	4.4	16	50.8	23.8
11. The following phrases best describe the attitude of the police during the events of May 1968.					
• Scandalous	3	14.1	38.8	29.7	9.9
• The police were provoked	5	15	35.6	36.2	4.2
• Opportunist	3.6	14.3	57	18.2	1
• Fascist	13.7	26.1	41.6	12.3	1
• Not hard enough	21.6	33.5	35	2.6	1.2
• The police were simply doing their job	4.8	19.2	34.7	29.7	6.3
12. The behaviour and attitude of the police during the events of May 1968 changed how they were perceived by the French.	2	13.3	37.8	38	4.2
13. The events of May 1968 were an exclusively Parisian revolt.	20	44	12.1	18	2.4

	SD	D	N	A	SA
14. The events of May 1968 have made it easier for students and lycéens to demonstrate on the streets.	1.6	6.1	10.1	60.6	18.8
15. The following groups/people should be held responsible for the events of 1968.					
• Students	2.4	6.5	10.3	54.1	23.8
• Workers	3	11.5	30.9	41.4	8.5
• Trade unions	2.4	6.9	25.5	51.9	8.3
• The government	1.8	8.5	25	41.5	13.3
• De Gaulle	2.6	9.1	41.8	32.3	8.5
• The Communists	2.4	7.9	55.4	24.6	4.4
• The Socialists	2.6	7.7	50.7	29.7	3.8
• International student movements	2.8	11.7	47.7	25.9	6.5
16. The following groups/people were the real victims of the 1968 events.					
• Students	3.2	20.4	28.3	33.1	6.3
• Workers	2.4	16.8	42.6	24	4
• Trade unions	4	19.2	49.7	14.5	2
• The government	4.4	17.6	38.6	25.5	3.2
• De Gaulle	4.8	15.8	36.4	25.3	7.1
• The Communists	4.2	20.6	53.5	8.5	1.2
• The Socialists	3.6	22.2	52.9	7.9	0.6
• The Bourgeoisie	8.1	20.8	39	18.4	3.2
17. A similar situation to the events of 1968 could occur in France.	4	21.2	19.2	41	9.5
18. The following groups/people did the most to resolve the crisis of May 1968.					
• Students	3.4	18.4	35	29.1	5.9
• Workers	2	15.2	47.7	21.2	3.2
• Trade unions	2.4	11.1	37.6	34.1	5.3
• The government	1.4	12.3	37.2	34.9	4.8
• De Gaulle	4.6	15.8	49.1	16.8	3.4
• The Communists	3.2	14.7	62.4	8.3	1
• The Socialists	2	13.1	55.4	17.2	1.6
• The Bourgeoisie	10.7	24.2	48.5	4.6	0.6
19. The crisis of May 1968 has been the most important moment in post Second World War French history.	10.3	28.7	19.8	30.3	6.9

Note: SD/D/N/A/SA – Strongly disagree/ Disagree/ Not certain/ Agree/ Strongly agree. An example of the questionnaire can be found in the appendix.

Table 3.4 The events of 1968 have been a positive experience for France

	Frequency	*Per cent*
Strongly disagree	4	0.8
Disagree	29	5.7
Not certain	89	17.6
Agree	300	59.4
Strongly agree	69	13.7
Total	491	97.2
Missing	14	2.8
Total	505	100

clashes throughout? Or, has the predominantly sanguine image propagated through a range of vectors over the years been translated in how the events are perceived?

The results in Table 3.4 confirm the assumption that the French consider the events of 1968 as a positive experience with almost three-quarters of those questioned either agreeing or strongly agreeing. Only a very small percentage disagreed. As Figure 3.2 demonstrates, the picture is consistent across the country with in excess of 60 per cent of respondents in agreement in each regional grouping.

In question 5 the respondents were asked whether they agreed or disagreed with the statement: 'The French should be proud of 1968 as an historic event.' Continuing from the theme in question 4, an assessment of whether or not the French are proud of the events of 1968 as a historical event will help prove or disprove the existence of an overall positive impression concerning them. Has the recent gloom surrounding 1968 and the debate on whether the events have been responsible for some of today's social problems affected the perception of the crisis? Or has the overwhelmingly popular idea of 1968 as a positive step for France, regardless of its seriousness and perceived negative consequences, created a certain pride in the events?

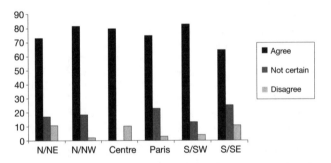

Figure 3.2 The events of 1968 have been a positive experience for France

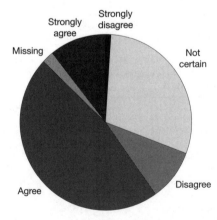

Figure 3.3 The French should be proud of 1968 as an historic event

As Figure 3.3 demonstrates, a majority of those questioned (58.2 per cent) either agreed or strongly agreed that the French should be proud of the events with slightly more than those in question 4 disagreeing (10.7). Despite confirming the affirmative response to question 4, the number of uncertain responses shows that respondents found it difficult to assert wholeheartedly that the events were a positive experience. This is arguably a direct consequence of the increasing negativity that has crept into the dominant narrative over recent years. Nevertheless, the overwhelming perception remains positive. The results are complicated somewhat when broken down according to regional groupings. As Figure 3.4 shows, whilst the groups N/NE, N/NW, Centre and Paris reflect the national picture, a comparison between S/SW and S/SE reveals a certain disparity across the south in relation to this question. Whereas in the S/SW the level of agreement is considerably higher than average, in the S/SE fewer than 50 per cent are in agreement and over one-fifth of respondents view the events as something they should not be proud of.

It is fair to assume that the events are overwhelmingly looked upon positively and with a certain degree of pride. By no means is it being suggested that this positive attitude and pride are misplaced. By all accounts, the events of 1968 have led to important, positive steps for France. However, the suggestion is that, by focusing too much on the romantic images of the events and ignoring the more challenging elements, the portrayal has facilitated the dominance of this positive perception. Consequently, those who were not present look upon it at some sort of petulant revolt at a time when the social and economic conditions were much more favourable. Furthermore, ex-'68ers reflect upon it – with some degree of embarrassment in many cases – as a time of insouciance and irresponsibility. Such factors have undoubtedly influenced the history and memory of the events and can help explain the progressively narrow nature of their portrayal. Several questions in the survey were chosen to measure to what extent this narrow portrayal had impacted on respondents' knowledge of the crisis of 1968. The results of these questions will establish whether young French people really understand what happened or whether their perceptions are simply based on the stereotypical attitudes shaped by the way in which the events have been portrayed.

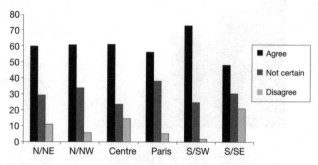

Figure 3.4 The French should be proud of 1968 as an historic event

Question 6 asked what expressions best describe the events of 1968. Covering a range of interpretations, ideas and representations discernible across the events' widespread coverage, the options ranged from 'Revolution' to 'Rush of blood'. This question would therefore enable an appreciation of the dominant image(s) of the crisis amongst young French people.

As the data in Table 3.5 and Figure 3.5 demonstrate, several options were much more popular than others. Top of the list are 'student unease', 'political demonstration' and 'generational conflict'. The options 'revolution' and 'rush of blood' received over 50 per cent in agreement. The more demanding elements (in terms of understanding) 'enough of de Gaulle' and 'left-wing opportunism' received a small percentage in agreement, with a high percentage of uncertain responses. Only 'party' received a majority in disagreement. The most obvious and stereotypical terms such as 'student unease' and 'generational conflict' were very popular. However, the high percentage afforded to 'rush of blood' and 'revolution' could be perceived as reflecting the negative impact of the coverage afforded to the events. Such interpretations are used by those, for the former, trying to play down the significance of the events and those, for the latter, claiming it was a genuine opportunity for

Table 3.5 The following expressions describe well the events of 1968 in France

	SD	D	N	A	SA	M
Revolution	4.4	15	14.1	47.7	15	3.8
Party	16.2	31.9	26.3	18	2.8	4.8
Political demonstration	1.2	3.8	12.7	59	19.2	4.2
Student unease	0.6	3.0	6.7	49.7	36.6	3.4
Generational conflict	1.2	5.3	15.2	48.3	24.6	5.3
Enough of de Gaulle	2.2	12.1	47.9	26.9	6.3	4.6
Left-wing opportunism	4.2	13.1	52.9	21	3.6	5.3
Rush of blood	2.4	7.9	25.5	48.1	11.9	4.2

Note. SD/D/N/A/SA/M – Strongly disagree/ Disagree/ Not certain/ Agree/ Strongly agree/ Missing.

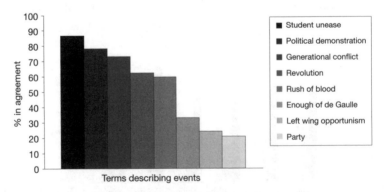

Figure 3.5 The above expressions describe well the events of 1968 in France. Note: results are a combination of agree and strongly agree responses.

revolution. May–June 1968 was certainly more than a rush of blood to the head, yet cannot be described as a revolution. The very low percentage of those agreeing with 'enough of de Gaulle' and 'left-wing opportunism' coupled with the high rates of 'not certain' responses show a lack of understanding of some of the finer details. The *ras-le-bol* of de Gaulle was unquestionably a major factor in the fervour of the 1968 movement. It is not by chance that one of the most memorable slogans of 1968 is *Dix ans – ça suffit!* However, and despite continual playing down of the events, a very small percentage agreed that 1968 could be described as a 'party' with almost 50 per cent in disagreement. Despite the dominance of a trend that reduces the importance of the events, such a result reveals genuine recognition of the seriousness of the events by young people today.

In question 13 the respondents were asked whether they considered the events to have been an exclusively Parisian revolt. As discussed in chapter two, one is struck by the huge emphasis put on what happened in Paris to the detriment of what happened on a more national scale.[3] However, one of the great strengths of the 1968 upheaval was its nationwide appeal. A complete understanding of May–June 1968 cannot be limited solely to what occurred in Paris. The results of question 13 will demonstrate whether young people are aware of the national aspect of the events or whether they believe them to have been exclusively Parisian.

The results in Table 3.6 show that a strong percentage of respondents disagree with the view that the events were an exclusively Parisian revolt. This is

Table 3.6 The events of May 1968 were an exclusively Parisian revolt

	Frequency	*Per cent*
Strongly disagree	101	20.0
Disagree	222	44.0
Not certain	61	12.1
Agree	91	18.0
Strongly agree	12	2.4
Total	487	96.4
Missing	18	3.6
Total	505	100.0

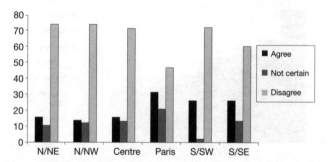

Figure 3.6 The events of May 1968 were an exclusively Parisian revolt

an indication that young people are aware of the nationwide element of 1968, thus demonstrating a certain degree of understanding. Nevertheless, it remains surprising that over one-fifth of respondents believe that the crisis was limited to the capital. When examined regionally it is possible to identify those areas where recognition of the events' nationwide impact is less obvious. Interestingly, as Figure 3.6 demonstrates, it is in fact Paris that bucks the national trend. Not only do 30 per cent of respondents agree that the events were indeed limited to the capital, what is more striking is that under 50 per cent were in disagreement.

The question 'The following groups/people should be held responsible for the events of 1968' tested further to what extent young French people are aware of some of the finer details of the events. As with question 6, all of the options have a case to be argued. However, by charting the most to the least popular responses we gain an appreciation of the level of understanding of what occurred.

As Table 3.7 and Figure 3.7 demonstrate, the categories, 'students', 'workers', 'trade unions' and 'government' all received over 50 per cent of responses agreeing or strongly agreeing. The other four options revealed considerable uncertainty. 'Students' and 'government' received over 50 per cent in agreement. It is worth noting that those surveyed demonstrated their

Table 3.7 The following groups/people should be held responsible for the events of 1968

	SD	D	N	A	SA	M
Students	2.4	6.5	10.3	54.1	23.8	3
Workers	3	11.5	30.9	41.4	8.5	4.8
Trade unions	2.4	6.9	25.5	51.9	8.3	5
The government	1.8	8.5	25	41.5	13.3	5
De Gaulle	2.6	9.1	41.8	32.3	8.5	5.7
The Communists	2.4	7.9	55.4	24.6	4.4	5.3
The Socialists	2.6	7.7	50.7	29.7	3.8	5.5
International student movements	2.8	11.7	47.7	25.9	6.5	5.3

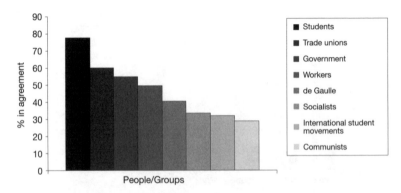

Figure 3.7 The above groups/people should be held responsible for the events of 1968

knowledge of the widespread nature of the events by alluding to the importance of 'trade unions' and 'workers', thus avoiding the pitfalls of the arguably
over-emphasized role of student elements. However, with those categories
demanding a fuller understanding of what happened such as the role of the
Socialists, the Communists and international student movements, uncertainty
prevails.

In a similar vein, question 16 asked respondents who they believed to have
been the true victims of the crisis. With certain groups quite clearly suffering
more than others as a result of May–June 1968, an appreciation of the level of
understanding could be ascertained.

Table 3.8 highlights how every category except for that of 'students' received
a majority of uncertain responses. Figure 3.8 demonstrates the high rate of
certainty yet shows how the four categories, 'students', 'de Gaulle', 'government' and 'workers' received more responses affirming that they were victims
than disagreeing. The other four categories, 'bourgeoisie', 'socialists',
'communists' and 'trade unions', show the contrary. Of these categories it is
quite surprising to note that the 'Communists' and the 'Socialists' revealed the
most uncertainty since these were two groups that really did suffer as a result
of the events.[4] Nevertheless, the fact that considerable percentages of respondents displayed some knowledge of the negative impact of 1968 for the

Table 3.8 The following groups/people were the real victims of the 1968 events

	SD	D	N	A	SA	M
Students	3.2	20.4	28.3	33.1	6.3	8.7
Workers	2.4	16.8	42.6	24	4	10.3
Trade unions	4	19.2	49.7	14.5	2	10.7
The government	4.4	17.6	38.6	25.5	3.2	10.7
De Gaulle	4.8	15.8	36.4	25.3	7.1	10.5
The Communists	4.2	20.6	53.5	8.5	1.2	12.1
The Socialists	3.6	22.2	52.9	7.9	0.6	12.9
Bourgeoisie	8.1	20.8	39	18.4	3.2	10.5

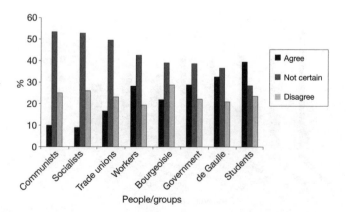

Figure 3.8 The above groups/people were the real victims of the 1968 events

government at the time (28.7 per cent) and de Gaulle (32.4 per cent) does again highlight some level of understanding. A similar look at the answers to question 18, 'The following groups/people did the most to resolve the crisis of May 1968', once again reveals the uncertainty surrounding certain elements of the events. Asking who the respondents believed to have done the most to bring the crisis to an end highlights just how deep young French people's knowledge of May–June 1968 goes.

Table 3.9 reveals how the 'students' category is that which is least character-ized by uncertainty. However, this time it is joined by 'government' and 'trade unions'. Figure 3.9 shows the vast rate of uncertainty with all options, whilst demonstrating the top four categories considered as having done the most to resolve the crisis: 'government', 'students', 'trade unions' and 'workers'. Not only do the four typical categories come out on top but, once again, the level of not certain responses reveals considerable ignorance of some, admittedly fine yet very important, details of exactly what happened in 1968. Particularly notable is the lack of understanding surrounding the role of the Communists in resolving the crisis. However, it could be argued that, with almost 40 per cent of respondents agreeing that the government and trade unions were important in bringing the crisis to a close, there certainly appears to be a fairly respectable level of understanding.

Table 3.9 The following groups/people did the most to resolve the crisis of May 1968

	SD	D	N	A	SA	M
Students	3.4	18.4	35	29.1	5.9	8.1
Workers	2	15.2	47.7	21.2	3.2	10.7
Trade unions	2.4	11.1	37.6	34.1	5.3	9.5
The government	1.4	12.3	37.2	34.9	4.8	9.5
De Gaulle	4.6	15.8	49.1	16.8	3.4	10.3
The Communists	3.2	14.7	62.4	8.3	1	10.5
The Socialists	2	13.1	55.4	17.2	1.6	10.7
Bourgeoisie	10.7	24.2	48.5	4.6	0.6	11.5

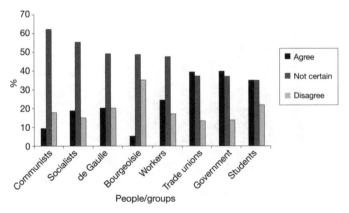

Figure 3.9 The above groups/people did the most to resolve the crisis of May 1968

With a certain idea of the events dominating the wide-ranging vectors of history and memory, the assumption was that there was a lack of genuine understanding, particularly of the least talked of, yet vitally important, aspects of the events. The results demonstrate that whilst an overall understanding of the crisis exists, key elements reveal a high degree of uncertainty. The impact of the narrow, stereotypical portrayal is, as suggested, discernible. In many respects this has to be expected as it is impossible for young people to be inter-ested in the finer details of historical events such as 1968. Nevertheless, the fact that, for example, such a significant proportion of respondents (20 per cent) believe the crisis to have been limited to the capital is symptomatic of their narrow portrayal. Many analyses ignore the nationwide aspect of the crisis of 1968 and this appears to have not been without significance for current attitudes. It has also been demonstrated that aspects of the revolt are unknown to young people, confirming the difficulties (as highlighted in chapter two) in forming a complete picture of the events.

One can begin to delineate a significant, two-pronged trend concerning the impact of the events' portrayal. One the one hand, the constant re-visiting of the events through the now traditional, periodic reassessments has ensured a certain prominence of them in the public eye. Consequently, and perhaps more so than other such historical moments, young people are actually quite familiar with what happened in 1968. However, such familiarity and know-ledge are based – as discussed previously – on a progressively narrow portrayal. As a result, there are clear and inescapable limitations on just how far levels of understanding can stretch. Whether or not such a trend extends to how the influence of the events is considered merits attention.

Specific areas such as feminism, education and morals are commonly perceived as being affected by the events. However, whether or not other areas – those that have seen more subtle developments or are less logically or commonly associated with the events – are considered as having been affected is another question altogether. The analysis of the following questions will gauge the level of understanding in regard to the extent of the events' influence. As has been already established in Table 3.4 and demonstrated in Figure 3.10, the results of question 4 of the survey, 'The events of 1968 have been a positive experience for France' are quite conclusive, with almost three-quarters of those questioned indicating that they considered the events a positive experience.

In question 7 the respondents were asked to reply to the following statement: 'The events of May 1968 brought about real changes to French society.' The events of 1968 undeniably led to wholesale changes to French society, some of which were rapid and highly mediatized while others took longer and were much more subtle. With such a sweeping majority agreeing that the events were a positive experience for France, this question would test to what extent the dominant representation concerning the influence of 1968 had permeated popular perceptions. The results, as Table 3.10 shows, are indeed conclusive.

The overwhelming majority of respondents either agreed or strongly agreed, with very few uncertain responses and even fewer disagreeing. Respondents were in no doubt that the events have been both a positive experience for

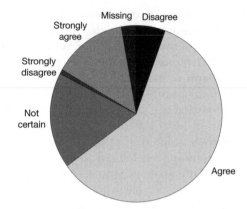

Figure 3.10 The events of 1968 have been a positive experience for France

France and that they have been important in the development of their society. As Figure 3.11 demonstrates, little or no significant differences are identifiable regionally with the high rate of agreement coupled with low percentages in disagreement reflected across the country. The results of questions 4 and 7 produced around 75 per cent positive responses, indicating recognition of the significance of 1968 in bringing about changes. Data on the statement 'The following sectors were most affected by the 1968 events' enables closer scrutiny

Table 3.10 The events of May 1968 brought about real changes to French society

	Frequency	*Per cent*
Strongly disagree	5	10.0
Disagree	28	5.5
Not certain	71	14.1
Agree	303	60.0
Strongly agree	82	16.2
Total	489	96.8
Missing	16	3.2
Total	505	100.0

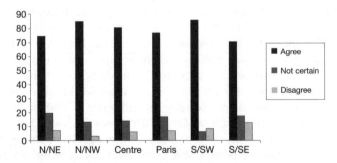

Figure 3.11 The events of May 1968 brought about real changes to French society

Table 3.11 The following sectors were most affected by the 1968 events

	SD	D	N	A	SA	M
Education	0.4	2	6.1	59.2	29.3	3
Trade unions	0.6	3.2	29.5	49.9	11.1	5.7
Working conditions	0.2	8.9	33.1	43.4	7.9	6.5
Politics	1	7.7	31.9	47.9	5.9	5.5
Judicial system	4	27.1	55.8	6.9	0.4	5.7
Regional movements	4	18.6	57.4	12.1	1.6	6.3
Media	1.2	9.1	33.3	41.2	9.1	6.1
Police	2	12.7	41.2	31.9	5.7	6.5
Feminism	1	4.4	18.2	46.3	25.9	4.2
Social mores	0.6	3.8	10.7	49.3	31.1	4.6

of where exactly those changes are perceived to have taken place. As Table 3.11 and Figure 3.12 show, the outcome was a long way off the clear-cut results of the previous two questions.

'Education', 'feminism' and 'social mores' come out as the areas believed to be the most affected by the events. Between 50 and 60 per cent point to 'politics', 'media', 'working conditions' and 'trade unions'. It appears that young French people are not sure as to the effect of 1968 on 'regional movements', 'the police' or the 'judicial system.'

As Figure 3.12 shows, although the majority of options given showed strong percentages in agreement, the results for other areas were far from conclusive. The most obvious sectors, or those more commonly associated with the events, received high percentages in agreement. Only the options 'regional movements' and 'judicial system' had higher percentages in disagreement than in agreement. However, there is also an extremely high rate of not certain responses in all areas except those that have become synonymous with the crisis of 1968.

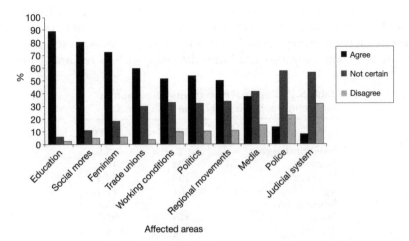

Figure 3.12 The above sectors were most affected by the 1968 events

This section began with the suggestion that certain areas would be considered as having been more affected by the events than others and that such areas would be those more commonly associated or those areas that characterize the dominant narrative, whilst some other important sectors are often ignored. The results of the question asking what areas respondents considered most affected by the crisis confirm that this suggestion is correct. The stereotypical areas such as education, feminism and morals come out with many in agreement. Those areas that have received considerably less coverage (such as regional issues, the justice system and the police) not only have very few in agreement that they have been affected by the crisis of 1968 but more importantly have extremely high rates of not certain responses. In fact, in almost all sectors, the rate of uncertainty is significant. Nevertheless, that considerable percentages agreed that the events had an impact on areas such as working conditions (51.3 per cent), trade unions (51 per cent) and the media (50.3 per cent) is a fairly strong indication of a certain degree of comprehension surrounding the widespread impact of the events.

Certain areas of the events that involved important institutions of French society were pinpointed for particular attention. In particular, the influence of the events in the regions[5] and how the events affected the willingness of students to demonstrate.[6] In question 8, respondents were asked to indicate what areas of French society they believed to have been most affected by the 1968 events. One of the ten proposed options was *Les mouvements régionaux.*

As Table 3.12 demonstrates, there is a substantial degree of not certain responses regarding the impact of 1968 on regional movements. Over one-fifth of respondents either disagreed or strongly disagreed that the events had had an impact in this area. In question 14 those surveyed were asked their opinion on the following statement: 'The events of May 1968 have made it easier for students and *lycéens* to demonstrate on the streets.'

As Table 3.13 shows, an overwhelming majority either agreed or strongly agreed. Only 7.7 per cent were in disagreement with 10 per cent uncertain. The difference between the two sets of results set out in Tables 3.12 and 3.13 demonstrates how the obvious areas such as education are believed to have been very much affected by the events. On the other hand, responses to questions on areas that are less commonly associated with the crisis, such as regional issues, are

Table 3.12 Regional movements were amongst the sectors most affected by the 1968 events

	Frequency	*Per cent*
Strongly disagree	20	4.0
Disagree	94	18.6
Not certain	290	57.4
Agree	61	12.1
Strongly agree	8	1.6
Total	473	93.7
Missing	32	6.3
Total	505	100

Table 3.13 The events of May 1968 have made it easier for students and *lycéens* to demonstrate on the streets

	Frequency	*Per cent*
Strongly disagree	8	1.6
Disagree	31	6.1
Not certain	51	10.1
Agree	306	60.6
Strongly agree	95	18.8
Total	491	97.2
Missing	14	2.8
Total	505	100

characterized by significantly higher percentages in disagreement and uncertainty. Figure 3.13 demonstrates the differences between these two areas.

A significant difference exists between perceived effects of the crisis of 1968 on regional movements and on the education system. The difference between the certainty concerning how one area has been affected compared to the uncertainty surrounding another is obvious in these results. It is easy to assume that because May 1968 is increasingly depicted very much as student orientated that it has been extremely influential in the educational domain.[7] However, due to the dominance of events in the capital, little coverage has been afforded not only to what occurred in provincial France but also what its impact has been on regional movements, for instance. Consequently, and as demonstrated, little appears to be known about this aspect of the crisis. Such disparity between these results is undoubtedly due to the way in which the events have been portrayed.

The aim of this section has been to assess whether or not young French people are aware of the influence of the events of 1968. It would be incorrect to claim that an underestimation of their importance exists with so many agreeing that important changes have resulted. Furthermore, these developments have been considered as progressive with so many agreeing that it was

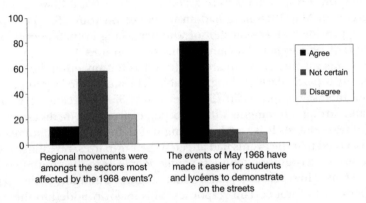

Figure 3.13 Comparison of results of questions 8 and 14

an altogether positive experience. There is evidently a broad recognition concerning the various areas that 1968 has influenced. Such levels of understanding, as was the case concerning the events themselves, reinforce the emerging trend that 1968 is in fact an area where young people clearly demonstrate some degree of understanding and are attributable to the strong and repeated presence of the 1968 events in popular discussion. Nevertheless, difficulties – and particularly uncertainty – became more obvious when respondents were asked to pinpoint the areas they perceive as being most influenced. Crucially, lacunas are discernable on those areas that have been airbrushed from conventional representations. Therefore, and logically, uncertainty as to the effects on the police, the justice system and regional movements exist and will persist until they are given the same attention as areas such as the education system, morals or feminism.

It has been established that, despite respondents' certainty that the events have been influential, the level of understanding concerning exactly where this influence has been most prominent is limited. Furthermore, such impressions appear to have been shaped, to a certain extent, by the stereotypical perceptions so heavily emphasized in the dominant portrayal of the events. In this section of the survey analysis, the aim is to establish whether or not young French people believe the crisis of 1968 to have had a direct effect on their own lives. The continual and still inconclusive debates on why the upheaval happened, its influence and its legacy have led to much uncertainty concerning its tangible effects. Whilst many young people may well accept that the events of 1968 have been extremely important, it could be argued that this assumption is based on the fact that they are a continual source of debate and that they have become a constant reference point. This section therefore aims to address two questions. Do young people believe that the events have influenced and continue to influence their own lives? Or do they have an image of May 1968 as a curious moment during which their parents revolted immaturely against the state, the result of which has been change that may well have been important thirty years ago but, in reality, no longer holds any importance?

In question 9 respondents were asked to reply to the following statement: 'The events of May 1968 have had an influence on your life.' This question aimed to provide a clear snapshot of whether young French people believed the events of 1968 to have had any bearing on their lives.

The results for this question are as divided as for any other, but the rate of uncertainty is particularly striking. As Table 3.14 shows, the largest proportion declared themselves uncertain (39.6 per cent), 35.8 per cent were in agreement and strong agreement, with 21.6 per cent either in disagreement or strong disagreement. It is worth pointing out that more respondents agreed than disagreed that the events had affected their own lives, revealing that there is some sort of recognition amongst young people as to the continued impact of the events. However, one statistic that requires attention is the high rate (39.6 per cent) of not certain responses. This majority added to the 21.6 per cent of those disagreeing brings to almost two-thirds the number of

Table 3.14 The events of May 1968 have had an influence on your life

	Frequency	*Per cent*
Strongly disagree	36	7.1
Disagree	73	14.5
Not certain	200	39.6
Agree	150	29.7
Strongly agree	31	6.1
Total	490	97.0
Missing	15	3.0
Total	505	100

respondents not sure or disagreeing that the events have had some sort of influence for them personally.

In question 10, the 35.8 per cent of respondents who agreed that the events had had some sort of effect on their lives were asked to indicate in exactly what areas. The results of this question would show what areas those believing that the crisis had influenced their lives felt have been specifically affected. By seeking more detail it would enable an assessment of the impact of those areas that have become synonymous with 1968 through their prevalence in the dominant discourse.

Table 3.15 shows how the categories 'politics', 'working conditions' and 'regional identity' received a considerable number of 'not certain' responses. The other four areas, 'education', 'social mores', 'feminism' and 'family relations', all came out with well over 50 per cent of respondents in agreement. As evidenced in Figure 3.14, when shown in a bar chart these results are much clearer. Whereas the four areas that have become most commonly associated with the events (and help strengthen the image of the events as portrayed by the 'official history') have substantial percentages in agreement, dwarfing the rate of uncertainty, the three remaining areas are dominated by not certain responses.

Of the seven options offered none received considerable numbers disagreeing. Whilst the most obvious and highly discussed areas, such as education and feminism, received substantial percentages in agreement, every option offered, except regional identity, from politics to family relations, received considerably more positive than negative responses. However, it must be

Table 3.15 The following sectors of your life have been most affected by the 1968 events

	SD	*D*	*N*	*A*	*SA*	*M*
Education	0.6	1.1	7.7	66.3	21.5	2.8
Politics	1.1	9.9	43.6	33.7	6.1	5.5
Family relations	2.2	7.7	25.4	45.9	12.7	6.1
Working conditions	2.2	6.6	45.9	35.9	3.3	6.1
Regional identity	4.4	21	60.8	5.5	1.1	7.2
Social mores	2.2	3.3	15.5	54.1	22.1	2.8
Feminism	1.7	4.4	16	50.8	23.8	3.3

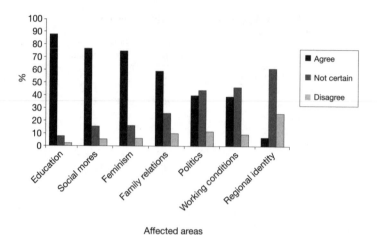

Affected areas

Figure 3.14 The following sectors of your life have been most affected by the 1968 events

noted that extremely high rates of uncertainty were recorded for the areas of politics and working conditions. Family relations also received a surprising 25 per cent of respondents declaring themselves uncertain. When one considers that those responding to this particular question were only those who accepted that the events had had an effect on their own lives, and that this was by no means a majority, the effect of 1968, especially in specific areas, remains uncertain.

The aim of this section has been to establish whether or not young French people consider the events to have directly affected their lives. There can be no doubt that the wide-ranging influence of what happened in 1968 has meant that very important sectors of French society, from the family to the education system, have been affected in some way. However, the results reveal a degree of uncertainty as to whether such an influence is felt by young people today. The high level of unsure responses in this area is indicative of the dominance of uncertainty amongst young French people as to the influence of 1968 on their own lives. Furthermore, the areas that characterize the stereotypical perception of the influence of 1968 are, predictably, those that are most popular amongst respondents. Conversely, the perceived impact on issues such as regional identity, working conditions and politics is minimal. Due to the complexities of the 1968 crisis and the wide-ranging and varying impact it had, it would be impossible for young people in general to be completely conscious of how the events have influenced their own lives. Nevertheless, the interest lies in what the perceived impact has been. This section has highlighted the dominance of stereotypical ideas as well as a lack of knowledge in areas not commonly associated with 1968. However, ironically, the only real certainty to be taken from these results is that young people are clearly uncertain of the effect of 1968 on their own lives. The fact that almost every single area, from education through to family relations, morals and feminism, received significantly more respondents agreeing than disagreeing that 1968 has been influential is revelatory of significant appreciation of the widespread and continued influence of the events. The fact that the issue of regional identity is dominated by over 60 per cent uncertain responses nevertheless reminds us of the shortcomings of how the events have been portrayed and consolidates the hypothesis that young French people generally underestimate the significance of the 1968 events.

In this final section the one question that was behind the original motivation to undertake this analysis of the attitudes of young French people regarding the events of 1968 is assessed. As discussed in earlier chapters and as expressed by several commentators, many look back on the crisis of 1968 as some sort of spectacular moment that created much fuss and trouble but in reality was not particularly important. Drawing on some of the results already established in the previous four hypotheses, the following section assesses whether or not young French people credit the events with the importance they arguably merit. An overwhelming percentage of respondents to question 4 agreed that the events have been a positive experience for France. It has equally been established that respondents were proud of the events as a historical event. However, a more detailed probing of respondents' understanding drew out a number of difficulties and revealed some interesting points. It becomes increasingly evident that a complete understanding of the events is absent, with the stereotypical ideas of the perceptions of the crisis coming out as those that dominate the majority of young people's ideas of what happened in May–June 1968. Whether it be concerning Parisian dominance in the crisis (see Table 3.6 and Figure 3.6), those who should be held responsible (see Table 3.7 and Figure 3.7), the true victims (see Table 3.8 and Figure 3.8) or those who did the most to bring the events to a close (see Table 3.9 and Figure 3.9), a trend becomes obvious. Great uncertainty surrounds key, yet little talked-of areas, with those ideas synonymous with the crisis receiving considerably higher percentages of respondents in agreement. Similar trends are discernible when attempting to gauge the extent to which young French people understand the events' influence.

Once again, a positive impression is generally prevalent. A significant majority of those asked believe the events to have led to real changes in French society (see Table 3.10 and Figure 3.11). However, as appears to be the case elsewhere, when asked to be more specific or when their genuine understanding of the events is put to the test, respondents' problems become evident. When they are asked what areas have been most affected, their responses reveal the same trends evident in previous results (see Table 3.11 and Figure 3.12). There is considerable uncertainty throughout. Those areas that have become closely related to the events once again come out on top. This trend is highlighted in the comparison between the effect of 1968 on students and on regional movements (see Tables 3.12 and 3.13, and Figure 3.13). Because 1968 began as a student protest and has been predominantly described as such over the years, many more respondents believe that the crisis has been more influential on the education system than on regional issues.[8] It is clear that, because analyses of what occurred beyond the capital and the influence of 1968 on the development of regional issues have been kept to a minimum, the assumption today is that 1968 has not been important in this area.[9] Similar trends can be highlighted when assessing perceptions amongst young people as to the impact of 1968 on their own lives.

The results of question 9 revealed massive uncertainty, with almost 40 per cent of those asked declaring themselves unsure as to whether the events had had an influence on their lives (see Table 3.14). When those agreeing that the events had affected their lives were asked to indicate in what specific areas, the high level of uncertainty remained constant (see Table 3.15 and Figure 3.14). It must be repeated that those areas that have become closely associated with being influenced by the events such as feminism, morals or education received considerably higher positive responses than less talked-of areas. On the one hand it could be surmised that young French people are – in the main – unsure of what influence 1968 has had on their lives. Those who identify some influence turn to stereotypical areas with levels of uncertainty remaining significant.

Whether in terms of the events themselves or their influence, it would be incorrect to suggest that a complete lack of understanding exists amongst young French people. Across the board, respondents demonstrated a considerable grasp of the major themes and ideas concerning what happened and what the consequences have been. Nevertheless (and this has been made evident through the scrutiny of the extent of understanding), the impact of the narrow, dominant narrative is clear to see. As discussed earlier, such a depiction has influenced how perceptions of 1968 in France have been shaped and can help explain why it is viewed so positively and with such pride. One would be forgiven when analysing the results of this survey, given the recognition of the impact of 1968 in so many areas (together with the positivity and pride so clearly associated), for drawing the conclusion that young people do credit the 1968 events with the importance they merit. However, when one considers the inevitable restrictions that are brought about by the narrow portrayal, one must be careful not to overstate the importance afforded. Young people do consider the events to be important, but such a reading is based on their understanding as drawn from conventional representations that, as discussed, have been progressively shaped to satisfy the needs of the present. It therefore becomes difficult to clearly define current attitudes to the 1968 events. Without the necessary tools to fully understand what happened, why and the consequences, and given the pressures exerted by the need to control and mould the collective memory of *mai 68*, it would be fair to describe current attitudes as being characterized by a certain degree of ambiguity. Such inconclusiveness is reflected when respondents were asked to put the events into some sort of historical perspective.

In question 19 those surveyed were asked to respond to the following statement: 'The crisis of May 1968 has been the most important moment in post Second World War French history'. The results were far from conclusive.

Table 3.16 The crisis of May 1968 has been the most important moment in post Second World War French history

	Frequency	*Per cent*
Strongly disagree	52	10.3
Disagree	145	28.7
Not certain	100	19.8
Agree	153	30.3
Strongly agree	35	6.9
Total	485	96.0
Missing	20	4.0
Total	505	100

As Table 3.16 demonstrates, there is little agreement over this statement. A similar percentage agreed (39 per cent) and disagreed (37.2 per cent), with almost 20 per cent uncertain.

Conclusion

By way of a conclusion, the following analysis of the 'any other comments' section of the questionnaire provides an overview of the results. The responses demonstrate to what extent ideas on the crisis of 1968 can vary. In addition, these comments give good indications that can help explain why such attitudes to the events actually exist. It has been established throughout the results that there is a lack of understanding concerning several elements of the 1968 events and this is confirmed in the final section of the questionnaire. The acceptance by respondents of the fact that they do not know much about the events is very frequent. As one Breton student declared:

In responding to this questionnaire I have realised that I have heard of May '68, the events, but that there is no real depth. I know 'May '68' but I am not really aware of the elements that triggered it, who the main protagonists were, the consequences. It is a pity. I will try to remedy the situation.[10]

This opinion is common. One Alsatian student declared: 'I realise that I do not know enough about the events of May '68.'[11] Or, as a young student from the Centre region pleaded: 'A class on May '68 please!'[12] As well as this acceptance by numerous respondents of their unawareness of the events of 1968, such incomplete knowledge of the crisis led to some striking examples of misunderstanding. One example is the young student from Poitou-Charentes who declared: 'For our generation, the events of May 1968 are not well known and covered little in school. It started out as a workers' movement before spreading to the students.'[13] Or the student from the Centre region who believes that the events have led to no changes whatsoever. 'I wasn't born in 1968 but these events on the face of it changed nothing.'[14]

Respondents themselves provided explanations for the fact that they are unaware of what happened or have certain misconceptions. In particular, the lack of attention paid to 1968 in school and in the media is cited as a reason why young people seem so uncertain of what happened in 1968 and what the impact has been. As one student from the Midi-Pyrénées declared: 'For young people of my age, little is known of this event and it is even unimportant. For those in the provinces, it is not discussed a lot and in history classes it does not feature. We hear about it from time to time on the news but without any explanations.'[15] Or there is the Breton student, critical of the educational system: 'The lack of information on 1968 in the education system at least at *lycée* level is lamentable.'[16] Another frequent explanation is that the events were so long ago that young people cannot be expected to have a complete understanding. One student from Auvergne made the point that the events being so long ago may help explain the fact that young people are unaware of their impact. 'My generation is perhaps exposed to the consequences of May '68, but we are not conscious of it.'[17] Or, the student from the Centre: 'Young generations have forgotten virtually everything about May '68 or maybe never even were aware.'[18]

When a subject is continually the source of debate as much as the events of 1968, many diverse opinions are bandied about. One recent trend has been the proliferation of negative attitudes. Increasingly, it has become common to hear that the crisis of 1968 is responsible for the *malheurs* of today's society. Such opinions have been expressed in this section, such as that of one student from Provence-Alpes-Côte d'Azur for whom 'May '68 is responsible for the French unease and that includes 21 April.'[19] A Corsican student goes even further declaring: 'The crisis of '68 is no more than a left-wing tantrum aimed at bringing down the right wing government; provocation to reduce de Gaulle's popularity. The French should be ashamed of these events.'[20] These examples show just how far attitudes expressed in the media and in literature can be influential. Another trend to be found in coverage of the events is the minimizing of their importance; an increasingly apparent development as the years have passed. Those who were opposed to what happened have expressed the idea that the crisis of 1968 was a petulant revolt by bourgeois students. The results of this section have shown that this attitude still persists today, as exemplified by a Parisian student: 'A rich kids' revolution who had nothing better to do with their time.'[21] Or the Poitou-Charentes student who declared that 'As far as the students were concerned May '68 was a "daddy's boy" movement.'[22] This more recent trend is matched by another interesting attitude that dates right back to the end and immediate aftermath of the events. It became common in some circles at that time for certain individuals, struggling to explain what was happening, to relate the events in France to some sort of international conspiracy.[23] Despite never being proven or really given any credibility this opinion still appears to be present today. As an Alsatian respondent stated: 'The events of 1968 are linked to a student alliance who, given their age, had no place at university. It was a US–China–Israel based collusion aimed at forcing de Gaulle from power.'[24]

Despite these examples of clear uncertainty, unawareness and negativity in the attitudes of those questioned about the crisis of 1968, there are those who demonstrate a genuine understanding of the events and an appreciation of their impact:

A failed political revolution brought about by students and taken on by workers on the ground, controlled by the trade unions and suppressed by the Gaullist government and the police. May '68 is more a moral revolution and a generational conflict. Unfortunately, this tradition is finished today, especially for the '68ers themselves, many of whom have become capitalists.[25]

This young student from Poitou-Charentes shows considerable knowledge of the events, as does another from Languedoc-Roussillon who states: 'For our generation, the achievements of May 1968 seem natural. They are movements that are not well understood but it is clear that they changed the general social mores of the French.'[26]

In question 17 respondents were asked their opinion on the following statement: 'A similar situation to the events of 1968 could occur in France.' The results are shown in Figure 3.15.

Over 50 per cent of respondents believe that a similar crisis could occur. One quarter of respondents do not believe that a repeat of the events is likely and almost 20 per cent declare themselves uncertain. This question provoked considerable reaction in the 'any other comments' section. Amongst those respondents demonstrating their knowledge of the crisis, one factor is quite frequent. Recognizing the considerable differences that exist between today's society and that of the late 1960s, several respondents expressed their belief that in no way could the events of 1968 recur today. As one Breton student declared: 'We will never see such a situation again because we are in a society of each for his own. There is no interest in the collective but only the individual.'[27] This attitude is backed up by the Parisian student who claimed: 'Nowadays it would be difficult to reorganise a movement of

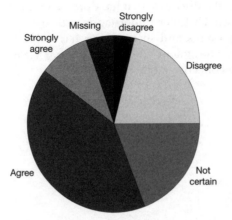

Figure 3.15 A similar situation to the events of 1968 could occur in France

such a magnitude. Mentalities and motivations are different.'[28] Despite the recognition of the great differences between the society of the 1960s and that of today and the fact that in today's conditions in no way could another 1968 happen again, there does appear to be a desire amongst quite a few young people to see a revolt on the same scale today. One Parisian student even declares: 'It would perhaps be a good idea to organise a second "revolution" to help get things moving in France'[29] – an attitude backed up by a student from Poitou-Charentes: 'May '68 was hopeful. Today we hope for another May '68.'[30] Such a desire for a repeat of the 1968 events reflects the positive perception concerning them amongst young people today.

This investigation has confirmed that the nature of the events' coverage and its progressively narrow perspective have shaped young people's reading of *mai 68*. As demonstrated across the results and as confirmed by several examples from the 'any other comments' section, the degree of understanding merits some recognition. In that respect, the unprecedented level of attention afforded to it has been positive, by giving young people sufficient information to formulate a comprehension of the broad outline of what happened, why and what the consequences have been. For an event that happened some forty years ago to be one that young French people are relatively knowledgeable of and interested in is indicative of the special place it has in the minds of the French in general. However, if one scratches below the surface it becomes clear that their ideas are based on a minimal understanding of the events. Deprived of the tools to further their understanding, knowledge of some areas is inevitably characterized by uncertainty whilst others are simply not associated with the crisis. This is true of the complexities of the events as well as the widespread nature of their influence. Therefore, the two-pronged impact of the events' coverage is clear to see. The paradox is that on the one hand the prominence of discussion on the events (characterized by the periodic reassessments that, as argued previously, are driven by the lack of consensus in key areas) has led to a familiarity surrounding the events, thereby ensuring a reasonable level of understanding. However, by propagating an increasingly limited perspective, the discourse that has dominated the decennial commemorations has prevented a fuller understanding of the true scope, magnitude and nature of the events and in so doing has helped shape what can be described as a very convenient consensus that has clearly not been without significance for the collective memory of *mai 68*.

Chapter Four
May/June 1968 and the French university system

Introduction

The majority of coverage of the university movement of 1968 is focused on the student fraternity in Nanterre and the Latin Quarter, with extreme left-wing students, their utopian ideals and revolutionary aspirations given pride of place. The crisis of the system of higher education is portrayed as a secondary issue in triggering student mobilization. The broader social malaise and the rebellious nature of young French people are given particular emphasis in explaining why the student world served as the spark of the 1968 revolt. Consequently, and as the overview below highlights, the crisis of the French system of higher education and the great desire for wholesale renewal amongst much of the university world during the crisis are downplayed elements of the 1968 movement. As a result, the subsequent university reforms receive little emphasis, which leads to a minimal appreciation of the legacy of 1968 for one of the institutions most affected.

Many aspects of the events have been subject to changing assessments, and the university crisis is no exception to this pattern. Of all the literature produced in the thirty years following the events, those texts written in their immediate aftermath place most emphasis on the significance of the numerous problems of the university system as fundamental in explaining the 1968 crisis. However, opinions are divided and there is evidence of the beginning of a trend that would see the role played by leftist elements dominating studies of the 1968 university movement. There are three types of analyses in such early texts. In accounts produced by prominent extreme left-wing militants there exists a clear desire to attach the university crisis to a broader social malaise.[1] The frustrations created by the weaknesses of the university system and the numerous problems ranging from sexual repression to archaic structures are described as giving militants the opportunity of politicizing the general student population with the aim of spreading the conflict beyond the walls of the faculties. The second type of early examination of the university crisis is represented by the important texts of two prominent Parisian university professors, Raymond Aron and Alain Touraine.[2] Both are unequivocal in highlighting the frailties of the university system, believing the events to have provided an opportunity for long-overdue reform. However, through their shared focus on those elements keen to extend the revolt more generally, Aron and Tourraine draw the similar conclusion that the opportunity provided was spurned.

Finally, Anzieu's text, examining the situation in Nanterre, is indicative of the emerging trend of the Parisian extreme left-wing minority dominating analyses of the university crisis of 1968.[3] Despite stressing the fact that militants were initially in the minority, it nonetheless describes how their ideas were crucial in mobilizing the student mass. Whilst indicating the split that existed between reformist and revolutionary factions, this analysis centres very much upon the latter.

In the years since the events, the details of the difficulties faced by the system of higher education as the reason behind the university crisis of 1968 have been increasingly minimized by a tendency to focus more on the revolutionary nature of certain elements. This is particularly evident in literature produced in and around the twentieth anniversary of the crisis. Such texts can be divided into two groups. The two *Génération* texts and *Que reste-t-il de Mai 68?* are those which best represent the first of these groups.[4] Despite outlining the existence of an important reformist movement in the years preceding 1968, *Génération 1* is limited due the fact that such details are described through the experiences of highly politicized, Parisian students (and in particular those at the Nanterre campus and the *Ecole Normale Supérieure*).[5] This narrow focus diminishes the importance of less spectacular yet important problems; a trend that continues in the second of the volumes which is an examination of the aftermath of the events through the experience of militants such as Bernard Kouchner, Jean-Pierre Goldman and Alain Krivine, none of whom demonstrated any particular concern for the plight of the system of higher education. A similarly limited view characterizes Weber's analysis which presents the events as an international revolt by the 1968 generation, whilst the problems experienced in the university are posited as only a secondary element in the general social malaise.[6] A second noteworthy trend is obvious in three other 1988 texts. Joffrin's *Mai 68, Histoire des événements* splits the upheaval into three separate crises – university, social, political – with the university movement receiving little coverage after the beginning of working-class involvement. The subsequent limitations of the assessment of the crisis in the university system are compounded with a specific focus on Paris through events in Nanterre and the Latin Quarter.[7] In a similar vein, Martelli's *Mai 68* pays scant attention to the events in the university world once the general strike takes hold. Whilst the implied monopoly of the role played by leftist militants in the student phase is somewhat reduced through references to similar movements in provincial towns, such revolts are described as merely following the trend set by Nanterre militants and in support of their ideas.[8] Martelli's analysis neglects the existence of reformist elements and fails to examine the legacy of the events on this institution. Capdevielle and Mouriaux's *Mai 68, l'Entre-deux de la modernité* is another study which highlights the independence of the university crisis from the subsequent social and political upheavals. The description of the student phase is dominated by utopian ideals and portrayed as having simply sparked off a general revolt that had been brewing for some time.[9]

By the time of the thirtieth anniversary, analyses of the university movement had been reduced, almost exclusively, to assessments of the role played by *gauchiste* militants. Consequently, notably less attention is paid to the reality of the critical state of the system of higher education at the time and the role of 1968 in shaping the development of this institution. The literature of 1998 can also be divided into two sections. The first is characterized by Tarnero's and Fauré's texts. In *Mai 68 – La Révolution fiction*, as the title suggests, little serious-ness is attached to the motivations of the 1968 movement. Describing student motivations as being brought about by a generation of young people drawing on extremist ideologies from around the world, Tarnero's analysis reduces the role of the protagonists of the events to being solely intent on playing a revolu-tionary game.[10] Despite being more detailed in terms of the numerous problems concerning the system of higher education and recognition of the Napoleonic nature of the structures, Fauré's *Mai 68, jour et nuit* is typical of the virtually exclusive focus on *gauchiste* elements of the university movement.[11] Concentrating on the more spectacular actions and ideas of Parisian – and in particular, Nanterre – students, it lacks a concerted focus of any serious reformist tendencies. Lavabre and le Goff's texts represent the second group of analyses. In *Les Mouvements de 1968*, significantly greater detail is offered in terms of the problems facing the system in the build-up to the events. Describing *mai 68* as part of an international malaise, Lavabre focuses heavily on radical elements in order to highlight common traits between the French student fraternity and their counterparts in other nations. Despite recognizing that one of the victories of the 1968 movement was forcing the government into reform through the Faure law, such concessions are described as minimal.[12] *Mai 68, l'héritage impossible*, focusing specifically on the extreme left-wing elements of the 1968 movement, offers a comprehensive analysis of the growing university malaise prior to May 1968 as well as a study of the Faure reform and its implementation. In addition to the plethora of difficulties analysed elsewhere, le Goff pays particular attention to the archaic nature of the structures that led to an inherent resistance to modernization in spite of a growing momentum behind the call for the adaptation of the system to the needs of society. Underlining the fact that extreme left-wing elements were very much in a minority, le Goff nonetheless describes the majority of the university world as being caught up in the moment, intent on having a good time or as he describes it, 'a bit of fun'.[13]

Whilst early literature focused on the extensive range of problems that were responsible for rendering the university the starting point for the momentous events of spring 1968, the seeds of the future portrayal of this area of the crisis were sown. As the years have unfolded, this reductionist view has gained ground as the abundance of difficulties that weakened the university system prior to 1968 have received considerably less attention than the utopian demands of the *groupuscules*. The serious difficulties of the system of higher education are pushed into the background, as is the importance of 1968 for the development of this institution. The details of the issues responsible for mobilizing students around the country are absent as is an appreciation of what impact – if any – the events have had on the French university system. The importance of students in triggering the events of 1968 explains why they are constantly at the centre of the portrayal of the crisis. As a result, the French university system is an obvious area to examine when investigating the influence of the revolt and the impact of the dominant discourse on current attitudes. Let us first of all consider current perceptions in this domain.

In question 8 of the survey, respondents were asked their opinion on the statement 'The following sectors were most affected by the 1968 events.' Table 4.1 indicates the breakdown of the results of those who singled out 'Education'.

Table 4.1 Education was one of the sectors most affected by the 1968 events

	Frequency	*Per cent*
Strongly disagree	2	0.4
Disagree	10	2.0
Not certain	31	6.1
Agree	299	59.2
Strongly agree	148	29.3
Total	490	97.0
Missing	15	3.0
Total	505	100.0

Almost 90 per cent of respondents either agreed or strongly agreed that education was affected by the crisis of 1968, with only 2.4 per cent disagreeing or strongly disagreeing. As highlighted in Figure 4.1, a comparison of those in agreement in each of the ten areas offered as options is revelatory of the assumed link between the events and education.

'Social mores', 'feminism', 'trade unions', 'politics', 'working conditions' and 'media' are considered as being very much influenced. However, it is 'education' that tops the results with significantly more respondents agreeing that this institution was most influenced by the crisis. In question 9 of the survey, respondents were asked whether or not they consider the events of 1968 to have had an influence on their own lives. Those who agreed or strongly agreed were then asked in question 10 to pinpoint the specific areas they believed to have been most influenced. Of the seven options offered, one was 'education'.

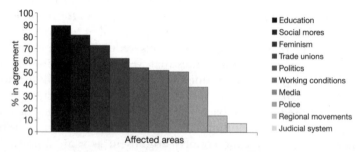

Figure 4.1 The following sectors were most affected by the 1968 events. Note: results are a combination of agree and strongly agree responses

Table 4.2 The events of May 1968 have had an impact on my own education

	Frequency	Per cent
Strongly disagree	1	0.6
Disagree	20	1.1
Not certain	14	7.7
Agree	120	66.3
Strongly agree	39	21.5
Total	176	97.2
Missing	5	2.8
Total	181	100

Table 4.2 shows how an overwhelming majority of respondents who believed the events to have had an influence on their lives agreed that their own education had been one of the areas affected. It is possible to rank those areas where respondents believe 1968 to have been influential in order to evaluate the relative importance attached to the impact on individual sectors.

As Figure 4.2 demonstrates, the areas of 'politics', 'working conditions' and 'regional identity' received below 50 per cent in agreement. 'Family relations', 'feminism' and 'social mores' all received significantly high percentages in agreement. However, it is once again the case that 'education' is most popular. Question 14 of the survey asked respondents their opinions on the following statement: 'The events of May 1968 have made it easier for students and *lycéens* to demonstrate on the streets.' As Table 4.3 shows, almost 80 per cent of those questioned were in agreement.

The results from the questions regarding 1968 and its impact on education issues allow for clear conclusions to be drawn. An overwhelming majority believe this domain to have been affected by the 1968 events. This is not only true in general terms. The fact that a similar percentage of respondents consider the events to have had an impact on their own education reveals a widely held opinion that the events have had a durable influence in this area. The fact that a majority of respondents mention it as one of the most affected sectors confirms the perceived correspondence between 1968 and education

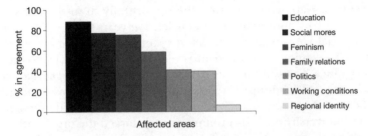

Figure 4.2 The following sectors of my own life have been most affected by the events of May 1968. Note: these results are taken only from those who declared their belief that the events had been influential on their own lives. The results are the combination of agree and strongly agree responses.

Table 4.3 The events of May 1968 have made it
easier for students and lycéens to demonstrate on
the streets

	Frequency	*Per cent*
Strongly disagree	8	1.6
Disagree	31	6.1
Not certain	51	10.1
Agree	306	60.6
Strongly agree	95	18.8
Total	491	97.2
Missing	14	2.8
Total	505	100

issues. Finally, that almost 80 per cent of young French people questioned believe that 1968 influences the French tradition of student protests is indicative of the significance they attach to the crisis and reveals another sphere of influence in this area. The following sections – by focusing on the system of higher education – aim to assess whether such opinions are well founded or whether the assimilation between education and *mai 68* is a misplaced amalgam resulting from the narrow portrayal of the events. It is therefore necessary to examine the years prior, what exactly the university movement was demanding and to what extent those demands and the nature of the crisis have gone on to be of influence.

The French university system: origins to 1968

The period between the creation of the first French university in 1208–9 in Paris and the Revolution of 1789 saw the founding of important characteristics of the system. In particular, it was during this era that the state took full control, bringing higher education under the tutelage of central authorities.[14] The Revolution was a particularly critical moment as universities were suppressed and professional schools, today's *Grandes Ecoles*, were created. Much discussion ensued as to how best to organize higher education but no concrete measures were put in place. Therefore, upon his accession to power at the end of the eighteenth century, Napoleon was given the opportunity to institute a system in accordance with his authoritarian tendencies. The years 1806–8 saw the creation of the Imperial University, an education system completely controlled by the Emperor.[15] The nation was divided into twenty-seven *académies*, each comprising various faculties. To assist the state, the *Conseil de l'instruction publique* was instituted. This council, made up of professors nominated by the government, played a significant role in the organization of the faculties and dominated every element of university life.[16] Its prominence reinforced the organization of the system along disciplinary lines. The early nineteenth century therefore saw the institution of one-dimensional faculties, strictly controlled and orientated by the central government and the *Conseil de l'instruction publique*, leading to a system characterized by 'dispersion and scattering'.[17]

Almost the entire nineteenth century passed without any concerted effort at reform. The only measures taken occurred beyond the faculties and further weakened their position. With the bolstering of the *Grandes Ecoles* system and the creation of the *Ecole Pratique des Hautes Etudes pour la Recherche* (1868), the training of the French elite and academic innovation were increasingly taking place elsewhere. With faculties progressively more independent of each other, it seemed that the absence of a true university system had been accepted in a period described as 'a blank in the history of the French university system'.[18] However, the beginning of the Third Republic heralded a series of reforms.[19] Faculties within each *académie* were grouped to form newly-founded universities. The status of 'student' was recognized, the first grants were awarded and an attempt was made to improve facilities with the construction of new university buildings.[20] Despite such an effort at reform, the previous period of prolonged stagnation meant that certain features were almost impossible to eradicate. The system remained strictly controlled by the central state, eminent professors maintained their powerful voice in the decision-making process and, whilst on paper universities had been reinstituted, the faculties continued to dominate. This *République des facultés*[21] was sustained, as was the mentality governing them; a characteristic that would prove extremely difficult to eliminate.[22] From 1896 to the beginning of the Fifth Republic, no groundbreaking reforms were undertaken. Whilst important, changes such as the introduction of the *propédeutique*[23] in 1948 or the *CAPES*[24] in 1950 did little to tackle the obvious weaknesses. In fact, the university system was further undermined during this period with the creation of the *CNRS* and the *ENA* in 1945.[25] It was equally at this time that the supremacy of Paris in the university world was confirmed. Housing the most prestigious institutions, the capital monopolized the system. This exaggeration of the importance of Paris would lead to a chronic lack of facilities and inhibit the development of regional faculties. As the Fourth Republic came to an end, the absence of university reform led to the emergence of a very particular system of higher education. The existence of a selective, well-funded family of *Grandes Ecoles*, assuring the training of the nation's elite, together with important research being conducted in bodies outside the faculties, left the latter in a precarious position. One-dimensional in terms of the courses on offer, with no control over intake and the principal objective of producing future teachers and low-level civil servants, the university system was to become the focus of much criticism.

De Gaulle's return to power in 1958 and the creation of the Fifth Republic saw many further calls for a renewal of the university system. However, as past experiences had demonstrated, this institution was highly resistant to reform.[26] It was this inability to change in the face of mounting pressure that would finally lay bare the weaknesses. The initial years of the Fifth Republic were dominated by the Algerian War. This issue led to a sharp politicization of the student environment in the early 1960s, reflected in the power wielded by the major student union – *L'UNEF* – at this time.[27] With the resolution of the Algerian crisis in 1962, the attention of militant students turned to criticism of the university system.[28] The weaknesses highlighted were certainly not new, but the rising number of student enrolments exacerbated them and increased calls for action to be taken.[29] Student organizations were not alone in calling for university reform. As early as 1956, a conference was held that led to the creation of the *Association pour l'expansion de la recherche scientifique*.[30] This group, made up of students, teachers, civil servants and even some important politicians (for example, Pierre Mendès-France and Valéry Giscard d'Estaing), came together in order to discuss a way forward for the French university system.[31] A second conference held by this group in 1966 would put further pressure on the government and was indicative of the desire for change that was mounting throughout the 1960s.

In 1962, Christian Fouchet was appointed Minister of Education. His attempts at university reform highlighted this institution's resistance to change and revealed the frustrations that existed. Fouchet focused on three specific areas: the necessity for the professionalization of higher education in order to adapt it to the needs of an ever-modernizing economy; a redefinition of the programme of studies within the faculties that would reduce the dropout and failure rates; and, most controversially, the introduction of a process of selection for entrance to university.[32] By 1966, the first two areas had led to important reforms. First, the *IUT*, offering a two-year programme of studies resulting in a professional qualification, was created.[33] Second, the *Propédeutique* was suppressed and replaced by two successive cycles: a two-year course resulting in the *DEUL* or *DEUS*, followed by a one-year course resulting in a *Licence* or a two-year course leading to the *Maîtrise*.[34] As a result of much opposition, Fouchet was forced to abandon any idea of selection, the *baccalauréat* being maintained as the sole requirement for entry to university. The implementation of these changes proved costly and difficult. The entire system was struggling to cope with the rising number of enrolments and Fouchet's series of reforms further complicated the organization of studies, putting the structures under even greater pressure. Instead of relieving the many tensions that had surfaced over the state of the university system, the Fouchet reforms gave those campaigning for wholesale change something to focus on and a cause with which they could stir the student masses.[35]

To help deal with the demographic explosion the government increased the number of new buildings, speeded up their construction and employed more university teaching staff. However, these measures created further difficulties. Students were forced to attend faculties on the outskirts of cities. New buildings were constructed in such haste that little consideration was given to the requirements of their users. It is no coincidence that the events of 1968 began at Nanterre, for this faculty represented everything that students detested in these new campuses. Isolated in the suburbs of Paris, Nanterre was not only difficult to get to. The depressing surroundings of shantytowns did little to alleviate the frustrations felt because of the lack of facilities, local amenities and the complete detachment from the exciting atmosphere of the Latin Quarter and general city life.[36] The arrival of a wave of new teaching staff also created problems in the prelude to 1968. In order to economize, many of those employed were young assistants leading (critically for 1968) to a 'divide [which] was widening with each year, between the older *professeurs* attached to university traditions and the often very young assistants who were a lot closer to the thoughts and feelings of students'.[37]

On the eve of the 1968 events, the university system was in a precarious position. It was, for Edmond Monange – who experienced the events in his first year as a university lecturer at the University of Brest before going on to have a long career in the same institution – an ideal place for the revolt to begin: 'The university is a place where we find young people who must reflect and in 1968 it was still ossified whilst at the same time subjected to problems linked to the massive influx of students.'[38] Christian Thibon – a historian at the University of Pau who experienced the events as a *lycéen* – flagged up an inherent contradiction that was inevitably to cause tension: 'We were in the most conservative institution with the most revolutionary population.'[39] The events of 1968 were much more than a protest for university reform. Nevertheless, whilst factors exterior to the university system were certainly fundamental in the emergence of the movement of 1968, the problems that existed within the system of higher education go a long way towards explaining just why it all began there, or as Philippe Blanchet – director of research at the University of Rennes who has clear memories of 1968 despite experiencing it as a child – put it: 'Because it was there that society was most out of sync. Students had the bread and the knife and they made their sandwich.'[40] It is important to clarify exactly what the motivations were that drove this university-based revolt.

The university movement of 1968

As le Goff comments, 'The university is a particularly revelatory example of the mutation of French society and the climate of insignificance towards which young people were particularly sensitive'.[41] A gulf had emerged between the baby-boom generation and its elders with the attitude of those in authority considered outdated and conservative.[42] The world was changing at a great rate and yet, the archaic nature of France's institutions and decision makers (personified by de Gaulle and university 'mandarins')[43] were seen to have prevented young people from benefiting fully from such developments. Furthermore, fears were increasing about the threat of unemployment amongst young graduates. The accumulation of these problems created 'a situation where material conditions were deplorable, contact with professors impossible, and enrolment opportunities available only in programs of studies that offered little chance of employment'.[44] The decline in the influence of l'UNEF – a drop from a membership of 50 per cent of students in 1960 to less than 10 per cent in 1967[45] – after the Algerian crisis is indicative of the demise of traditional political organizations within student circles in the 1960s. It was, however, the demise of student support for the PCF – in particular the 1965 split – that led to the creation of extreme left-wing groups that would play such a significant role in 1968.[46] The *gauchistes*, inspired largely by revolutionary figures such as Marx, Mao, Castro, Trotsky and Lenin, considered the

university system in France to be an example of the overwhelming dominance
of the consumer society, providing 'teaching based on the consumption of
knowledge, not humane education'.[47] Using the growing tension within the
universities and the issue of the ongoing Vietnam War, these militants awak-
ened the consciousness of the silent student mass and were thus fundamental
in triggering the 1968 events.

However, as Fischer indicates, 'The majority of French students showed
their reticence if not their hostility towards the leftist model'.[48] Whilst the
actions of this minority sparked the initial riots that began the entire movement of 1968, university reform was not their principal preoccupation.
Furthermore, the first phase of the events, that saw the emergence of a united
and determined movement, flared up in protest against the repressive attitude
of the police and the state and was fixed on three clear objectives in no way
related to the *gauchiste* agenda.[49] This initial mishandling allowed the crisis to
escalate and led to the increased involvement of those outside the university
system. When Pompidou yielded to the three demands of the student movement on 11 May, the existence of a very real malaise within the faculties
became evident. As attention turned (both at the time and importantly in the
dominant narrative since) to the spreading of the crisis to other sectors of
society, interesting developments were unfolding in the recently occupied
faculties. In universities around the country, committees, workshops and
commissions were formed. For example, Monange describes how the situation
developed in Brest: 'There we had, almost immediately, an absolutely extraordinary collaboration between students and teachers.'[50] The issue of inevitable
reform of the university system inspired many of the debates that so characterized the university movement of 1968.[51]

It was at this point that the intense diversity of the university movement
became obvious. The lack of unity that gave it its dynamic strength has also
been cited as one of its fundamental weaknesses.[52] The role of the *gauchiste*
elements and – in particular – their utopian, revolutionary stance and icono-
clastic slogans cannot be overlooked. Nevertheless, an over-emphasis on their
role often disguises the existence of a real reformist movement in the occupied faculties. Beyond the colourful utopian debates on how to revolutionize
society, the symbolic barricades, the riots and the desire to see a convergence
of the working class and student strikes, existed a national movement made up
of students and members of the university teaching staff (particularly young
assistants) who discussed and formulated clear sets of proposals for the reform
of the system of higher education. Both elements were present, active and
important; and in some cases provided the grounds for tension within the
'student movement'.[53] However, what is more striking is the monopolization of
the collective memory of the student movement by the *gauchiste* elements.
Those with more serious and realistic demands that clearly were not lost on
influential people such as Edgar Faure[54] and that arguably best capture the
general spirit of the 1968 revolt, have been progressively airbrushed from
memory.

Pierre Mendès-France argues that the events of 1968 included almost every sector of French society and that this reveals the existence of a common desire for change.[55] The aspiration to have a say or a role to play in the decisions that governed one's life is perhaps the best possible way to sum up the feelings of the time that led to the widespread nature of the 1968 revolt. The difficulty in explaining what brought so many diverse elements out in protest is similar to the difficulty in finding a clear set of proposals that could best summarize what the university movement was calling for by way of reform. If we concentrate on the demands formulated in commissions and committees of the occupied faculties, whilst leaving the unrealistic wishes of some *gauchiste* elements to one side, a collection of common demands is decipherable.[56] The fact that such demands are in accordance with the general spirit that arguably sums up the aspirations of the entire movement of 1968 gives them greater validity and explains why they would go on to be so influential in the formulation of the government's response to the university crisis.

State control of the university system and the dominance of high-ranking professors in the decision-making process help explain why students and assistants were so eager to occupy the faculties during the crisis. However, this desire was not to be confined to the period of the events and was in fact something the movement wished to see become an integral part of the newly reformed university institutions.[57] This demand to have a role to play was accompanied by a call for greater autonomy. Without a break from the uniform control exercised by the central state, any part played by students in the decision-making bodies of their institutions would prove to be only symbolic.[58] There was a call for greater adaptation of the system. This stemmed from the belief that lack of reform had prevented universities from dealing with the explosion in numbers. Consequently university diplomas were devalued and graduates were ill-prepared for an increasingly competitive job market.[59] As a result, there were calls for the university to become more open, for regional issues to be taken into consideration and for the promotion of new interdisciplinary courses, more in line with the demands of the modern economy.[60] Beyond these broader issues concerning the functioning of the university system, more specific areas, and in particular those concerning teaching and assessment methods, were the focus of much debate around the idea of 'a profound lack of adaptation'.[61] Despite the obvious reliance on lectures (*cours magistraux*) in order to cope with the sharp rise in student enrolments, there were constant calls for them to be replaced. It was claimed that they widened the gulf between students and lecturers, making the latter 'as elusive as a star'.[62] In addition, the use of end-of-year examinations was criticized as an unfair method of assessment – little more than a *loterie*.[63] During the occupations, both teaching and assessment methods were so widely criticized that their renewal became one of the major demands of the university reformist movement.[64] Finally, although Fouchet had dropped the option of selection two years previously, it was feared in university circles that de Gaulle believed it to be the logical solution to the problem of growing enrolments. The reiteration of wholehearted opposition to this 'threat hovering on the horizon' was an unremitting feature of reformist demands.[65]

Prior to 1968, the university system had been allowed to stagger along without any serious reform for over a century and a half. But in the years preceding the events the institution was faced with pressures it had never been exposed to and was to prove incapable of dealing with. The exceptional circumstances of the general 1968 crisis arose from a desire for people to take greater control of their lives. This extraordinary atmosphere led to the occupation of faculties around the country, with concrete proposals for reform of the system the focus of many assemblies. The spectacular actions of extremists dominate the portrayal of the student phase of the 1968 events. However, the university movement was made up of much more than far left-wing elements inspired by utopian ideals. The following section demonstrates how it was the *réformistes* and not the *révolutionaires* that would have a more durable impact on the development of the university system.

The Faure reforms and their implementation

Following the resounding Gaullist victory in the general election of June 1968, Edgar Faure was handed the task of formulating the government's response to the university crisis as the new Minister for Education.[66] This institution's inherent resistance to reform together with several other factors made Faure's undertaking an unenviable one. With the distinct possibility of the movement picking up where it had left off in June, it was paramount that an acceptable series of proposals be prepared in time for the autumn *rentrée*, a problem Faure recognized yet refused to accept as an excuse standing in the way of the successful drafting of his proposals.[67] His task was made even more complicated by the absence of 'a coherent representative of these views among the student organizations, the teachers' unions, or the universities in general'.[68] Finally, whilst reform was unavoidable, it was imperative that any changes considered the diverse groups within the university system.[69] In order to overcome such difficulties (and as well as sounding out the opinions of students),[70] Faure surrounded himself with advisors, committees and representatives of the various elements of the university world. He was also aware of the existence of the *Association pour l'expansion de la recherche scientifique* that had been behind the Caen conferences of 1956 and 1966. The ideas that had received consensus within this movement provided him with a basis for his proposals and would prove influential in his eventual law on university reform.[71] On 12 November 1968, after having received an almost unanimous backing from the National Assembly, *La loi d'orientation de l'enseignement supérieur* detailed the government's response to the 1968 crisis.[72] The main principles of the reform were to emerge from new structures. The faculty was abolished and replaced by the *Unité d'enseignement et de recherche*. The UERs were invited to come together and form universities (Article 3, Titre II).[73] Each region would have a *Conseil régional de l'enseignement supérieur et de la recherche*, comprising representatives of each of the region's universities (Article 8, Titre II). Finally, headed by the

Minister of Education, the *Conseil national de l'enseignement supérieur et de la recherche* would coordinate the university system on a national scale (Article 9, Titre II). The principles of pluridisciplinarity, autonomy and participation governed the way these new structures functioned and were the most pertinent concessions to the spirit of 1968.

In terms of participation, each UER would have a council composed of teaching staff, students, non-academic personnel and figures from outside the university world (Article 13, Titre II) – 'chosen on the basis of their competence and their role in regional life'.[74] Elections would be held to determine who sat on the council, which would then elect a director for a period of three years and who would go on to represent that UER on the university council. This body would in turn elect a president with a five-year mandate. The importance of eradicating the previous dominance exercised by high-ranking professors in the decision-making process was made all the more significant due to the increased autonomy afforded to the UERs and universities. The reform gave each university the freedom to determine how it spent its own budget (Article 29, Titre V). In terms of pedagogy and organization, course content, teaching methods and assessment procedures were left up to the individual UERs, through their elected councils, to determine (Article 19, Titre IV). Through the grouping of different fields within each university and the support of co-operation between different disciplines, the notion of *pluridisciplinarité* was encouraged (Article 6, Titre II). Other changes outlined in the reform – and clearly inspired by the demands of the 1968 university movement – included an insistence on the need for continuous assessment of studies as opposed to the previous reliance on end of year examinations (Article 20, Titre IV). By allowing universities to seek funds from private organizations and the presence of persons exterior to the university on the various councils, the desire to eradicate the previous narrow objectives was clear (Article 26, Titre V). The demand for the system of higher education to be more adapted to the needs of society was dealt with by the promise of closer links with the private sector and the insistence on the need for regional factors to be taken into consideration in the organization of individual establishments (Article 22, Titre IV). This measure was also aimed at breaking down the heavily centralized administration of higher education. In order to combat the problem of escalating failure and dropout rates, provisions for greater guidance for students were detailed in the reform (Article 21, Titre IV). Finally, the lack of freedom of political expression that had been such an important issue at the beginning of the crisis was addressed with the cautious acceptance of students' right to a degree of political activity within the newly founded institutions (Article 36, Titre VII).

The Faure reform was indeed very ambitious. Under this new system, a clear attempt at eradicating the previous dominance of faculties was attempted; paving the way for 'a greater degree of flexibility, it also allows for a general restructuring of university relations'.[75] To further encourage cross-disciplinary studies, a flexible credit system was introduced. Students could now choose courses in various disciplines, each corresponding to a certain number of points with a specific total to be reached in order to progress.[76] Due to the greater autonomy afforded to the new university bodies, students were given the opportunity to have a say on decisions such as the budget, course content, teaching methods and the general organization of their studies in what Faure described as 'a serious experiment'.[77] Not only was the use of continuous assessment encouraged in the law but also the new level of autonomy in terms of pedagogy meant that the application of innovative teaching methods was possible.[78] The elitist decision-making procedures that had existed beforehand were eradicated and replaced with a democratic process aimed at eliminating the conservative mentality that had prevented universities from moving with the times. In theory, Faure's *loi d'orientation* satisfied many of the demands of the 1968 movement and marked an important turning point in the history of the French university system.[79] However, the reform was not without its weaknesses. The fact that each university's budget was allocated by the Ministry of Education meant that the Faure reforms did little to reduce the overall financial control exercised by the central government. As such, the call for financial autonomy was not met with real change. Equally, although the UERs were granted a degree of freedom in terms of pedagogy, the government maintained control, as it awarded the qualifications that remained uniform throughout the state.[80] Furthermore, despite being given a role to play in the running of their UERs, students were required to reach a certain quota of votes in order to ensure full use of this new role (Article 14, Titre III).[81] This would lead to students exercising only a limited influence on the councils.[82] In terms of pluridisciplinarity, the long-standing organization of the system along faculty/discipline-orientated lines would prove extremely difficult to overcome.[83] A considerable transitional period would be required before the impact of such a change could be felt on the ground.

Despite these weaknesses, the *loi d'orientation* provided a significant opportunity for renewal of the university system. However, the real test lay in its implementation. The university *rentrée* of 1968 saw sporadic attempts by various student groups to renew the agitation of the previous spring.[84] However, their lack of unity and inability to propose a coherent alternative to the Faure proposals ensured a marginalization of such activity.[85] Both the government and student militant groups recognized the importance of the first elections to the UER councils as the yardstick that would measure the success of the *loi d'orientation*.[86] As a result, university authorities tried hard to thwart any attempt by militants to jeopardize the election process. Such militants saw the elections as no more than an attempt by the authorities to turn the crisis to their advantage.[87] However, despite a call for a complete electoral boycott, the high rate of participation demonstrated how 'The Faure law successfully survived the baptism of the polls'.[88]

Over the course of the next five years, the weaknesses of Faure's reform were exploited and changes in the political, economic and international landscape led to a reduction in the overall impact of the *loi d'orientation* of 1968. Perhaps the most important example of how the Faure reforms did not to live up to expectation comes from the failure of one its most important elements – the renewal of the university structures. It was hoped that the archaic composition that saw the dominance of the faculties, preventing any real crossover between disciplines, would be eradicated. However, giving each *UER* the freedom to decide with what others it would form a university did not lead to the creation of the type of establishments Faure had intended particularly as 'most often, professors would collect on personal, political, or disciplinary basis'.[89] This not only prevented the creation of universities on cross-disciplinary lines, it also led to universities being created strictly on the grounds of political tendencies.[90] One such example concerns the two Lyon universities where as a result of 1968, Lyon II emerged to accommodate the demands of the more radical students and Lyon III the more reactionary; a split that still exists today. Despite the initial success of student participation in the new decision-making bodies, persistent squabbling between increasingly diverse student groups prevented the emergence of a united front and curtailed their potential influence. As the 1970s passed, lack of influence created apathy resulting in ever-lower participation in elections.[91] Less than five years after being offered a part to play, students appeared to have lost all interest in an issue that was at the heart of the 1968 crisis.[92] This downturn in student enthusiasm for reform coincided with important changes within the government. De Gaulle's resignation in 1969 resulted in Faure being replaced by the much more conservative Olivier Guichard; 'the season for reforms, like the season of protest, was very short'.[93] The fear of a repeat of the 1968 events was one of the major driving forces behind the formulation of the *loi d'orientation* of 1968. The marginalization of extreme left-wing movements (due to the irresponsible actions of groups such as the GP[94] and the undermining of the ideological inspirations of so many *gauchiste* groups)[95] in the early 1970s significantly reduced any likelihood of a re-emergence of the revolutionary tendencies that forced the state into such widespread concessions. Such changing external factors worked against Faure's reforms.[96] Finally, the impact of the 1973 oil crisis resulted in a major shift in priorities.[97] This change in perspective led to students focusing more on getting a job than dedicating their time and effort to political activism because for them 'The priority was hitherto situated beyond the university'.[98]

By the mid-1970s, the *loi d'orientation* had been implemented throughout the nation's newly founded universities. However, its impact was not that hoped for by Edgar Faure or the university reformist movement of 1968. Changes in perspective, due to economic and political developments, exposed weaknesses and led to few concrete results despite the initial promise. The structures intended did not emerge and the notions of pluridisciplinarity, autonomy and participation were struggling to prevail. Nevertheless, and as Tarrow argues, the Faure reforms 'were an advance on the situation they replaced, where there had been no structure even resembling the university system common to other advanced countries'.[99] It was the most substantial reform of education undertaken since the end of the nineteenth century and the most tangible impact of the 1968 events on the university system. Whilst remaining secondary in coverage of the events, it was the actions of the reformist elements of the university movement in

1968 that appeared to have had more of an impact on what followed. In any case, the influence of their actions certainly seemed to be more durable than those of the extremist elements that have come to dominate the portrayal of the events.

The French university system and the legacy of 1968

As demonstrated earlier, current students overwhelmingly singled out education as the aspect of their lives most affected by the 1968 events. When one considers the very narrow, stereotypical representation which will have been influential in the formation of such impressions, one is left wondering exactly where such an influence is discernible. However, a clue can be found when one considers that almost 80 per cent of those surveyed agreed that the events had facilitated the tendency of French students to come out in protest. That 1968 has been influential in this domain is not in question. In fact, many current-day lecturers who experienced the 1968 events and/or their aftermath within the university system point to the revolt as providing a durable example. Despite the absence of any upheavals on the same level, it has remained a constant reference and as such indirectly influenced the system's development. As Jean-Pierre le Goff argues, each time a significant protest movement has emerged since 1968 the inevitable question follows 'are we going to experience a new May '68?'[100] Any replication of the events may well be impossible but they nevertheless demonstrated that students have a powerful voice. Monange declared how he believes 1968 to have had a subtle influence in this area: 'I think that unconsciously May '68 created a tradition of university demonstrations.'[101] Others point to a more direct influence claiming that students were made more aware of their strength and recognize that the crisis has been influential on their ability to protest against reforms that they consider inappropriate.[102] As Alain Collange – current-day lecturer at the University of Mulhouse and student in the same institution in 1968 when he was active in opposition to the revolt – commented: 'It is clear that it unleashed things. Students know that they have a voice and they can have an influence.'[103] Others like Jean-Pierre Barraqué, who has no strong memory of the events themselves but as lecturer at the university of Pau has certainly experienced their consequences, claims that whilst some of the ideas of the 1968 movement are no longer applicable, the way in which protests are conducted, managed and led today has been influenced by the events: 'In the ritual, but the motivations are different; in the form but not the content. It demonstrated the practise that we follow now.'[104] It could be argued that the demonstration of strength by students in 1968 is something the government has taken note of. As Jean-Jacques Alcandre – who was highly active in 1968, a student at Nanterre, had close relations with Daniel-Cohn Bendit and is a current-day lecturer at the University of Strasbourg – indicated, successive administrations have been aware of what can happen and have certainly been cautious in their dealings with this area: 'A Minister for Education can no longer consider starting a reform process without taking into account the student reaction.'[105]

However, despite providing an example and arguably a source of inspiration, it would be incorrect to consider 1968 in isolation.

In reality, the events are just one further example of a long tradition that fits the 'old tradition of popular movements, street protests and the right to strike'.[106] Whilst they unquestionably strengthened and updated such a trend, it is difficult to consider them as having fundamentally changed the nature of protest movements. As Blanchet explained: 'there is an old tradition of popular movements [. . .] I do not think that '68 invented anything new in that respect.'[107] Such a sentiment is shared by Mme O'Dea – lecturer at the IUFM Lyon who experienced the events as a twelve-year-old child yet vividly remembers her parents' fears of the time – who saw 1968 as part of 'a tradition, and not only student, but more generally, and that existed before '68'.[108] Given the focus on the spectacular elements of the university movement, it is hardly surprising that young people today perceive the events as a demonstration of potential strength from which they can draw some inspiration. However, and despite an unquestionable degree of influence drawn from 1968 as an example to be followed, as argued, the power of *la rue* cannot be attributed solely to this set of events. A much more significant, tangible and durable legacy can be identified by turning our attentions away from the stereotypical representations and focusing on the impact of the reformist elements.

It is possible to highlight one fairly spectacular failure to undermine the impact of the reforms brought about by the events on the university system. The one element of the Faure reform that best encapsulated the true spirit of the 1968 university movement has not been backed with the same level of enthusiasm that forced its introduction. Despite early promise, taking part in university elections never really captured the imagination of students and the participation rate has continued to diminish since. As Collange described, a constant battle is fought within his UFR[109] by the teaching corps 'so that students become more involved'.[110] However, such efforts are often in vain. And when one considers that 'we scream for joy because we are able to reach a participation rate of 12 per cent'[111] one can understand the opinion that students have 'nothing to gain'.[112] The majority of those standing for election are not considered as representative of students in general but instead considered as 'a handful of students who participate and not always in the interests of all students, they are sometimes sectarian'.[113] Others are much more critical: 'the majority of students do not give a damn.'[114] The vehicle through which the true essence of the 1968 university movement was offered its greatest possible expression has never really been utilized by those concerned. However, in order to fully understand why today's students appear to ignore one of the most important advantages gained as a result of the 1968 protest, one has to consider the changes French society has experienced since.

The ideas that emerged during the crisis of 1968 were specific to that exceptional era. The culmination of several factors facilitated the emergence of what Jacques Gozart – an ex-communist who experienced the events first-hand whilst a student at Tours – described as 'an immensely rich time [. . .] an unleashing of all active forces that existed within society',[115] that seems unreasonable and inapplicable today. The authoritarianism that existed at all levels, the presence of what seemed viable political alternatives, the exceptional international circumstances, the cultural changes of the time, the effects of the baby-boom and, perhaps most importantly, the economic prosperity being enjoyed in France are all factors that merged to produce a particular atmosphere that is so hard to put into perspective today. As Gérard Binder – a student in Mulhouse at the time of the crisis, very much involved in the events and who has gone on to become the Director of an UFR in the same institution – explained, 'It was a time of full employment; conditions for young people were therefore easier, which is not the case today.'[116] For current students, in an institution whose prestige has been constantly weakened and with the perpetual fear of unemployment, the idea of participation and the need to have a say in the running of their university is no longer a priority. As Barraqué explained: 'In '68, students did not want to integrate the system whereas today, students say "I *want* to integrate the system".'[117] Such developments came along quite quickly after the events and as Jean Dewitz – member of the Strasbourg branch of the UNEF in 1968, very much involved in the movement and current-day lecturer in the same institution – argued, 'students quickly realised that it was in their interests to have qualifications.'[118] Students are increasingly preoccupied with finishing their studies in the minimum time possible in the hope that their qualifications will be enough to secure employment. This is in stark contrast to the possibilities open to the generation of 1968 'who were extraordinarily fortunate [. . .] all we needed to do was have a haircut, put on a suit and we found a job'.[119] Such preoccupations are discernible – as described by Blanchet – through the manner in which current-day students conduct their protests: 'Recently during the strikes, students were writing slogans on the walls. However, they wrote them in an orderly fashion with chalk so that we could clean them away. That is not at all the spirit of '68.'[120] Huge contextual changes have led to significant shifts in priority that distance today's generation and university system from those of 1968 or, as Blanchet put it, 'they do not have the same political consciousness; citizens' intuitions take other forms and channel other objectives than in previous generations'.[121] Such changes help explain why the notion of participation, as held then, is different (and less important) today. Nevertheless, the influence of the 1968 reformist movement cannot and should not be reduced to this factor alone.

In order to make sense of the evolution of the university system until today, one cannot ignore the influence of the 1968 events as having started what Guy le Moigne – a current-day lecturer at the University of Brest who experienced the events in the same institution as a student – described as 'a process of university reform that is still unfinished'.[122] An institution that, until 1968, had been characterized by a chronic lack of substantial reform since the end of the nineteenth century, would, after the crisis, undergo a process of continual restructuring. The events finally put an end to the idea that the system was beyond reform and helped eradicate the rigidity that had previously prevented it from adapting. As Mme Ducol – a student in

Tours in 1968 and today a teacher at the University of Tours – outlined, the changes implemented were widespread:

> *The end of year exams were changed; the university has become more open, more transversal, more professional with other streams; there has also been the massification of the university; coursework, etc; all of this stemmed from '68.*[123]

Furthermore, despite the many problems that continue to plague the French university system, the process of reform initiated in the aftermath of 1968 has unquestionably led to a much-improved system, an opinion shared by current-day university lecturers such as Binder for whom, as a result of 1968, '[the university system] is better. This change was necessary. It is better even if problems remain.'[124] The increased autonomy of contemporary universities is a vast improvement on the pre-1968 situation characterized by an overbearing dominance of central authorities: 'The pyramidal system collapsed little by little giving way to a more horizontal network for exchanging knowledge.'[125] As Brigitte Dumortier – current-day lecturer at the Sorbonne who experienced the events as a schoolgirl – outlined, together with the structural changes: 'May '68 changed the organization of classes [with] the introduction of coursework assessment and a democratization of the university system.'[126] The introduction of democratically elected councils, comprising all elements of the university world, has meant that 'The "mandarin" era is in the past'.[127] The poor teacher-taught relations that characterized the pre-'68 situation began to change as 'After '68, students and teachers spoke to each other'.[128] Such changes have been bolstered by the fact that 'May '68 led to the opening up of the university system',[129] thereby increasing the involvement of local authorities and helping the development of provincial universities in accordance with their specific regional requirements. As such, and as highlighted by Cadène – lecturer at Jussieu who, only 13 in 1968, did not experience the events proper but has certainly lived through their consequences in the university system – the influence of 1968 is evident: 'The university system was immersed and May '68 saw the adaptation of the system to the needs of society.'[130]

The post-'68 creation of 'true' universities – where the previous faculty-dominated organization was replaced through the eradication of 'disciplinary compartmentalisation'[131] – has given students the chance to undertake multidisciplinary studies, thus making diplomas more adapted to the increasingly diverse demands of a modern economy. A much fairer and transparent system has consequently come into being, or, as Blanchet put it, 'for those who believe the university's mission to be more than the training of the elite, '68 is a clear improvement'.[132] Such a positive outlook is not widespread. Some believe that things have gone from one extreme to another: 'We were really in a mandarin regime and we moved to a system which is sometimes close to chaos.'[133] The current system is clearly not without flaws with some behind a return to the pre-'68 situation: 'Prior to '68, the university system was coherent, that is no longer the case. We went too far.'[134] Others

such as Jean Bastié – retired university lecturer and by his own admission, a
'mandarin' at the Nanterre campus in 1968 – perceive the events of 1968 as
having completely destroyed the university system creating what could be
described as 'a shambles'.[135] Nevertheless, for others, change was simply
unavoidable: 'Considering the manner in which things were organized at the
time, it is inconceivable that it would have continued any longer.'[136] Whether
or not the changes introduced by Faure were the direct result of the 1968
events is debatable, with some believing change to be inevitable in what was an
'untenable' situation.[137] Others are of the opinion that the 1968 crisis acceler-
ated an inevitable process of reform that 'would have been done more subtly
or otherwise'[138] or that 'it would have required a long time for them to tran-
spire'.[139] In response are those who believe that 'an event like '68 was necessary
to change things'[140] because 'without the strength of the street protests, things
would have changed less and much slower'.[141] For Ilari, the events, having
created a specific set of circumstances, forced the government into unprecedented reforms: 'it is the direct result, it is clear. The administration would
never have given away so much, not at that time.'[142] The fact that the *loi
d'orientation* of 1968 *was* the government's reaction to the events is an argument much stronger than any form of speculation: 'The changes did not
happen without '68. I do not think we would have had them without '68 or
something similar.'[143]

The continued absence of any significant alteration of the structures instituted by Faure in 1968 underlines the importance of this moment in the
history of the French university system and its continued influence today. As
Binder argued, despite constant tinkering, the principles introduced under
the Faure reforms 'gave the university the face it has today'.[144] That such a
series of reforms was the government's direct response to the 1968 events –
and in particular to the demands of the reformist elements of the university
movement – and that such a framework remains in place today is a reflection
of the true heritage of 1968. Whilst the spirit of 1968 is inapplicable in the
current socio-economic climate, the events' legacy in universities is not
completely discarded. Recognition of the role of 1968 in the institution of the
structures that govern the contemporary university system is recognized as it is
a system that continues to 'live with the consequences of '68'.[145]

Conclusion

It has been demonstrated how the events have remained influential through
the example they provided for the government and the university world alike.
Students questioned signalled their belief that the events of 1968 have facilitated their tendency to demonstrate in the streets – a view shared by both
analysts and those well-placed to comment. The events have unquestionably
bolstered a long-standing tradition of street demonstrations in France. As
such, they have arguably shaped the way in which students, lecturers and
successive governments have approached reform of the university system.
However, the 1968 events were just one more in a succession of such protest

movements and any legacy in this domain must be considered with this long-term tradition in mind. That young people today consider the events to have had an impact on education is hardly surprising given the widespread depiction of them as a student revolt; the link is therefore easy to make. However, one must drill down even further and ask what has been the dominant portrayal of the student movement. As argued throughout, the progressive dominance of the *gauchiste* elements over the period 1968–98 has seen reformists pushed to the background. Any association is therefore based on this limited portrayal. It would therefore be reasonable to suggest that the results of the survey (that saw an overwhelming majority of respondents indicating education as being the area of their life most affected by 1968) are intrinsically linked to the narrow depiction of the university movement. The focus on the spectacular and most radical elements can explain why so many of those surveyed pointed to the events as helping the tendency of French students to come out in protest. This limited level of understanding is related directly to the image of 1968 created via the dominant narrative; as Cadène argued, 'for them it is a myth and the media and the actors of '68 are responsible for the creation of the image of the events. It seems to me that they have no idea of what happened.'[146]

The most significant legacy can be found beyond the stereotypical narrative. This chapter has examined the true nature of the movement and its short- to long-term influence on the French university system. Instead of the stereotypical extremist elements, it was those more pragmatic and realistic trends that made up the bulk of the numbers, best encapsulated the overall spirit of 1968 and whose influence has been much more significant. This is true in the short term through the Faure reforms which reflected many of the ideas of the more moderate elements of the university revolt. The same arguments are applicable to the long-term impact, as highlighted by the continued relevance. Whilst the *gauchiste* influence quickly faded and has become – due to huge socio-economic changes – increasingly irrelevant and almost incomprehensible for today's youth, that of the reformist elements has been shown to remain relevant. This is true in terms of the continued importance of the principles and structures introduced under the 1968 *Loi d'Orientation* and the fact that 1968 unquestionably marks a turning point in terms of attitudes to the reform of the university system. On the surface, it may appear that current-day students (with the survey results in mind) are fully aware of this influence. However, with the nature of the event's portrayal in mind, one would be surprised if the reformist elements were at the forefront of how young people today consider *mai* 68. The link between the two could well be a simple consequence of the telescopic focus on the 1968 events as a university movement, allowing many people to draw a logical correlation between 1968 and education. The next chapter examines an area that is much less commonly associated with the 1968 events.

Chapter Five
May/June 1968 in the regions

Introduction

The events of 1968 in France saw upheaval across the nation. Whilst Parisian students were instrumental in triggering the crisis, the subsequent widespread revolt, culminating in the general strike, revealed the existence of a general social malaise throughout the country. Every region experienced the events in its own way with varying motivations behind its diverse demands. However, literature concerning the crisis is largely dominated by events in the capital. Consequently, the true magnitude of the nationwide insurrection and the driving forces behind provincial revolts are given scant attention.

By describing the crisis of 1968 as principally Parisian in *Les Années orphelines*, Jean-Claude Guillebaud highlights the tendency just described.[1] Nevertheless, the majority of analysts stop short of describing the revolt as exclusively limited to Paris. However, many texts simply do not give any credence to the regional impact through their overemphasis on what occurred in and around the *Quartier Latin*. Whilst evident in some important early texts, the absence of provincial analyses is identifiable across the commemorative periods.[2] For example, Debray's 1978 *Modeste contribution* makes no mention of regional revolts and Balladur's *L'Arbre de mai* of the same year is equally devoid of provincial coverage.[3] Important twentieth-anniversary texts forego any analysis beyond Paris. Weber's *Que reste-t-il* pays specific attention to the Paris-based generation of 1968, portraying the entire 1968 movement under the banner of *gauchisme* revolting against a homogenous set of political, social and cultural circumstances.[4] Such a reductionist view of the 1968 movement is equally notable in Rotman and Hamon's *Génération 1*. Focusing specifically on highly militant students and the politicized atmosphere of the Latin Quarter, this analysis is limited to a select band of Parisian *soixante-huitards*.[5] The same approach is adopted in Jean-Pierre le Goff's 1998 *Mai 68, l'héritage impossible*. Despite acknowledging that they were by no means exclusively Parisian, le Goff nonetheless leaves events in the provinces to one side, preferring to focus on the more extreme left-wing student elements particularly prominent in the capital.[6] Such a telescopic focus is equally notable in several other thirtieth-anniversary texts with *Mai 68 à l'usage des moins de vingt ans* particularly exemplary. In the preface, Jean-Franklin Narodetski calls into question the misconstrued notions of the 1968 events in what he describes as 'falsifying literature'.[7] After detailing his personal experience of the crisis, he provides a collection of tracts, songs and slogans. Depicted as representing the true spirit of 1968, every single example is taken from the Parisian movement.[8]

Whilst the texts above highlight an almost complete disregard for events in provincial France, it would be incorrect to suggest that all analyses are limited solely to what occurred in Paris. However, even when featured, the focus is minimal and secondary. Philippe Labro's *Les Barricades de mai* is indicative of the understandable dominance of the spectacular Parisian events in early texts. However, even at this stage, there is recognition of the extension of the crisis beyond the capital with reference to parallel movements in Nantes, Strasbourg and Lyon.[9] Similarly, in *La Révolte étudiante,* prominent Paris-based student militants acknowledge the nationwide impact of the crisis and the importance of provincial support for their struggle.[10] Two 1969 texts reveal a growing recognition of the full magnitude of the 1968 events. In *Le Gauchisme, remède à la maladie sénile du communisme,* the importance and novelty of events elsewhere from both a student and working-class perspective are underlined.[11] Finally, Alain Griotteray's *Des Barricades ou des réformes,* in its criticism of the centralized nature of the French state, reveals recognition of the nationwide nature of the movement and the problems it posed for the authorities.[12]

Again the decennial anniversaries provide useful plotting points. For example, conferences held by the two major trade unions at the time of the tenth anniversary show a heightened perception of the nationwide impact of the events. The CFDT analysis pays particular attention to the widespread nature of the general strike, the role played by provincial factories in launching it, as well as the exceptional nature of several regional strike movements where the CFDT was prominent.[13] In a similar vein, the CGT conference, highlighting the significance of the strike, underlines its widespread nature with the existence of specific regional difficulties brought to the fore, as well as an insistence on innovative action in movements in Nantes and Montreuil.[14] Another noteworthy 1978 text is Alain Delale and Gilles Ragache's *La France de 68* which focuses heavily on the nationwide aspect of the events, with particular reference to the spreading of the general strike.[15] Three twentieth-anniversary texts indicate the growing importance attributed to regional participation in the events. For example, Martelli's *Mai 68,* despite being mainly in relation to the general strike and important moments such as 13 May demonstrations and the extreme violence of 24 May, nevertheless affords a certain degree of importance to the role of provincial movements.[16] Reiterating Griotteray's reference to the highly centralized nature of the French state as crucial in spreading the crisis, Joffrin's *Mai 68, histoire des événements,* despite focusing heavily on the Parisian student movement in the initial phase of the crisis, highlights considerable working-class tension beyond the capital in the years and months preceding May 1968 and the importance of provincial factories in precipitating the general strike.[17] The *décalage* in prosperity between Paris and the rest of France (with particular reference to Brittany) as fundamental in the existence of serious working-class frustrations in the build-up to the revolt is a particular focus in *L'Entre-deux de la modernité.* However, whilst accepting the diverse nature of regional 1968 movements, Capdevielle and Mouriaux nonetheless point to the prevailing dominance of events in the capital.[18] The monopoly of the 'student phase' by Paris had, by 1998, become a recurrent feature. For example, in *Les Mouvements de 1968*, whilst the problems regarding university halls of residence and students' freedom to visit members of the opposite sex are examined as a national phenomenon, the overall focus remains centred on Paris, Nanterre and figures such as Cohn-Bendit, with the characteristics of the spectacular Parisian movement held up as representative of the national student mentality. Only when the analysis moves to the general strike do differences, such as particular regional difficulties and the exceptional provincial movements (in particular Nantes), come to the fore.[19] Finally, whilst Fauré's *Mai 68, jour et nuit* largely confirms this trend, by using the capital as a reference point to show how each major event (13, 24, 30 May, for example) was mirrored in provincial towns and by including tracts from movements in Strasbourg, Toulouse and Nantes, it nevertheless highlights the heterogeneous nature of a movement not without significance outside the capital.[20]

Recognition of the nationwide impact is clearly not entirely absent and in fact has been gaining prominence over the years. Nevertheless, little is known of the intricacies of such movements and few texts offer a concerted analysis of the diverse motivations of provincial revolts. However, those that do reveal significant and interesting contrasts between the provincial experience and the dominant narrative. For example, Danielle Tartakowsky's *Le Pouvoir est dans la rue* explains how many regions, exposed to mounting tension and upheaval before the student revolt in Paris, experienced movements portrayed as independent and dissimilar to those in the capital. Describing events in Paris as considerably more politically orientated, Tartakowsky emphasizes the importance of demonstrations in all major French cities, the violent nature of several provincial movements and the characteristics that set provincial towns apart from Paris. Not only described as fundamental in the exceptional nature of May/June 1968, regional diversity is highlighted as playing a prominent role as an obstacle to a unified movement thus facilitating a peaceful conclusion to the crisis.[21] In *L'Aubépine de mai*, François le Madec offers a detailed account of the famous strike movement in the Nantes Sud-Aviation factory. Revealing the prominence of heightened tension amongst employees concerning their future as early as 1967, this account underlines the process – driven largely by local issues – that led to the emergence of such a significant movement. Nevertheless, there is recognition of a growing influence from what was occurring in the capital. Inspired by the huge 13 May demonstrations, the discussions that led to the factory being occupied as well as the sequestration of the *patron* bring to light the calculated nature of this regional strike movement. The organization of this occupation, the respect for premises and the existence of productive worker/student relations are highlighted; revealing the distinct nature of the Sud-Aviation revolt that was unyielding in the face of developments on a national scale.[22] This account, concentrating on one provincial factory, turns the spotlight on the existence of individual movements around the country, the specific problems that spurred such mobilizations and the novel forms of action put into practice. George Chaffard's depiction of the *Vendômois* 1968 events in *Les Orages de mai* highlights the impact of the crisis in an area where such an upheaval would not have been expected to be so significant. With working-class population minimal, trade union membership virtually non-existent and no traditional inclination for political matters, the *Vendômois* landscape is portrayed as having been severely shaken by the events.[23] Detailing the contrast between the disorder in Paris and the rejection of revolutionary tendencies amongst the conservative population, such wholehearted involvement is explained by the proximity of Paris, local rivalries and the prominence of the PSU and CFDT in the area. However, it is the portrayal of the uncharacteristically intense electoral campaign of June 1968 that reveals the true impact of the events on this commune. *Les Orages de mai* shows how the events of 1968 spread throughout the nation, bringing participation from even the most apolitical of citizens, and demonstrates how the crisis was able to influence the political status quo of areas unaccustomed to political upheaval.

Due to the heavily centralized nature of the state, the predominance of Paris over the rest of the nation in almost every sector is a permanent feature of the French landscape and to a certain extent explains why examinations of provincial 1968 revolts remain very much in the minority. Despite a growing importance attached to the significance of events in provincial France, the dominant perception is one that ignores the underlying characteristics of regional student and social movements and portrays the provincial events as evolving strictly in relation to the unfolding developments in the capital. Such a portrayal has unquestionably led to important consequences in the way in which provincial 1968 movements are considered today.

One of the most glaring gaps in the dominant narrative is therefore the lack of an adequate view of how the events were experienced in different regional contexts. Ross comments thus on the lack of regional coverage: 'By some accounts, provincial France saw more violent and sustained demonstrations than did Paris during May and June, but this is not represented in the official story.'[24] Sommier points to the dearth of focus beyond the capital as just one of three characteristics (alongside a telescopic focus on the month of May and the student contribution) that have seen the events stripped of their complexities.[25] Vincent Porhel commented on how the Parisian focus has monopolized representations of May–June 1968: 'In the commemorations, things still have not changed; it is May '68 in Paris – it begins rue Gay Lussac and finishes at the Ministry of Work.'[26] The importance of Paris as the spark that would bring about revolts around the country is not in question. As Edmond Monange comments: 'There would not have been a May '68 in Brest without the Nanterre *gauchistes*, the clashes at the Sorbonne or the barricades on the boul'Mich.'[27] Nonetheless, Bernard Boudic, president of the *Association générale des étudiants brestois* (AGEB) in 1968, a prominent member of the Brestois branch of the UNEF and a major protagonist in these regional events, fails to recognize his 1968 in the way the events are commonly portrayed, lending weight to the argument that this 'official history' does not tell the whole story. As Boudic commented when asked how he considered the current over-emphasis on Paris:

Historically, it is an error. It is a mistake which falsifies the interpretation of these events. Not all elements are taken into consideration. It is therefore only logical that a false image of the events prevails. It is surprising. It is shocking from a logical perspective.[28]

An examination of the conditions that led to revolts in two provincial cities (Brest and Strasbourg), together with an analysis of their nature, will help in assessing to what extent Boudic's claim is justified. First let us consider how current attitudes have been shaped in this domain.

It is worth beginning by reiterating the result of question 13 of the survey concerning whether or not respondents agreed that the events of 1968 were an exclusively Parisian revolt. Whilst the majority of those questioned disagreed, that over one-fifth of respondents agreed that it was largely restricted to the capital is indicative of the influence of the stereotypical portrayal on an understanding of the nationwide nature and impact of the crisis. Question 8 of the survey asked respondents to indicate what areas they considered to have been most affected by the 1968 events. Ten sectors of French society were proposed as options, one of which was 'regional movements'. As Figure 5.1 demonstrates, by comparing the rates of agreement in each of these areas, the perceived importance of 1968 in this domain can be put into perspective.

'Regional movements' received a minority of positive responses. Only 'judicial system' proved less popular as an area perceived as being affected by the 1968 crisis. The results outlined in Table 5.1 show the breakdown of responses concerning the influence of 1968 on regional movements.

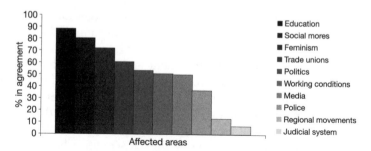

Figure 5.1 The above sectors were most affected by the 1968 events

Table 5.1 Regional movements was one of the sectors most affected by the 1968 events

	Frequency	Per cent
Strongly disagree	20	4.0
Disagree	94	18.6
Not certain	290	57.4
Agree	61	12.1
Strongly agree	8	1.6
Total	473	93.7
Missing	32	6.3
Total	505	100

The rate of not certain responses (57.4 per cent) was considerable. Over 20 per cent of those questioned do not believe the crisis to have affected regional movements, with only 13.7 per cent agreeing that it has been influential in this domain. The results illustrated in Figure 5.2 show a comparison between the national picture and that of the two regions that provide the focus of the subsequent case studies.

In terms of the high level of not certain responses, the regional and national pictures are without any significant differences. The one slight, yet notable divergence concerns the levels of agreement and disagreement. There are clearly more Bretons than Alsatians of the opinion that the 1968 events were important for regional movements. Whether or not respondents believed the events to have had an influence on their own lives was the subject of question 9 of the survey. Those in agreement were asked to pinpoint specific areas, one of which was 'regional identity'. Figure 5.3 demonstrates how the rate of those in agreement that 1968 has been an influence on their regional identity compares to other areas regarded as having been affected.

Of all the areas, 'regional identity' is clearly that which is perceived as being least affected. Table 5.2 outlines the results of those who believe 1968 to have had an influence on their lives and regard their regional identity as one of the affected areas.

Over one-quarter of respondents either strongly disagreed or disagreed that the 1968 events have influenced their regional identity, with an insignificant

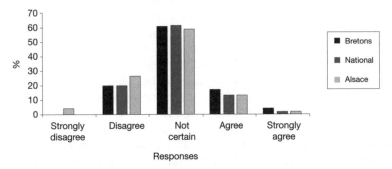

Figure 5.2 Brittany/France/Alsace: regional movements was one of the sectors most affected by the 1968 events

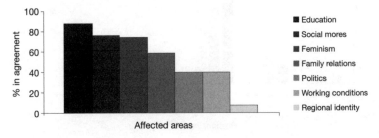

Figure 5.3 The above sectors of my own life have been most affected by the events of May 1968

Table 5.2 The events of May 1968 have had an impact on my regional identity

	Frequency	*Per cent*
Strongly disagree	8	4.4
Disagree	38	21
Not certain	110	60.8
Agree	10	5.5
Strongly agree	2	1.1
Total	168	92.8
Missing	13	7.2
Total	181	100

6.6 per cent in agreement. However, most salient is the extremely high rate (60.8 per cent) of uncertainty. Figure 5.4 flags up any differences between the national and regional outlook.

Once again, the high level of uncertainty nationally is reflected in both regions singled out for attention. Whilst the number of Breton respondents agreeing that 1968 had had an impact on their own regional identity was quite small, most noteworthy is that fact that not one single Alsatian respondent was in agreement. This difference is equally evident when one compares the higher rates of disagreement in Alsace than in Brittany.

The national picture clearly reveals how young people see no significant correlation between 1968 and regional issues. What must be noted, however, is that such a perspective is not the result of a clear rejection of the idea that a connection indeed exists. Instead the high degree of not certain responses highlights a certain void in how the events are perceived. This gap in how 1968 is appreciated is replicated from a regional perspective. Results from Brittany and Alsace mirror the high rate of uncertainty. There is in fact very little regional deviation in the results; the only noteworthy difference being the (very small) degree of recognition amongst Breton respondents of the importance of 1968 for regional matters. When one considers the nature of the events' portrayal over the 1968–98 period that has airbrushed the regional dimension from history, the lack of correlation between 1968 and regional

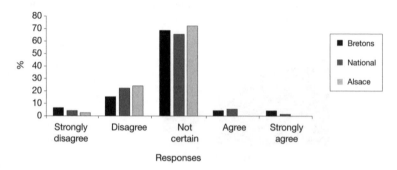

Figure 5.4 Brittany/France/Alsace: the events of May 1968 have had an impact on my regional identity

questions is hardly surprising. The following analysis turns the spotlight away from the capital and on to the cities of Strasbourg and Brest in order to challenge the Paris-centred narrative.

Local circumstances

The telescopic focus of the dominant narrative on Paris does not simply impact on perspectives of how the events themselves were played out. The circumstances from which the crisis emerged are often reduced to the notion that it was somewhat of a bolt from the blue,[29] the implication being that the great political, economic and social stability that the 1968 revolt disturbed was nationwide. However, a closer look at regional circumstances in Brittany and Alsace prior to 1968 reveals why such a simplistic generalization falls short of telling the whole story.

Independent from France until annexation in 1532, Brittany's isolation, underdevelopment and cultural differences were long a feature of its special relationship with Paris. Material destruction coupled with the presence of collaborationist elements during the Second World War only served to heighten the region's detachment. Together with an exodus of young people – a problem since the mid nineteenth century – a severe blow had been dealt to the reputation and morale of all things Breton.[30] The history of the Alsace region is characterized by a high level of flux. Between 450 BC and the 1648 Treaty of Munster, control of the region passed from Celts to Romans, from Romans to Franks, from Franks to Germans before it became part of the Holy Roman Empire in the later tenth century. The Peace of Westphalia of 1648 signalled the beginning of a direct two-way power struggle between France and Germany as over the next three centuries the region changed nationality five times.[31] A recurring feature each time the region changed hands was a determined effort on the part of the new 'masters' to impose a cultural hegemony mainly through the eradication of all traces of the former's cultural imprint.[32] This trend had obvious connotations for the regional identity and was one that was given even greater strength and resonance in the aftermath of the Nazi occupation.[33]

In Brittany, post-war reconstruction and government delocalization programmes (due in large part to lobbying on behalf of the *Comité d'étude et de liaison des intérêts bretons* – CELIB) saw the beginning of a turnaround for the region.[34] However, frustration was evident as in the 1950s and 1960s Brittany experienced many violent protests by the farming sector over the pricing of produce[35] and the re-emergence of extremist elements with terrorist groups such as the *Front de Libération de la Bretagne* (FLB).[36] Basic amenities were lacking, unemployment was high and, as Jean-Luc Poussier describes, a real gap in prosperity between Brittany and the rest of France was evident with Breton salaries 30 per cent less than the national average.[37] The principal concern was regional unemployment, and it was this issue, more than any other, that would bring about the most important action. This was exemplified by the mass march and meeting on 8 May 1968 under the title *L'Ouest veut vivre*. This rally, supported by all trade unions and attracting participants from across the entire region, had been organized independently of the forth-coming events of May. In fact, the objectives of this day of action were set out in a meeting between representatives of the working class, farmers and teachers on 13 March 1968, calling for 'The defence of jobs. The guarantee of resources. The increase of spending power'.[38] Mass rallies against poor economic prospects hardly tally with the commonly held idea that the 1968 events exploded during a period of widespread economic, political and social stability. Indeed, the element of surprise that is said to have greeted the crisis of 1968 was almost completely absent in Brittany. As Jacqueline Sainclivier argues: 'In the Breton case, you could say that the scale of May 1968 should not be a surprise. The events in Paris resonated but the Breton '68 was not a bolt from the blue. Problems of all sorts and in numerous areas were present.'[39]

During the same period in Alsace, economic difficulties were not a major source of concern. Nevertheless, whilst the region was benefitting from *les trente glorieuses,* its regional identity was experiencing serious difficulties. From 1945 to 1968, the process of imposing a French identity was afforded an added impetus as a result of the need to exorcise any German (thus Nazi) influences from French soil.[40] Importantly, the duality that underpinned Alsatian culture and society became more commonly viewed in a pejorative light by the native population. In this period described as 'the collapse of regional cultural life',[41] anyone proclaiming the need to foster and maintain this identity was associated with those pushing the autonomy agenda, thus collaborators. German was forbidden in schools and Vogler's description of perceptions of the dialect gives some idea of the position the Alsatian identity found itself in during this period:

> *The dialect, little by little, tends to be considered as a defect, a shameful illness, as behaviour that is threatening the francophonie, as the expression of an under-developed culture just about good enough for the farm hand, a Sunday rhymester or any other such amateur of slapstick comedy.*[42]

The difficulties faced by both regions in the years leading to 1968 reveal similarities and differences. On the one hand, such difficult pasts, and the consequences they led to, created a specific way of life and attitudes in each region in relation to regional identities and their place in the nation. On the other, the diverse economic situations further underline the inadequacy of the commonly held idea that the 1968 events exploded during a period of wide-spread economic stability and growth. Such factors would be crucial in determining how the revolts were experienced. An examination of Strasbourg and Brest on the eve of May 1968 provides a valuable insight into how local specificities brought about upheavals that do not fit the stereotypical view.

Brest was, in 1968, a microcosm of the general difficulties of Breton life at the time. The city had been almost entirely destroyed during the Second World War because of its strategic military position. In the immediate after-math of the war, the rebuilding of the city provided employment for the population. However, once the hasty reconstruction programme was completed, unemployment became a permanent feature.[43] Geographical isolation made it harder for the region to keep pace with a rapidly modernizing France. With Georges Lombard (from the centre-right formation *Progrès* and *Démocratie Moderne*) as mayor since 1959, Brest had benefited from some important examples of decentralization (in particular, the establishment of the *Compagnie de télégraphie sans fil* (CSF) factory). However, despite these improvements, the city remained under-funded, isolated and under-equipped. Emigration was endemic throughout Brittany but was particularly prominent in Brest. In 1968 the population of the Finistère department was 768,929 – 4,000 below the 1901 total of 773,014.[44] Edmond Monange, whose first year as a university lecturer in Brest happened to coincide with the events, outlines the problem as follows:

> *Freedom from isolation remained incomplete. Decentralisation, which was vigorously pursued at the beginning of the decade, had run out of steam and jobs appeared under more threat than elsewhere. A great number of young people had resigned themselves to an exodus in order to find work.*[45]

Much more in keeping with the dominant narrative, in Strasbourg there were little or no obvious signs of the upheaval that was just round the corner. Jean Dewitz described how, even as an activist with L'UNEF prior to the events, he and his comrades had no idea of what was coming: 'I have always been surprised because we were aware of nothing [. . .] there was never a question of what was about to happen, of what was brewing, we were focused on the usual things.'[46] Such apparent calm was both reinforced by and reflected in the great stability that characterized the economic and political landscape. Economically, Strasbourg was in a relatively strong position. Having benefitted from the government-sponsored *délocalisation* programme, together with the advantages associated with its proximity with Germany, unemployment was amongst the lowest in the country. In comparison with the rest of France, both Strasbourg and the Alsace region in general were in good economic health.[47] Such stability was equally evident in terms of the political landscape. Since coming back to power in 1958, Gaullists had completely dominated the region with the general held in very high esteem as the saviour of French Alsace.[48] The economic and political stability enjoyed since de Gaulle's return fed into, and was arguably shaped by, an inherent conservatism often described as a prominent feature of the Alsatian mentality.[49]

The conditions concerning higher education in both cities are notably important. At this time, Brest lacked a university. It did have a CLU (*Collège littéraire universitaire* – created in 1960) and a CSU (*Collège scientifique universitaire* – 1959) both of which were dependent on the University of Rennes. The student corpus was made up mostly by people from relatively modest backgrounds, many of whom were the first from their family to be given the opportunity to go to university. This was critically important in determining their attitudes towards the system and thus influenced their behaviour during the events; 'For them, university is a means to finding employment – and fast.

The profile is not at all the same as the Parisian student. They are not at university to be involved in a revolution.'[50] This profile, together with the relative novelty of the establishment, meant that there was little in the way of militant student activity. There were student associations such as *L'Union des Etudiants Communistes* (UEC), *La Jeunesse Etudiante Bretonne* (JEB) or *La Jeunesse Etudiante Catholique* (JEC). However, such groups had very few members and little influence. The one organization that seemed to provide a common denominator was L'AGEB. This regional branch of l'UNEF, headed by Bernard Boudic, was the most influential of student organizations and would go on to play a pivotal role in the events of May–June 1968. The CLU de Brest had distinct difficulties but was also experiencing the effects of the general frustration making itself felt in universities around the country.[51] Critically understaffed and lacking in facilities, the Brestois CLU – like many higher education establishments elsewhere in France at the time – was struggling to meet the demands of the baby-boom. However, on top of these more general complications, it was grappling with other difficulties including incomplete courses and the frequent absence of teaching staff – problems that were attributed to the over-dependence on the University of Rennes.[52] The Brest situation is a perfect example of the two-pronged problems that beset Brittany. The coming together of local and national tensions would create a fertile ground for revolt; but one that problematizes commonly held perceptions: 'In Brest, just as in Paris, student unease exists. But the dynamite and the fuse were not of the same nature and the explosion would have different effects.'[53]

A quick glance at the University of Strasbourg of the 1960s reveals similar experiences to elsewhere in the country.[54] The number of students was growing exponentially, courses were seen to leave graduates ill-prepared for the modern world of work, and the government reaction to the baby-boom (i.e. the hasty construction of new buildings (namely *l'Esplanade*)) was both protracted and perceived as falling short of meeting growing needs.[55] However, the one episode that does point to some degree of divergence relates to the famous *Situationniste* scandal of 1966. Throughout the 1960s the University of Strasbourg had one branch of the *International Situationniste* (IS). Marginal and made up of a handful of highly militant students, the Strasbourg branch nevertheless created a huge controversy when it managed to take control of the *Association Fédérale Générale des Etudiants de Strasbourg* (AFGES) at the beginning of the 1966 academic year. In so doing they were handed a say in the management of the university restaurant, a Corsican holiday camp and given control of a two-million franc budget.[56] Such responsibilities in the hands of a group that – via its outrageous pamphlet *De la misère au milieu étudiant* [57] – made clear its intentions to destroy every element of the university system, created panic amongst the authorities and thus became the focus of sustained national media attention.[58] Tension mounted as the *Situs* pursued their inflammatory tactics through increasingly provocative texts and actions. The scandal was eventually brought to a head when they decided to close down the *Bureau d'Aide Psychologique Universitaire* (BAPU).[59] This move provided ample ammunition for the university authorities to step in, strip them of their responsibilities and exclude some prominent members from the university for life.[60] There then followed a long period where the case was brought before the courts.[61] Despite this process continuing until the spring of 1968, in the meantime any *Situationniste* influence had dissipated with the Strasbourg branch riven with conflict and even excluded from the IS.[62] Georges Foessel, who was a young archivist in 1968 and is responsible for the outstanding collection of material on the 1968 events in Strasbourg available in the Archives de la Ville, described the lack of influence of this movement by 1968; 'In the student milieu, *Situationnisme* was not very well known. One was aware that it was an extremist movement with fairly surrealist ideas, but no more than that.'[63] Locally, this episode had, by the eve of 1968, exacerbated the national phenomenon of indifference amongst the student mass.[64] The silent majority of students increasingly perceived political issues as the domain of an excitable minority intent on wreaking havoc via extremist ideology. Largely apathetic, they preferred to concentrate on their studies despite grounds for discontent with the system.[65] As a result of such local specificities on the eve of *mai 68*, the events that subsequently took place, their mobilizing factors and the composition of the movements in Brest and Strasbourg were to be very much in contrast to those usually considered today as vital.

Activism

Upon hearing news of what had been happening in Paris at the beginning of May, the then generally apolitical Brestois student population followed the AGEB call for a strike on 6 May in protest against police brutality in the capital. To everyone's surprise, this initiative was strongly supported, with teaching staff particularly active alongside students.[66] Attention then turned to the mass demonstration organized for 8 May. As headlines in the local press reveal, the success of the demonstration was not limited to Brest with 'Over 100,000 workers, farmers, students [who] protested for the survival of their region'.[67] As explained by Annie Jeffroy, despite the level of frustration, the demonstration was marked in particular by its discipline and lack of violence: 'At 2pm, Brest returned to normal: the typical traffic problems started up, 8 May unfolded in an orderly fashion from beginning to end.'[68] This show of strength hardened the resolve of the Brestois students who continued their strike in support of their Parisian comrades.[69]

However, from 8 May, inspired by the success of the 'L'Ouest Veut Vivre' rally, the students in Brest, initially influenced by what was happening in Paris, soon began to focus on local issues – in particular, the predicament of the CLU.[70] After *La nuit des barricades* in Paris on 10 May, occupations began in Brest with contacts being made between the striking students and university staff as well as with workers and their trade unions. As at a national level, the one-day strike on 13 May in protest against police brutality soon took the form in Brest of an all-out general strike.[71] Over the course of the next three weeks, Brest was gradually brought to a standstill with daily rallies, general assemblies and the politicization of the movement. The 1968 events in Brest also saw the participation of the farming community, a sector of the society that until then had preferred to remain independent and certainly would not have wanted to be aligned with any student movement. However, when the strike began to create major practical difficulties, particularly in terms of food supply, the farming community was on hand to donate some of its produce and to participate in its distribution.[72]

In Brest neither the Grenelle accords nor de Gaulle's second address reduced the determination of the Bretons to keep their movement alive.[73] Interestingly, as in the capital, a huge pro-Gaullist demonstration took place in Brest following the general's radio address on 30 May. This demonstration of support of the Gaullist regime took place on 1 June and provided an opportunity for the 'silent majority' to claim back the streets. The fact that it coincided with another demonstration in favour of the movement reveals a further example of the restrained nature of the revolt, from both sides. Meticulous planning allowed the opposing sides to march around the streets of Brest without a hint of trouble.[74] Nonetheless, as a return to work began in Paris and around the country, it was only a matter of time before the movement in Brest followed suit. Slowly but surely, workers began to drift back to their factories. The strike ended when, on 21 June, the workers at the CSF returned to work.

The Strasbourgeois events were equally triggered by news from Paris. However, the trajectory was soon to differ between what took place in the Latin Quarter and on the Esplanade.[75] On 6 May in reaction to the events of the previous three days in Paris, a minority of students in the Arts faculty quickly brought together 500 people in the *Aula* (the grand reception hall) of the *Palais Universitaire* (PU) in a strike that spread to the seven faculties where students, teachers and senior figures in the university milieu focused on the need to discuss and organize a coherent movement.[76] Lucien Braun, a young lecturer at the time, described his very own involvement alongside colleagues and students: 'There were young teachers, my colleagues, who in the evenings contributed to critical texts and we founded the critical university [. . .] We worked in commissions at night time during the occupation.'[77] On 10 May the Strasbourgeois students occupied the PU, declared the university autonomous and then flew the red flag from what has been described as the 'symbol of the university'.[78] The university movement, which established many *commissions paritaires* and formulated proposals for the reform of the university system, was given a significant boost when Alain Peyrefitte (Minister for Education) granted it official permission to undertake an experiment in autonomy.[79] Lucien Braun, who was privy to the actual conversation with Peyrefitte, described how the minister 'said that we could carry out an experiment and draw up conclusions at the end'.[80] An important shift in the events in Strasbourg took place on 18 May when, in both the public and private sectors, the strike movement began to take hold.[81] However, this period also saw what had been a relatively contained and measured university movement overstep the boundaries of the acceptable in a series of actions that ultimately would trigger the beginning of its demise.

On 21 May, the Strasbourgeois population woke to the news that in the early hours of the morning the word *révolution* had been daubed on the *Monument aux Morts* in the city centre.[82] The student movement was immediately held responsible for this 'mistake to avoid'.[83] On 24 May students marched to the *Pont de l'Europe* on the border with Germany to welcome Daniel Cohn-Bendit back to France following his famous *interdiction de séjour*.[84] The impression amongst the conservative population that Strasbourg was being subsumed into the anarchic fervour of the Latin Quarter was exacerbated later that same evening. Following de Gaulle's failed address, the students decided to take to the streets where they were faced with local police and CRS who were not keen on seeing the violence of Paris replicated in Strasbourg.[85] The students nevertheless managed to build a barricade and prepared to defend it.[86] During the inevitable police charge, there was minimal violence, only a handful of arrests and little damage. However, the fact that the students had dared construct a barricade in an affront to local authority was clearly a step too far. From this point the student movement had lost all credibility in the eyes of the local population and the tide was beginning to turn against it. By 28 May, the strike had reached its high point.

The combination of the concessions offered at Grenelle and the *chienlit* of the previous week spurred a push for a return to reality. Gaullist supporters signalled their desire to finish with this movement during a gathering at the now symbolically charged location that was the *Monument aux Morts*.[87] This backlash was given even greater impetus when, on 30 May, de Gaulle's defiant speech struck a chord with the local population and inspired them to take matters into their own hands. Whilst some of the biggest and most important factories voted for a return to work, the general's call for defence committees to be established around the country to protect the Republic was immediately met through a 'political counter-offensive'; the students were becoming increasingly isolated.[88] Then on 1 June, another pro-Gaullist demonstration ended with an attack on the occupied PU. The subsequent clashes were eventually brought under control before a stand-off between the students and their assailants. Negotiations on the possibility of removing the red flag were eventually brought to a close when it was agreed that the tricolour and the European flag would accompany that of the students.[89] This extraordinary episode signified the divide between the student movement and the general population that had had enough of the defiant attitude towards authority experienced for almost four weeks. The rest of the month would see the gradual decline and demise of the university revolt. Despite hosting firstly a national *assises* on 8–10 and a European meeting on 15, the month of June saw the Strasbourgeois movement dealt a number of critical blows that would gradually erode its support and force it to an end. Slowly but surely, the numbers dwindled and the occupied buildings emptied. On 23 June, the first round of legislative elections saw the Gaullists sweep to huge victory without the need for a second round: all 13 sitting deputies were re-elected.[90] The students were on holiday and the Strasbourgeois '68 was over or, as one anonymous tract ironically put it, 'If the movement dissipates and the occupations stop, it is because the vacation of great values has fallen foul of the value of a long vacation'.[91]

As well as being heavily centred on Paris, the dominant narrative is charac-terized by several concerns, one of which is the depiction of a lack of student/working-class fraternization. Many analyses refer to the turning away of students at the gates of the Renault factory at Boulogne-Billancourt – the fiefdom of working-class militancy and bastion of the Communist CGT – as indicative of the complete failure of students and workers to unite.[92] The impression given is one of a highly fragmented movement. In the case of Strasbourg, this narrative is confirmed. Such was the detachment between the university and the general population that Foessel described what happened as 'a volcano on an ice field'.[93] Dewitz confirmed this feeling of isolation by indicating how his involvement in the movement gave him the impression of having 'lived in a bubble'.[94] The conservative nature described above is a significant factor in making sense of the degree of isolation felt by the student movement in Strasbourg. Despite a certain degree of effort, there was a profound mistrust on behalf of the workers that stood in the way of any fruitful contacts.[95] In fact, and despite some sporadic strikes, the general disunity and dispersion that characterized the strike movement in the region reflects the reluctance of the working class to become involved. For Roger Siffer – student in 1968 and a very well-known figure in the Alsace cultural movement – what happened in Strasbourg was essentially perceived as a student movement:

> *The strike in Alsace was not followed strongly. In comparison with the working class on the outskirts of Paris who were in solidarity with and got involved in the movement, here it was seen as disorderly. Here the movement was followed much more timidly; it remained on the whole an intellectual, student-based movement.*[96]

Whilst Strasbourg perhaps confirms the commonly held idea, the case of Brest problematizes any nationwide generalization. The mistrust between the CGT and Parisian students was not a significant factor in Brest where the revolt was characterized by the unity of all those involved. A vital element in explaining this factor was the relative dominance of the CFDT in the region. It was, in Porhel's words, 'the dominant trade union'.[97] Jean le Roux (general secretary of the AGEB in 1968) explained that, due to the flexible attitude of the CFDT regarding the student movement, working-class–student relations were generally much more productive: 'Contact between us was easier, we were more in step with the CFDT.'[98] Henri Didou (General Secretary of the CFDT in Brest in 1968) highlighted the existence of such close relations: 'We were quite open. We worked well with the left-wing students. There was a good understanding and even a good level of co-ordination. There were not two separate movements, only one.'[99] All demonstrations in Brest were conducted on a unified basis, with workers, students, teachers, farmers and trade unions marching together and holding joint meetings. As one tract calling on the Brestois population to back the 13 May demonstration indicates: 'Workers demands and their struggles are those of teachers, students and other categories of the working population. [. . .] Long live the union of workers and students.'[100]

In Brest, in order to defuse the possibility of problems between rival trade unions, joint meetings were presided over by a student representative (in particular by Bernard Boudic), highlighting the close student/worker relationship described as absent elsewhere during the crisis. As he later explained: 'As the workers, farmers and teachers' unions found it difficult to agree on who should chair the meetings, it was left to the students.'[101] Students were made to feel welcome in occupied factories as were workers visiting the CLU where everyone was encouraged to have a say as all sides attempted to form a common platform for their demands. The workers managing the strike and occupation in the Brestois CSF factory detailed how they considered student/worker contact:

> *Even before E Descamps called for the students and workers to join each other's struggle, it had already happened at the CSF. The workers there had as many discussions with the student representatives of the AGEB as they did with the non-affiliated students. After having explained their motivations and the reason for their struggle, they listened to the workers' point of view. Each time the following conclusions were drawn: We no longer want to be like the managers of today; We must mutually support each other; We must increase our contacts, conferences and mutual explanations.*[102]

Overall, the unity that characterized the 1968 Brest movement is in stark contrast to the animosity between the Communist-led union (CGT) and some of the extreme left-wing elements in Paris that has come to represent student-worker relations during the events. Furthermore, as Le Roux notes, in Brest the convergence of workers and students revealed their common objectives: 'The worker demanding the right to participate (not simply to give his opinion) in the organization of the workplace and the management of companies, the students having the same demands in regard to the university.'[103]

The Brestois revolt fits the commonly held view that the events of 1968 brought the country to a standstill with, as discussed above, a strike movement that incorporated all sectors from farmers to students. However, the same could not be said for Strasbourg where the strike never matched the exploits of other cities.[104] Jean-Michel Mehl – a student at the University of Strasbourg in 1968 whose father was dean of the theology faculty at the time – sums up precisely how this set Strasbourg and the entire region apart: 'When the '68 movement started on a downward turn within France, the trade unions asked the question of how they could bring the strike to a close. In Alsace the question was rather "Are we going to go on strike?"'[105] Consequently, at no stage was there ever any sense that the city was on the verge of paralysis. Two reasons in particular help explain why this was the case. First, as mentioned previously, the Strasbourgeois population was inherently conservative and one that found comfort in the stability and order that characterized Gaullist France. One only has to consider the great upheavals experienced across the region's tumultuous history to understand the population's desire to maintain some degree of stability. Local historian and journalist Hervé de Chalendar summed up the impact of the past: 'Alsace has a distinctive history. Its population has suffered somewhat, most of the time twice as much as anyone else. The fear of chaos is therefore even stronger here than elsewhere.'[106] Therefore, there was not the general propensity for radical change so prominent elsewhere, which explains why the movement very rarely stepped over the boundaries or showed very little tolerance for those elements that did. The impact of the proximity of the German border was also not without significance. Whilst other parts of the country soon found difficulties in providing the basics, and in particular petrol, such a degree of shortage was not to be experienced in Strasbourg. Anything running short, as Foessel explained, could simply be bought across the border: 'There was no shortage of food; neither petrol nor cash were lacking, and all that thanks to the proximity of Germany.'[107] One specific anecdote in relation to this geographical circumstance and the electricity supply for the region is particularly revelatory. Georges Foessel explained how his concern for the impact of a strike by *Electricité de Strasbourg* (EDS) was tempered when he visited their headquarters during the revolt. He was brought to an area where he was shown a lever that permitted the regional grid to be switched to the German system in the event of a strike.[108] This sums up just how the proximity of Germany and the cross-border ties created over the years provided the grounds for specific characteristics that set Alsace apart and as Foessel argued 'meant that, in the end, the movement came across as more irritating than anything else'.[109]

The diversity of these provincial movements in terms of composition, spread and magnitude highlights the difficulty of generalizing how the events of 1968 were experienced across the nation and, in so doing, problematizes the stereotypical narrative. The inadequacy of the latter is underscored even further when one considers how commonalities in Brest and Strasbourg run contrary to the conventional representation. The student movement is commonly depicted as irresponsible, based on utopian ideals with no serious consideration for an alternative to the system it was opposing. Such an image of the 'student '68', during which out-of-control elements only interested in having a good time and carrying out hopelessly idealistic discussions in occupied faculties, is certainly not applicable to the situations in Brest or Strasbourg. Brestois students were extremely pragmatic and realistic in what they hoped to achieve. When the strike began on 6 May in the CLU, it was very much in line with the nationwide protest concerning the Parisian events. However, as the crisis unfolded, the Brestois student movement distanced itself from what was occurring in the capital. A *commission paritaire* was set up comprising students, teachers and non-teaching staff, with the aim of discussing and putting together suggestions on future reform of the university system. It had specific objectives from the start, concentrating on 'issues related specifically to higher education: organisation of teaching; exams; technological and pedagogical training; jobs [. . .]; problems with the structure of the university system'.[110] The Brestois proposals were based around three key principles: freedom, autonomy and joint management. Their ideas included the scrapping of end of year examinations, the introduction of continuous assessment, the dismantling of the strict hierarchy that so dominated the archaic system of the time and the adaptation of higher education establishments to the needs of local economies.[111] For

Edmond Monange, this added a particular edge to events in Brest: 'There is something more concrete, I would say more realistic, even much more materialistic than Paris, and that includes the student movement.'[112] The utopian ideals that are said to have so dominated the atmosphere – as Boudic commented – held no sway in Brest: 'Anything of the sort "sexual revolution", "it is forbidden to forbid" or deliberate police provocation was completely alien to us.'[113] University occupations only took place during the day, there were no all-night debates and no slogans painted on walls or damage to the university buildings. This 'more respectful attitude'[114] was not restricted to Brest.

One only has to consider the quantity of declarations, proposals and general output of the university reformist movement in Strasbourg to understand where its priorities lay.[115] As Alphonse Irjud – a journalist in 1968 – explained 'There was a marginal group who wanted to be in charge, those involved in the « *Manifeste* » that were known as leftist anarchists, but the rest were reformist much more than revolutionary'.[116] The numerous *Commission Paritaires* from the seven different faculties benefitted from the genuine interest in formulating proposals to improve the existing system as well as the active participation and close alliances with significant members of the teaching corps. As Jean Dewitz explained 'The involvement of a good number of teachers [. . .] gave the movement an almost official aspect which meant that Strasbourg became a centre that was taken seriously'.[117] This aspect, in many respects, can help explain one of the most interesting developments of the Strasbourgeois '68. The fact that the then Minister for Education Alain Peyrefitte gave permission for the University of Strasbourg to carry out an experiment in autonomy is, as François Igersheim argues, what sets the Strasbourgeois '68 apart.[118] Following a lengthy conversation between Peyrefitte and representatives of the university, the minister seemingly conceded to one of the principal demands of the student movement.[119] There are several possible explanations for this extraordinary set of circumstances, unique in 1968. It could be argued that Peyrefitte was simply appeasing the students in such a huge city by giving the impression of offering them what they wanted in order to prevent them from joining the more radical elements of the 1968 revolt, or, as Foessel described it, 'A bone to chew on'.[120] Braun, present when the experiment was given the go-ahead, supported such an analysis: 'It was a way of getting out of it, Peyrefitte had nothing political in mind, it was to keep them occupied for the moment.'[121] This interpretation is given even greater weight when one considers the government's desire to see such a symbolic and dangerously located university kept out of the seemingly uncontrollable movement developing in Paris. As Foessel explained:

At the time, no one was quite sure what was going to happen in Germany. There was a fear that the German movement would triumph leading to thousands of revolutionary, German students in Strasbourg. Such a scenario haunted the authorities.[122]

There is also the question of the significance of the term 'autonomy' for this region. Could the choice of this term – laden with pejorative historical significance – have been a strategic choice on behalf of the minister to conjure up the spectre of past errors and in so doing discredit the movement in the eyes of the general population? For, as Siffer explained:

> *The fact that it was Strasbourg that decided to become autonomous was taken very badly at state level. The amalgam autonomy and « autonomisme » was quickly made – therefore, separation of Alsace from France, a return to the 'grand' Germany, the pan-Germanism. The old hereditary hatred of 'Germany the enemy' re-emerged in Paris.*[123]

One could also argue that the movement in Strasbourg was at the very front line of the reformist elements of the national 1968 movement. The serious nature of the movement and the determination to focus efforts on future reform was so obvious that Peyrefitte genuinely saw what was happening there as providing fertile ground for the discovery of possible solutions to the undeniably problematic system of higher education.[124]

Such measured approaches with direction, aims and objectives can help explain another important element that sets the Brest and Strasbourg movements outside the commonly held perception of the events. Despite the great frustration felt by the Breton population concerning their predicament and the wholeheartedness with which they embraced the 1968 movement, there was virtually no violence.[125] Daily rallies were conducted with dignity and were extremely well marshalled, any signs of disruptive elements being dealt with swiftly. As Didou remarked: 'It was not the atmosphere, there was no need to look for trouble.'[126] A clear distinction can be drawn when we consider the serious clashes that took place in Paris and other cities that have come to characterize representations of the revolt. Breton participants, recognizing what their movement stood for and the strength emanating from their great unity and discipline, had no need for wanton violence. Trade union leaders (such as Henri Didou) who had become accustomed to organizing peaceful demonstrations took the situation in hand. Consequently, there was an element of coordination between union leaders and the authorities in a bid to avoid clashes leading to a situation whereby 'during the '68 events there were no CRS in Brest'.[127] Both sides wished to avoid the violence that had marked the 1950s and 1960s in Brittany, instigated by frustrated elements within the farming sector and the FLB. Whilst perhaps for different reasons, in Strasbourg such a lack of violence was replicated. The most prevalent impression is that 1968 in Strasbourg was experienced with a certain degree of *sagesse*. Mehl explained how 'We demonstrated that we were more mature, we participated in '68 but in a calmer, more tranquil manner',[128] or as one tract from 10 June put it, 'Strasbourg, forever at the avant-garde of the return to order'.[129] In fact, there was very little tolerance of any excesses in terms of street protests. As Siffer explained: 'The aim of the movement was not to attack the police, it was to reflect and bring about change.'[130] On the one occasion that students did overstep the mark, the revulsion of the general public was matched only by the hard line of the local police chief who declared the next day: 'I gave the order to charge and to do so vigorously. I take full responsibility. There are limits to be respected. We will not tolerate Strasbourg becoming a city of barricades.'[131] Such an attitude is often described as emanating from the prevailing conservatism of the Alsatian population. One can understand – given the history of the region – those who were reluctant to support a movement that challenged a system that brought about a long-overdue period of stability. However, as Lucien Braun explained, such conservatism is equally a consequence of the hybrid nature of Alsatian identity: 'It's German, the German spirit is in Alsace [. . .] we like order here [. . .] it is a German tradition.'[132]

Therefore, in terms of the actual events of 1968, it is clear that whilst Strasbourg and Brest cannot be considered in isolation to what was happening nationally and in particular in Paris, it is equally true that the capital cannot be considered as representing these provincial revolts. When one juxtaposes the dominant narrative of the 1968 events with a close regional analysis it becomes clear that important differences and elements are being squeezed from the history of 1968. One very symbolic example of this in terms of what happened in Strasbourg concerns the extraordinary events of 1 June. In the stereotypical image of 1968, the students are often framed in direct opposition with the police and, in particular, the CRS. On 1 June in Strasbourg the students were actually protected from attack by a crowd of marauding Gaullists by the CRS at the steps of the PU.[133] Describing what happened, one journalist pointed out that 'It is paradoxical to see the CRS and the forces of order preventing Strasbourgeois citizens from removing the red flag flying from their university.'[134] This is indeed May 1968 *à l'envers*. Events of the same day in Brest that saw pro-Gaullist and those on strike parade at the same time around the narrow streets of Brest are equally notable but for different reasons. As Monange describes: 'It was a surprising to-ing and fro-ing where each side took care to avoid the other and in so doing demonstrated how from both camps, prudence and wise heads took precedence over fanaticism and exaltation.'[135] The diversity with which this same day was experienced in two different cities problematizes the progressively diluted history of these events and flags up the inadequacy of the dominant narrative in reflecting the heterogeneous nature of the national 1968 movement.

Contribution

While the specificities of these provincial revolts might suggest that they were isolated sets of events, the Strasbourgeois and Brestois movements did not go unnoticed and were not without consequence on a national scale. The CSF factory in Brest had the longest-running strike of the city, concluding on 21 June. However, as Le Roux pointed out, it was not just the duration but the nature of the strike and occupation which was important: 'There were factory occupations, undoubtedly less than in other regions, but there were particular occupations such as that at the CSF-Thomson factory in Brest.'[136] Upon seizing control of their factory on 20 May, the CSF workers were not content simply to down tools and bring all activity to a halt. Determined to maintain the factory in pristine condition, they organized it along democratic lines, set up commissions and produced the results of their deliberations in a journal, *Notre combat*. As Monange told me, they established links with farmers and students, holding joint meetings during which they discussed future plans and action: 'There was even a joint meeting between arts students and Thomson-CSF Trade union representatives.'[137] The striking CSF workers focused on the issues of control and participation, demanding a greater say in the overall running and management of the factory. The second issue of *Notre combat* would see the raison d'être of the commissions explained and was responsible for this factory becoming the focus of much attention: 'The creation of workers' commission is only a first step. They will allow those workers to want to go further down the road of self-management.'[138] One of the workers' major concerns was to demonstrate that they were capable of running the factory themselves and at one stage they were close to reopening it under their control.[139] Although this failed to happen, their strike was of particular significance as one of the first examples of *autogestion*. In the years following the 1968 events, this became a buzzword and formed the bedrock of the CFDT's policy with the Brestois CSF factory remaining a significant reference point.[140] Despite questions surrounding just what those concerned actually understood by the concept of *autogestion*,[141] the Brestois factory set an example that many workplaces and trade unions would follow during the crisis and in the ensuing years (e.g. Lip (Besançon) in 1973).[142]

The significance of the Brest movement can be measured in other ways. The prudent and purposeful attitude of students, teaching staff and service personnel in the CLU de Brest as regards university reform was not without significance. From the outset, there was a determination on the part of the *Commission paritaire* to come up with what Porhel describes as 'a credible reform project'[143] – this, arguably, was what it achieved. As well as proving to be a success in harnessing the energy of participants in Brest, the influence of the Brestois *Commission paritaire* was not limited to the local perspective. On 17–19 June 1968, the various student–teacher commissions that had been established around the country during the crisis organized a meeting in Clermont-Ferrand during which they compared each set of proposals in order to determine which could best serve the cause of the university reform movement. A team of Brestois representatives, including Fanch Broudig who was not only an extremely important member of the Brest student movement, but has also gone on to become a highly respected and famous member of the Breton language movement, most notably known for his regular news programmes in Breton on France 2, was in attendance and presented the work of their *Commission Paritaire*.[144] From the wide-ranging proposed reforms, 'The representatives from the different universities at this meeting had decided to use the Brestois project as the basis of preparation for the next meeting to be held in Grenoble. That proves that the work carried out in Brest was of a serious nature.'[145] In the meantime, Edgar Faure, the newly appointed Minister for Education, was steadfast in his drive to complete the *loi d'orientation*. Nationally, the importance of the reformist element of the university movement – often overshadowed by the actions and ideas of *gauchiste* elements – was significant in prolonging the crisis and influential in the ensuing Faure reform. Faure himself did take ideas from student groups on board – such as greater student participation and the reduced importance of examinations – and listened to what students thought.[146] The successful work of the Brestois *commission paritaire* was clearly an important feature of this reformist drive. Thus, both in terms of the working-class and the university revolt, the movement in Brest provided an important model for activists elsewhere. The lack of coverage or attention paid to the events in Brittany has obscured these facts. While this relative lack of interest is perhaps due to the absence of both violence and utopian politics in the Breton case, the importance of the reformist 1968 and of Brest's contribution to it should not be ignored.

It would be wrong to state that the Strasbourg 1968 is ignored in the dominant representations of 1968. In fact, due largely to the influence of *Situationniste* ideas and language on the spectacular elements that dominate the stereotypical image of the French 1968, one could be forgiven for interpreting the events in Strasbourg as very much fitting the mould of the conventional representation.[147] However, this is not the case because as Amman explains: 'Wishing to attribute the *Situationnistes* in Strasbourg a major role [is] an abusive judgement, which incidentally also fits the most fantasised of speculations.'[148] By 1968 the main protagonists of the *Situationniste* movement in Strasbourg were no longer around and as Philippe Breton – militant *lycéen* in 1968 and current-day university professor in Strasbourg – explained, their influence was minimal: 'A small, elitist, intellectual movement that was only discussed in intellectual circles that was at the origin of nothing at all.'[149] Those present were extremely critical of what was happening;[150] in one tract claiming that 'students have clearly understood nothing at all'.[151] Such criticisms stemmed from the fact that the Strasbourgeois student population – contrary to popular myth – was, from the outset, dedicated to putting together a serious movement whose aim it was to work on proposing reform of the system. It was this element that had the most significant impact in terms of a contribution to the national revolt. All too often, the *Situationniste* past in Strasbourg leads to an easy assimilation of the 1968 events there with the dominant narrative. However, as Daniel Coche, who was a first-year history student at the University of Strasbourg in 1968, pointed out:

> *It is somewhat of a pity from a historical perspective to only speak of the situationnistes. In '68, they were representative of nothing at all; they enjoyed themselves, they did their thing and moved on to something else. It is practical vis-à-vis the image, but historically false.*[152]

Such an over-emphasis on the *Situs*, as Foessel explained, inhibits a true understanding of events in Strasbourg: 'In the end, the *situationnistes* gave the 1968 movement a folkloric edge and there has been no attempt to uncover the serious and more profound aspects of the movement.'[153]

As discussed previously, there was a considerable investment on behalf of all seven faculties that made up the University of Strasbourg to concentrate their efforts on producing detailed and realistic proposals for reform of the system. Such involvement was not limited to the student body but saw active participation from across the academic spectrum. Such a focused and serious approach would be influential in a number of respects. First – and as discussed above – one cannot emphasize enough the significance of Alain Peyrefitte's exceptional decision to grant the Strasbourgeois movement permission to undertake an experiment in autonomy. There are, as we have seen, numerous arguments to explain this unprecedented decision. Nevertheless, one can assume that the prominence of reformist elements and the thoroughness they demonstrated from an early stage cannot have been without significance in this step. From this point on Strasbourg would assume a prominent role in the national movement for university reform. This is reflected in the presence of Strasbourg representatives as guests at other occupied faculties around the country during the events. Such a leading role was underscored even further when Strasbourg hosted an *Assises Générales* in June 1968 which brought together fourteen universities from around the country to discuss the future for university reform. Finally, it is also true that Edgar Faure, the minister responsible for reforming the system of higher education in the aftermath of 1968, consulted a number of people prominent in the various *commission parit-aires* around the country with Strasbourg once again playing a central role.[154] As Bernard Carrière, describing some of the key elements of the reformist drive in Strasbourg, argued, 'To some extent, the Faure law and others that have followed have taken on these concepts.'[155] The dominant narrative tends to focus on the spectacular elements and thus (through an overemphasis on the role of the *Situs*) portrays Strasbourg as a hotbed of student radicalism. The reality, as indicated above, is that the most prominent, focused and influential trend that emerged from the Strasbourgeois 1968 was in fact that which was focused on reform not revolution.

Conclusion

While studies of regional movements are not completely absent and many of the more complete analyses of the events highlight some important regional developments, the quasi-monopolization of the history of the 1968 events by the capital has led to an assumption that what happened in Paris was typical of what happened elsewhere. The revolts in Brest and Strasbourg stemmed from wholly different sets of circumstances – not only from each other but also from those propagated by the dominant narrative. Hence, the manner with which these provincial revolts were played out were particular to each region. It would seem increasingly obvious that the very selective memory of a Parisian 1968 does not do justice to a highly diverse, nationwide revolt. The evidence from Brest and Strasbourg suggests that a more complete understanding of the 1968 events is predicated on a more thorough consideration of what happened around the country. Such a de-centring of the analysis would go some way to addressing the situation lamented by Monange, who continues to regret that 'people have more of a tendency to focus on the surface rather than what lies beneath what was happening at the time; the spray rather than the waves'.[156]

Conclusion
2008 – 'Liquidate', consolidate and innovate

The 1968–1998 period saw the emergence of a dominant narrative on *mai 68*. This doxa has been shaped by a convenient consensus driven by a very unlikely tango. On the one hand, former *gauchistes* – who have monopolized (particularly during the decennial commemorations) how the story of 1968 is told – have perpetuated the reductive lens that focuses almost exclusively on their own contribution. This has ensured their place as representatives of these iconic events and all the advantages they have been able to reap as a result. On the other, the state, which has happily looked on as this conventional representation has taken root, safe in the knowledge that its narrow perspective would be pivotal in reducing the potential influence of 1968 as an example to be followed.

The fortieth anniversary was always going to see the continuation in the trend of decennial commemorations of the 1968 events in France. This tradition, as discussed, has long been in place and the 'industry' was not to watch the golden opportunity of the fortieth anniversary pass it by. As such, it provides an excellent opportunity to assess to what extent the developments outlined across this study have continued, developed or completely diversified. As usual, the context from which the 2008 commemoration would emerge was all important. Nicolas Sarkozy's September 2007 election campaign speech was to be of particular significance at this juncture.[1] By declaring the need to 'liquidate' the spirit of 1968, the future president only served to further heighten the level of interest and guarantee a blockbuster year. In some respects, his attack gave the green light to an early start to the commemoration as the number of analyses from late 2007/early 2008 demonstrate.[2] What is clear is that by singling out the *soixantehuitard* generation for such criticism, Sarkozy was sure to receive a response from both those involved and a general population that, as demonstrated, very much holds the events in a positive light.

This concluding chapter will examine a sample of the material produced to coincide with the fortieth anniversary. A number of questions will be the focus of attention, providing opportunities to draw appropriate conclusions to some of the questions raised throughout the study. First of all, to what extent does the 2008 commemoration compare with those previous? Does it continue the narrowing trend as identified and discussed in chapter two? Does the *mai 68* industry continue to impinge on the type and quality of material produced? Has the context had any significant impact on the nature of this commemoration? And, if so, has it forced a recalibration of the typical portrayal of the events? Finally, has the forty-year juncture seen the emergence of any new approaches that challenge the stereotypical nature of coverage? And, if so, what are, if any, the implications for the collective memory? In order to provide answers to these questions, the nature of coverage across a number of mediums (academic studies, television programmes, filmic representations, press coverage, etc.) will be assessed.

First of all, it is important to note how 2008 fitted the trend of a huge surge in interest. This was evident in a number of typical areas and some new sources. In terms of the literature produced, one only had to visit any French bookstore during the period late 2007–late 2008 to take stock of how much interest 1968 had generated.[3] Such was the volume of output that large areas of floor space were dedicated to the *mai 68* section, with material that, as will be discussed later, ranged from cobblestone shaped books to groundbreaking studies.[4] The outpouring of material was mirrored in national and local press coverage. Each of the major newspapers and weekly magazines dedicated significant column space to special editions or daily 1968 sections.[5] The coverage ranged from discussions on straightforward accounts of what took place to analyses of the major questions of debate. Television also proved to be a prolific source of output. Old films were re-screened alongside new studies as well as a number of programmes debating the legacy of 1968.[6] French radio equally dedicated a lot of airtime to the anniversary commemoration. From *RTL* to *France Inter*, there were innumerable debates and documentaries that gave a prominent place to this medium so important in 1968.[7] The academic community also bought into the commemorative fervour. The number of conferences in France and abroad was such that some of the 'big names' of '68 studies were on a constant tour of the country,[8] whilst a large number of academic journals also featured special editions on 'Mai 68'.[9] Such was the plethora of events taking place with film screenings, exhibitions and plays adding to the conferences, that one website in particular, set up by the *Collectif des centres de documentation en histoire ouvrière et sociale* (CODHOS), became a necessity for anyone trying to keep up with what was happening.[10] The internet itself really came into its own in terms of the 1968 events on the fortieth anniversary. The number of hits on a simple Google search is indicative of just how much the web has become a valuable tool and innovative site of output for this area of research.[11] Furthermore, the basic modern-day necessity for all media outlets to have a web presence meant that television and radio stations, newspapers and magazines as well as other independent sites have offered a new medium through which 1968 is analysed, commented on and one that offers a democratization of accounts put forward.[12] The sheer magnitude of material and interest suggest that 2008 even saw a consolidation of the commemorative trend.

Moreover, 2008 saw this surge expand and move on to a completely different level with the depth and breadth of output far outstretching any previous commemorative period. In many respects, one could argue that Sarkozy's attack had a lot to do with focusing interest. However, it is also worth noting the progressive building across the decades which has seen *mai 68* become a commemorative growth industry. Another indication of the endurance of a certain perspective comes from the dominance of the usual suspects that up until this point have been so crucial in shaping how the events are portrayed. Whether in terms of the texts produced, the press coverage or television appearances, the same faces that have dominated from the start continue to do so forty years on. The omnipresence of Daniel Cohn-Bendit in a range of areas is perhaps most exemplary of this.[13] It cannot be without some irony that the undisputed *mai 68* poster boy advises us to 'Forget '68' while his omnipresence makes it clear that he patently has no intentions of doing so.

In quite a lot of the material produced, it is clear that there has been no attempt to do otherwise than confirm and consolidate the conventional representation that is typically prominent in such anniversary coverage. There continued to be too much attention afforded to the *gauchiste* elements and not enough to the working class and the strike. June remains absent and the events continue to de depoliticized. Instead, 1968 continues to be considered as a moment of petulance that has – as Sarkozy's 2007 speech demonstrates – become increasingly blamed for the ills of twenty-first-century France. Indicative of this trend are the nature and results of a *Nouvel Observateur* survey entitled '*Que reste-t-il de mai 68*' carried out in March 2008.[14] The very questions posed confirm the narrow optic through which the events continue to be analysed.[15] Furthermore, the responses given confirm the results of chapter three by highlighting how respondents, whilst demonstrating a certain degree of knowledge and sympathy vis-à-vis 1968,[16] nevertheless show clear signs of being heavily influenced by the narrow portrayal.[17]

The question relating to the obvious sympathy for 1968 in France in relation to Sarkozy's speech also added a certain tint to the nature of some of the material produced. In some cases the desire to respond to the speech was picked up and used by analysts. For example, Raphael and André Glucksmann's *Mai 68 expliqué à Nicolas Sarkozy* argues that the very rupture the president was so keen to promote during the campaign would not have been possible without 1968.[18] Patrick Rotman's *Mai 68 expliqué à ceux qui ne l'ont pas vécu*, which begins with a preface entitled '*La faute à Nicolas*' is further indication of just how important this speech was for this anniversary in urging people like Rotman to produce such works.[19] Gérard Filoche's *Mai 68, Histoire sans fin* is another text that exemplifies the need to respond to the president's speech with a concluding section entitled '*Liquider mai 68. Même pas en rêve*'.[20] It is worth pointing out that not everyone used Sarkozy's speech as an opportunity to defend *mai 68*. For example, Mathieu Grimpret and Chantal Delsol's collection of essays *Liquider Mai 68?* clearly demonstrates how the president is not alone in wanting to exorcise the ghost of 1968.[21] However, perhaps the most striking trend in terms of assessing how the discussion has progressed or not is the number of republished studies that clearly took advantage of both the anniversary window and the heightened interest generated by the *faut-il liquider* debate to trot out the same analysis from ten, twenty, thirty and in some cases forty years previously.

For example, Alain Griotteray's *Des Barricades ou des Réformes* makes a reappearance four decades after it was first published.[22] There are some new
additions to the text but for the most part it is simply a reproduction of the
same analysis initially commissioned by Valéry Giscard d'Estaing back in 1968.
Not only does this highlight the static nature of the debate, it also contributes
to the consolidation of a core discourse that, as discussed previously, was
grounded very early on and has continued to be prominent across the years.
Another example is Régis Debray's *Mai 68, une contre-révolution réussie.*[23] First
published in 1978 under the title *Modeste contribution aux discours et cérémonies
officielles du dixième anniversaire*, it confirms the idea that a thirty-year-old analysis continues to be considered relevant. Or, as the author himself puts it, this
book 'has become more, rather than less, relevant'.[24] Perhaps even more
exemplary of this thread running from 1968 through to 2008 is Morin,
Castoriadis and Lefort's *Mai 68, la brèche.*[25] Originally published in 1968, it
reappeared in 1988 with some updates. Its third outing in 2008 is indeed indicative of the stagnant nature of the discussions surrounding the 1968 events
from the very outset.

It is by no means being suggested that such famous analyses do not warrant
their place forty years down the line. However, the sheer number of texts does
add weight to the suggestion that a certain consensus has been reached. For
example, Laurent Joffrin's *Les événements de 68*, first published in 1988, and
then in 1998, once again finds its place in 2008.[26] The same *parcours* can de
delineated with Henri Weber's *Faut-il liquider mai 68?*[27] This is in fact the
republication under a different title of his 1988 *Que reste-t-il* study that also
made a reappearance in 1998. Other important works that were rolled out for
2008 include the collection of articles from the journal *Le Débat* brought
together for *Mai 68, le débat.*[28] These articles appeared between 1981 and 1998
and chart the development of analyses surrounding 1968. *Les Années 68; Le
temps de la contestation,* a groundbreaking study first published in 2000, is
another example of an important text that reappeared to coincide with the
fortieth anniversary.[29] On the positive side, the fact that old studies are republished means that new generations are able to take stock of how the debate has
evolved over the years. However, it does suggest that a lack of progress in
studies has maintained a place for recycled analyses where they are able to
continue to contribute to the ongoing discussions. The great difficulty with
this situation is that the commemorative periods have become so swamped
with material that is only there to take advantage of the commercial opportunity that some quality, groundbreaking works that question the dominant
narrative must compete with a plethora of material that does little more than
consolidate the doxa.

So, for example, three texts that have already been identified in 1998 as
doing little to challenge the conventional representation were republished in
2008.[30] The fact that they remain largely unchanged means that they do
nothing to shift the focus away from what one has come to expect, i.e. the spectacular, Paris-centric perspective. They were, however, not alone in attempting
to cash in on the commemorative industry. The number of photography

books, poster collections, as well as comics, quiz books and even *pavé*-shaped books are all indicative of just how much of a gimmick, souvenir industry the 1968 events have become.[31] The general upshot of these factors is the continuation of the dominant perspective or the convenient consensus. As discussed in chapter two, the paradox between the consensus and disagreement has been critical in shaping the place *mai 68* occupies in the French collective memory. The fortieth anniversary revealed that those areas devoid of consensus continue to be a major source of doubt. A number of episodes of the 1968 events in France were and have remained shrouded in mystery and intrigue. The lack of consensus over how to interpret the events, how to describe the role of the police, the debate surrounding the rejection of the Grenelle accords and de Gaulle's mysterious disappearance were highlighted as amongst the reasons that could help explain just why the events remain such a focus of discussion. It was also intimated that a lack of agreement over such areas has been important in preparing the ground for the dominance of the conventional representation. A number of 2008 publications demonstrate how this process has continued and how questions remain. There is perhaps no better example than the notorious Baden-Baden episode.

As outlined in chapter two, de Gaulle's trip to the French army base in German territory was not only a critically important moment in the unfolding events. Since 1968, much discussion has centred on the motivations for this mysterious visit to General Massu. Patrick Rotman's *Mai 68 expliqué à ceux qui ne l'ont pas vécu* recalls two hypotheses, reminding us of the unresolved nature of this episode.[32] The fact that he does so is revelatory of the continued intrigue as well as underscoring the stagnant nature of the debate. However, it would be wrong to suggest that no new studies emerged. On the contrary, two texts in particular were published in 2008 that add to the complexity and the inconclusiveness surrounding this episode. Henri-Christian Giraud's *L'Accord secret de Baden-Baden* examines this turning point in the events.[33] Emphasizing de Gaulle's 'duo-duel' with the Communist Party as the most significant source to help gain an understanding, Giraud's text nevertheless does little to help bring us any closure on the debate. In fact, he charts how the episode has been the focus of many different hypotheses that have emerged, been challenged and replaced over the years.[34] He even goes as far as to suggest that de Gaulle and those supporters involved in the lengthy and inconclusive discussion have deliberately maintained an air of intrigue in order to conceal actions that could run against the 'official history'.[35] Benoît d'Aigullhon and José Lenzini's 2008 *Mai 68, Baden la mort du Gaullisme* is another study that takes the iconic Baden-Baden episode as its focus.[36] Once again, the possible interpretations are presented, demonstrating the continued contention on the motivations behind the general's disappearance. However, the central thesis of the study is not an attempt at resolving any such debate but rather an effort to frame the president's trip as the confirmation of the end of Gaullism that 1968 has been interpreted as representing. One of many documentaries released to coincide with the fortieth anniversary was the France 2 programme *Droit d'inventaire* fronted by Marie Druker with the participation of a number of special guests.[37]

Organized around a number of themes, this programme singled out the Baden episode for particular attention in a dramatic reconstruction accompanied with the title *Le jour quand le pouvoir était à prendre*. The dominant picture that emerges is that which favours the notion that de Gaulle went to check that he had the support of his army. In the discussion that follows, the confusion surrounding the motivation of this disappearance is examined as is the existence of the three theses that exist. Those present certainly appear to lean towards the idea that the whole thing was a well-calculated ruse by de Gaulle in order to jolt the population back to reality. That the Baden episode continues to be shrouded in mystery and intrigue and the focus of such persistent debate is just one example of how the 2008 commemoration has continued a long-standing trend. Further examples can be found in other areas where disagreement exists.

One of the major sources of contention discussed earlier concerns the role played by the forces of order. On the one hand, there are those who hold the police and, in particular, the CRS responsible for the spread of the crisis. On the other, there is the official line that sheds a positive light on the police arguing that they behaved professionally and with cool heads given the difficulties faced. This tension is the focus of one section in the *Droit d'Inventaire* documentary entitled *CRS stars de 68*. The opening scenes provide footage of serious violence and suggest that the CRS were heavy handed and out of order in 1968. However, after describing how much of the tension that was present at the time came from accusations based on exaggerated and false rumours, the film compares the French events to what was happening elsewhere suggesting that *mai* 68 was in fact very well managed. In order to emphasize this point, this piece focuses on *l'autre coté de la barricade*. By giving former CRS officers their say, we learn of the difficulties they faced, the insults, the inadequate uniforms and the number of injuries. The common accusation that the CRS were extreme right-wing thugs is countered and instead the behaviour of these 'ordinary French men' in the opening week of May 1968 is explained by poor decision making that exposed them to unmanageable pressures. Maurice Grimaud is then described as taking the events in hand and almost single-handedly ensuring the success that 1968 is described as being for the CRS. The film ends by suggesting that the missed chance of a revolution for the students nevertheless resulted in a revolution for the CRS, as they experienced great progress and improved facilities as a result of the crisis. Such a line is replicated in another 2008 piece. *Liasons*, the official magazine of the police, published a special edition to commemorate the fortieth anniversary.[38] Here, just as in *Droit d'Inventaire*, the emphasis is on the other side of the barricades. Again, the difficulties faced by the police are detailed and the overall performance of the forces of order is unsurprisingly given a positive spin with Maurice Grimaud again held up as a hero. Generally speaking, the image of Grimaud the negotiator, the cool-headed, open and balanced chief of the Parisian police is very much thrust to the fore; arguably to counter the notion that the forces of order were somehow responsible for the spread of the crisis in

1968.[39] The fact that Grimaud released a text late 2007 with the ironic title *Je ne suis pas né en 68* gives some sort of indication just how much of an emphasis has been placed on the former prefect's role over the years.[40]

These examples demonstrate a clear desire from the official side to challenge the perception that the police were somehow culpable in 1968. This need to get their side of the story across only really serves to confirm that another interpretation exists; one that paints a less flattering picture of their role. The battle over how the part played by the police should be interpreted continues some forty years on. The Baden episode and the role of the CRS are but two examples of how certain aspects of 1968 are still the focus of contradictory discussions. The fortieth anniversary also confirmed the malleability of a number of other areas. For example, the reasons behind the sensational rejection of the Grenelle protocol of 27 May remains a serious source of tension for one of the most important protagonists of this episode. In *Résister. De Mauthasen à Mai 68*, Georges Séguy confirms the unresolved nature of this episode.[41] The fact that he attacks a Swiss journalist for having suggested that he could have somehow misinterpreted the mood of his troops would suggest that the wounds remain open.[42] More generally speaking, the continued debate over such elements, together with the polemical discussion over the legacy of the events, feeds into the lack of overall consensus over just how the events as a whole should be interpreted. This continued debate is obvious in the plethora of re-edited texts released on the fortieth anniversary that effectively perpetuate the questioning on how to interpret 1968. Also, one could point to the multitude of diverse studies that instead of bringing us any closer to consensus only seem to further underscore the unlikelihood and difficulty of such a thing.[43] Amongst this continued level of discussion that does little to resolve enduring questions, it is the dominant image that continues to shine through. Quantity, it appears, continues to outweigh quality. The same figures that have been so pivotal across the decennial commemorations of the past remain the stars of the show. They have continued to trot out the same discourse that has proven critical in shaping the conventional representation of what happened, why and what the consequences have been. Their continued presence has and will continue to make it difficult to see any real shift in how the events are portrayed. This is perhaps the single most important reason why *mai '68* continues to be framed in a stereotypical manner as is evidenced by the film *Nés en 68*.[44]

This 2008 film, starring Laetitia Casta, follows a band of friends who, involved together in the 1968 events, are forever influenced and united by their experiences. Their development is charted from their post-1968 commune to the election of Francois Mitterrand in 1981 before concluding on Sarkozy's 2007 speech on his intent to liquidate the spirit of 1968. The representation of the events is fairly typical. The opening scenes focus on Paris, the Sorbonne and the student milieu. The clichés are all there; the posters, the CRS, the music and even the reconstruction of two iconic scenes (first, the reading of Marchais 3 May *Humanité* article and second a fleeting reference to the *La reprise du travail aux usines de Wonder* film that was the focus of Le Roux's *Reprise*). As the band of friends go through their life from this point on, one cannot help but discern a certain degree of irresponsibility; the issue of sexual liberation is to the fore as are the utopian ideals that continue to set this generation apart. As a result, this film does little to challenge the dominant discourse that has emerged over the years. Whilst it does give some indication of the impact that these events have had on people throughout the rest of their lives and there was a decision by the directors taken to use anonymous characters and thereby avoiding the focus on the usual suspects, the emphasis on the stereotypical clichés means that this film sits very comfortably with the conventional representation.

Up until this point, it has been argued that the fortieth anniversary has very much seen a continuation in the trend as discussed in chapter one. In other words, the fourth decennial commemoration has seen the consolidation and confirmation of what can be described as a narrow portrayal of the 1968 events. The convenient consensus is therefore able to continue. This is facilitated by one half of the 'unlikely tango' (the usual suspects) – as described in chapter one – continuing to play a prominent role in telling the story of *mai 68*. However, there was evidence of some movement in terms of focus that suggests that 2008 could be a turning point in just how the events are studied, analysed and presented. The grounds are arguably being laid for a potential decoupling of the unlikely tango with obvious connotations for the collective memory. Amongst the plethora of material produced to coincide with the fortieth anniversary that fits the conventional representation, there were a number of studies that Robert Gildea describes as widening 'the historical lens to situate it [1968] in a larger chronological and geographical context'.[45] Such analyses would suggest the emergence of a new generation of researchers or at least a new approach that runs against the grain and contributes to a much more rigorous examination of what happened, why and what the consequences have been. These shifts can be demonstrated through a number of themes.

As described throughout, the doxa surrounding the events presents them very much from a Paris-centred perspective. In chapter five, the cases of Brest and Strasbourg demonstrated how this capital-focused representation ignored the existence of regional protests, effectively undermining the nationwide nature of the crisis that clearly made it so exceptional. Furthermore, by only really briefly suggesting how provincial revolts followed what was happening in the Latin Quarter, one is left with the impression that what happened beyond the capital simply replicated it or lacked significant importance. However, as argued, not only did 1968 take place in regions such as Brittany and Alsace, but the movements there, whilst certainly triggered by events in Paris, were of a different nature, focused on different demands and with different consequences. Some of the protagonists interviewed even discussed how they felt their regional 1968 was absent from the conventional representation, so much so that they did not consider their own movements to be part of how the 1968 events were commonly portrayed.

However, 2008 has arguably marked the beginning of a trend at de-centring the analysis. There have been a number of studies that set out explicitly to demonstrate how 1968 was experienced in provincial France and how they did not necessarily follow the Parisian model. For example, Gisèle Lougart's *Pays Basque Nord: Mai 68 en memoires* aims to challenge the notion that nothing happened in the Basque country in 1968.[46] Drawing on archival resources and interviews with former activists, Lougart demonstrates how the area experienced not only a significant movement but also one that was based on serious and concrete demands. Furthermore, she highlights how both students and workers were involved in important strike movements that included instances of fraternization between the two elements. The significance of the revolt as well as the feeling amongst those interviewed that it was a major turning point, together with the regional specificities, effectively underscore the inadequacy of the dominant narrow portrayal. Lougart's study demonstrates the sheer diversity of contexts, events and consequences, so often airbrushed from conventional representations. In a similar vein, Pierre Robin's *Mai 68 en Lot-et-Garonne* seeks to challenge the stereotypical angle so prevalent during commemorative periods.[47] It aims to avoid the opposing notions of celebration and condemnation, instead underscoring the fact that May 1968 was and remains a significant turning point throughout France; the Lot-et-Garonne department included.

This desire from within provincial France to highlight how 1968 was experienced locally was also evidenced in the huge interest in local press. Most provincial newspapers dedicated significant coverage both in the daily papers but also in online dossiers.[48] A common trend was the push to encourage those who had experienced 1968 to recount how their '*mai*' unfolded. Such a regional push could be interpreted as a focused effort to dilute the dominance of the stereotypical clichés within the history and memory of 1968 in France and give more coverage of the diversity of this *national* movement. Furthermore, one only has to consider the number of provincial conferences, debates, exhibitions, etc., to get a sense of the desire within the regions for people to have their say.[49] This de-centring process was not simply evident within the provinces. More generally, 2008 saw a drive to see beyond Paris and the Latin Quarter. So, for example, whilst many provincial events took place focusing on local circumstances, national conferences examining 1968 saw more emphasis on events outside the capital.[50] Another critical medium is television. Often, the lack of TV coverage beyond the capital during the events is posited as one of the major reasons to explain why so little attention is afforded to regional 1968 revolts. The stereotypical and spectacu-lar images of the barricades, the CRS or Daniel Cohn-Bendit have been so prevalent that they have become etched in the minds of anyone considering the events. However, and in keeping with the 2008 de-centring focus, *l'Institut National de l'Audiovisuel* released a DVD entitled *Mai 68. Les images de la television* that affords much attention to beyond the Latin Quarter with sections such as 'José en Alsace', 'Qu-est-ce qui ne va pas dans le nord?' or 'La Maison de la Culture à Amiens'.[51] Perhaps even more significant was the *France 3* initiative that saw seven documentaries each diffused simultaneously across the regional network.[52] Each film presents a specifically regional perspective that, taken together, provides some indication of the great diversity that characterizes nationwide experiences of the events of 1968.

The need to present what was a mosaic of experiences is equally evident in a number of key 2008 texts. For example, the edited collection *Mai Juin 68* avoids the Paris-centred approach in what is an extremely wide-ranging examination of the 1968 events. Instead, it offers numerous examples of how the provinces were involved and affected before, during and after the events.[53] In *Le Moment 68* Michelle Zancarini-Fournel highlights the inadequacy of the typical geographical framing of the 1968 revolt.[54] In a chapter that highlights how 1968 has been progressively reduced over the years, one of the most striking features is described as the overemphasis on Paris. In another significant 2008 study – *68. Une histoire collective* – which Fournel co-edited with Philippe Artières, the national aspect of 1968 is equally present. Throughout this vast study, there is a clear desire to place as much emphasis on how the period leading up to the events as well as the revolt itself and its consequences were experienced throughout the country.[55]

This recalibration of the geographical focus has equally been evident in terms of a trend to examine the transnational nature of 1968 and how the French events fit. All too often, the international dimension has been used to express the sentiment that what happened in France was no more than some sort of typically Gallic over-reaction to a strange sequence of international events. Such an approach strengthened the emphasis on a select band of *gauchiste* students caught up in some revolutionary fervour drawing on issues such as the Vietnam War, the US civil rights movement, the Cuban revolution or the Chinese Cultural revolution. In so doing, such an approach served to highlight the exceptionalism of what happened in France in comparison to other western European nations whilst at the same time ignoring any deeper international pressures that may offer a more fundamental reason to explain why so many nations experienced such similar revolts and how the French events should be considered in such a perspective. A number of examples of 2008 material suggest the emergence of a more rounded approach to this question.

The lack of French studies specifically focused on the idea of an international 1968 is perhaps some indication of how the tendency has been more towards what Daniel Gordon describes as the continuation of a 'certain francocentricity'.[56] One can point to a number of non-French studies to highlight a more general move in recent years towards examining the transnational aspect of this year of revolt.[57] Nevertheless, and as exemplified by one of the few French studies of 2008 that focused specifically on the international question, the fortieth anniversary did see a change in how the French 1968 was perceived from this perspective.[58] There were, for example, a number of special editions dedicated to framing the 1968 events in a more international optic.[59] Furthermore, a number of the many conferences during the commemorative period focused on or included panels examining the international dimension.[60] Television coverage was also keen to examine how 1968 was played out beyond France, as evidenced with the screening of a number of documentaries that took a more transnational view.[61] Finally, whilst much new and republished material continues to focus exclusively on a French- (and even Paris-) centred perspective, the shift in other significant works towards a more global view exemplifies the trend that has seen 2008 mark a turning point. For example, in *68. Une histoire collective* there are four sections across the time-periods examined dedicated to analyses of what was happening beyond France. With twenty chapters ranging from studies on, amongst others, the US, Japan, Mexico, Prague, Italy, Chile, Iran and Poland, the desire to broaden the geographical lens is evident.[62] Boris Gobille's *Mai 68* tackles the difficulty of examining the question of contact between international students[63] whilst Damamme, Gobille, Matonti and Pudal's edited collection *Mai Juin 68* contains a number of chapters which give some insight into the impact of the international circumstances on the movement in France.[64] Finally, in *Le moment 68*, Fournel discusses the shifting focus towards a more international approach arguing that this is a necessary shift but one that is not without difficulties.[65]

So from a geographical perspective, there is evidence of a shift in focus within the material produced in 2008. From both a national and an international angle, horizons have been broadened, enabling a presentation of 1968 as more than some sort of Parisian tantrum in reaction to a series of dangerous international influences.[66] This widening of the perspective has also been traditionally absent in terms of portrayals of those people involved in the 1968 events. As demonstrated throughout, the dominant image of 1968 is one that has seen it become perceived largely as a student revolt. There can be no question that students were fundamental in triggering the crisis in France. However, the over-emphasis on a select band of Paris-based *gauchiste* students has been fundamental in shaping the narrow portrayal of the crisis. Chapter four demonstrated how, even from a university perspective, this overemphasis on what was a minority element fails to portray the complete picture with significant reformist movements left out. However, the limited view extends beyond the faculties. For example, despite the fact that 1968 saw the largest-ever strike in French history, the involvement of workers, their motivations and the nature of their strikes are all features that have been progressively airbrushed from the dominant perspective. The involvement of the working class has increasingly been depicted as simply profiting from the opportunity to extract long-held demands from the *patronat*. With (a minority element of) students stealing all the limelight and the working class given some (limited) attention, little coverage has been afforded to the rest of French society. What happened beyond the Sorbonne and Boulogne-Billancourt is given scant coverage. However, here again, 2008 has witnessed moves that suggest an attempt to go beyond the conventional representation, of which several examples are indicative.

Groups that have not had their voice heard above the stereotypical clamour were given a prominent place in 2008. For example, the role of immigrants in the 1968 events is given attention.[67] Other areas brought into the narrative that demonstrates just how widespread the events were include the Church, the farming community, the ORTF and even footballers.[68] As indicated earlier, and mainly through local press and via the internet, there was a concerted effort to leave the usual suspects to one side and give a voice to the foot soldiers of 1968 in a bid to gather their personal accounts and experiences; Nicolas Daum's *Mai 68, raconté par des anonymes* is an excellent example of such a trend.[69] One could also highlight a number of chapters in more general 2008 texts that further exemplify this widening optic with the involvement of actors beyond the Latin Quarter given some attention.[70] However, perhaps most notable are two texts that manage to widen their analysis geographically as well as providing a much more thorough analysis of one of the most important groups whose role has so often been minimized – the working class. Xavier Vigna's *L'Insubordination ouvrière dans les années 68* tears up the stereotypical representation of working-class involvement in 1968. His study goes beyond the Parisian bastions and into the provinces, the roles of oft-forgotten elements such as women and immigrant workers are examined and the typically oversimplified relationship between workers and extreme left-wing militant students is problematized.[71] In a similar vein, Vincent Porhel's *Ouvriers Bretons. Conflits d'usine, conflit identitaire en Bretagne dans les années 68*, by focusing specifically on one region, demonstrates how complex, diverse and varied tensions were experienced and how revolts are remembered.[72] Drawing on five different industrial conflicts in the region at the time and with a particular focus on interviews with former prominent protagonists, Porhel's study drives home the inadequacy of the dominant discourse on how the working class experienced 1968.

Together with a much more fragmented picture from a national perspective, Vigna and Porhel's texts challenge the simplistic narrative that pitches the events as little more than a student revolt. Such a more holistic approach to examining the crisis has also been discernible in terms of the time period under examination. As discussed in chapter two, the very title *mai 68* highlights a major drawback in the period of time commonly taken to represent what happened in France. All too often, coverage begins with the police intervention in the Sorbonne on 3 May and ends with the pro-Gaullist demonstration in Paris on 31 May.[73] As discussed, the month of June is given little coverage with important events glossed over or ignored. Such minimization has been yet another feature adding to the narrow portrayal of the French 1968. Here again, 2008 has seen a marked increase in the number of studies affording more attention to a *mai–juin 68* analysis.[74] However, perhaps even more significant has been the trend – as demonstrated in both Porhel and Vigna's texts – that has attempted to place 'May–June 1968' in a much longer timeframe. This shift in focus emerged from a four-year project launched in 1994 by Geneviève Dreyfus-Armand, Robert Frank, Marie-Françoise Lévy and Michèle Zancarini-Fournel. Entitled *Les Années 68: événements, cultures politiques at modes de vie*, this Institut d'Histoire du Temps Présent venture culminated in the 2000 publication of *Les Années 68. Le temps de la contestation* which was subsequently republished for the fortieth anniversary. It is clear that this shift away from the simple 'May' and in particular the singular '1968' has been of significant importance in '1968 studies'. In so doing, the idea that what happened was some sort of unfathomable blip that came and went without any tangible short-to-medium-term consequences is challenged. Furthermore, such a perspective has very much been consolidated and confirmed as is evidenced by the number of important 2008 studies that employ this framework.[75]

Alongside the widening geographical lens and the wider view of those who participated in the events, the move to expand the time period helps under-score a much greater understanding of the 1968 events. For example, the debate surrounding the unpredictability of the crisis is illuminated by seeing what happened in 1968 as a result of building tensions across French society in the years preceding. Also, by continuing the analysis beyond 31 May, beyond June and into the mid-1970s enables a much greater appreciation of the direct influence of the events in the years that followed, subsequently bridging the gap in our understanding of how and why these events have been and continue to be influential in such a diverse variety of areas. Overall, the trends outlined above could be described as emerging from a generally more critical approach to ''68 studies'. Perhaps as a result of the time distance, the *recul* offered has allowed previous researchers and a new generation of younger academics to look at the events in a new light. Whatever the reason, and as has been demon-strated, 2008 certainly spawned a different approach that has led to the publication of a number of studies that provide a new angle on the 1968 events in France. Such a shift is important in terms of the conventional representa-tion. Whereas some of these explicitly question the dominant narrative, others do so implicitly. By going against the grain and presenting areas that challenge long held notions they step out of the narrow framework and force a reconsid-eration of how 1968 is presented and could ultimately force a change in perceptions.

Chapter one discussed the role of commemorations in shaping the collec-tive memory and the idea that one commemorative period cannot take place without continuing on with trends previously evident. Each commemoration that comes along therefore picks up the dominant threads of the preceding discourse and reshapes them according to any contextual changes. In this respect, 2008 has very much fitted the model. The thread running through 1978, 1988 and 1998 has continued on until 2008. This has been evident in the persistence of the dominant narrative presenting the narrow, Paris-focused, student-led perspective. However, as with each commemoration, new elements clearly impinged on the nature of the fortieth anniversary. In particular, Nicolas Sarkozy's attack is certainly a pertinent example of how a new factor can come along and inflect a commemorative period. The response to the future president's comments confirmed that *mai 68* holds a special place in the psyche of the French but also revealed the continuing tension surrounding just how 1968 and its legacy should be interpreted.

Sarkozy's speech, as evidenced by the reaction it provoked, is significant for a number of reasons. This was the most overt attempt by any French president to date at intervening in the debate over how the events of 1968 are remem-bered. It is worth pointing out that this intervention was just one of a series of clumsy attempts by Nicolas Sarkozy to shape the French collective memory of past events.[76] However, it does beg the question as to why he felt it necessary to do so and why at this point. In response, one cannot ignore his desire to capture the support of a certain section of the electorate for the 2007 presidential elections. Nevertheless, there was clearly something more fundamental underpinning his motivations. It is arguable that he felt that the convenient consensus – which thus far had managed to play down the true magnitude and reduce the potential influence of the events – was losing its grip on how the narrative was being transmitted or that it was time to reduce its scope even further. He perhaps feared the emergence of *mai 68* as an iconically important moment that could be held up as an example of how the French population is capable of potent, collective, mass mobilization. For someone aspiring to be elected on a *rupture* ticket, promising the strength and courage to make difficult choices and sacrifices, Sarkozy could ill afford the events of 1968 to be considered beyond the parameters set by the dominant narrative thus far and it was perhaps an opportune moment to reconsider the extent of such parameters.

One could argue that the content of Sarkozy's speech was in fact an acceptance of the importance and widespread impact of the events. However, in reality, the '1968' that he blames for almost every social ill facing contemporary French society is the '1968' as portrayed by the conventional representation. In other words his attempt to dismantle the legacy of *mai 68* drew exclusively on the stereotypical, narrow image and focused on the most utopian and irresponsible elements and ideas involved. In so doing, he may well have marked a shift in how the state approaches the convenient consensus. However, his objective was not to put an end to it but rather an attempt to head off any challenge it may face. Consciously or not, this speech fits the forty-year-old trend that has shaped the collective memory and permitted the dominance of the conventional representation. By airbrushing the strike and by focusing on the few to the detriment of the many, the magnitude of 1968 has been constantly and progressively reduced and Sarkozy's speech can be viewed as the continued participation of the necessary second half of an unlikely tango that has thus far facilitated the emergence of the convenient consensus. Where Sarkozy's intervention potentially marks a shift is in his attempt to further reduce the scope of the consensus. He unquestionably perpetuated the notion that *mai 68* was a largely utopian, libertarian movement punctuated by radical excesses. However, the underlying motivation of his speech was an attack on the French spirit of protest. The dominant narrative has thus far framed 1968 as belonging to a typically Gallic tradition whereby periodic jolts accompany and assist reform and modernization. By rejecting this notion, Sarkozy aimed to narrow the focus of the conventional representation and, in so doing, lay the grounds to facilitate pushing through a series of difficult measures without having to face the traditional backlash from *la rue*. Despite his success in implementing the highly contentious pension reforms in October 2010, the magnitude of revolt and protest in the weeks and months beforehand would suggest that his mission to liquidate the spirit of 1968 in a bid to delegitimize street protest was a failure.

The response to the speech is one thing and certainly suggests how the general view is reluctant to accept that 1968 should be held responsible for the social ills of twenty-first-century France. This need to rush to the defence of 1968 is certainly an example of how the context of a commemorative period is shaped by present-day concerns. Nevertheless, and as has been identified, perhaps the most significant difference with the fortieth anniversary has been the emergence of more rigorous, broader analyses that challenge the dominant narrative. Such approaches are perhaps indicative of what is to come. However, and in keeping with the Olick–Schwartz model on the persistence of a core discourse as discussed in chapter one, whilst 2008 may have seen an increase in studies that question the conventional representation, the dominant trend has continued. Numerous studies, TV programmes, press coverage, films and so on continue to focus on the narrow perspective. Certain areas remain devoid of sufficient coverage; for example, the role of university reformist elements continues to be largely absent. The convenient consensus remains in place and the plethora of material that consolidates its position is some indication of how this image is anchored within the collective memory of the French. There is no suggestion that there has been overt collusion between the state and the extreme left in bringing about the dominant narrative. Its prevalence is more the fortunate consequence of a convenient set of circumstances. The result of the authority bestowed on 1968's 'memory custodians'[77] has suited both sides. On the one hand *les soixantehuitards* par excellence have been able to shape how the events have been recounted so that whatever 'they become throughout their lives can be then projected retrospectively back on May'.[78] The fact that – in the main – their post-'68 trajectories have meant that the overriding impression is that *mai 68* was no more than a 'benign transformation of customs and lifestyles that necessarily accompanied France's modernization'[79] has understandably met little resistance from the state. However, such circumstances can only continue as long as the 'memory barons'[80] maintain their grasp on how the events are recounted. Their dominance, as discussed in chapter one, resides in a culmination of factors that affords them what Wertsch describes as a 'privileged position' in shaping our understanding of the past.[81] As the years go by this will become impossible and the void left as that generation passes on and the influence of their autobiographical memory dissipates will require filling. The shifts outlined above in the coverage around 2008 are perhaps an early indication of what differences we can expect. Nevertheless, given the depth of the imprint left by forty years of the dominant discourse, many more studies and anniversaries will be required before the balance can be redressed and the convenient consensus brought to an end. Regardless of whether this indeed could ever be possible, the fortieth anniversary nevertheless offers some degree of hope.

Appendix

LES EVENEMENTS DE MAI 1968: UN QUESTIONNAIRE

Q 1. Age: 15–18 ☐   19–25 ☐   26–35 ☐   36–50 ☐   51+ ☐

Q 2. Région

Nord Pas de Calais	☐	Haute Normandie	☐	Basse Normandie	☐
Picardie	☐	Champagne Ardenne	☐	Lorraine	☐
Alsace	☐	Bretagne	☐	Paris Ile-de-France	☐
Franche Comté	☐	Bourgogne	☐	Centre	☐
Pays de la Loire	☐	Poitou Charente	☐	Limousin	☐
Auvergne	☐	Rhône-Alpes	☐	Aquitaine	☐
Midi-Pyrénées	☐	Languedoc Roussillon	☐		
Provence-Alpes Côte d'Azur	☐	Corse	☐		

Q 3. Métier ou Profession

Etudiant ☐   Fonctionnaire ☐   Ouvrier ☐   Agriculteur ☐
Profession libérale ☐   Autre ☐

	Fortement en desaccord	En desaccord	Neutre	En accord	Fortement en accord
Q 4. Les événements de mai 1968 furent une expérience positive pour la France?	☐	☐	☐	☐	☐

	Fortement en desaccord	En desaccord	Neutre	En accord	Fortement en accord
Q 5. Les Francais devraient être fiers des événements de mai 1968 en tant qu'événement historique.	☐	☐	☐	☐	☐

Q 6. Les expressions suivantes décrivent bien les événements de mai 1968.	Fortement en desaccord	En desaccord	Neutre	En accord	Fortement en accord
Révolution	☐	☐	☐	☐	☐
Fête	☐	☐	☐	☐	☐
Manifestation politique	☐	☐	☐	☐	☐
Malaise étudiant	☐	☐	☐	☐	☐
Conflit des générations	☐	☐	☐	☐	☐
Assez de De Gaulle	☐	☐	☐	☐	☐
Opportunisme de la Gauche	☐	☐	☐	☐	☐
Montée de fièvre	☐	☐	☐	☐	☐

	Fortement en desaccord	En desaccord	Neutre	En accord	Fortement en accord
Q 7. Les événements de mai 1968 ont provoqué de réels changements dans la société française.	☐	☐	☐	☐	☐

Q 8. Les secteurs suivants ont été les plus touchés par les événements de mai 1968.	Fortement en desaccord	En desaccord	Neutre	En accord	Fortement en accord
L'Education	☐	☐	☐	☐	☐
Les Syndicats	☐	☐	☐	☐	☐
Les Conditions de travail	☐	☐	☐	☐	☐
La Vie politique	☐	☐	☐	☐	☐
Le Système judiciaire	☐	☐	☐	☐	☐
Les Mouvements régionaux	☐	☐	☐	☐	☐
Les Médias	☐	☐	☐	☐	☐
La Police	☐	☐	☐	☐	☐
Le Féminisme	☐	☐	☐	☐	☐
Les Moeurs	☐	☐	☐	☐	☐

	Fortement en desaccord	En desaccord	Neutre	En accord	Fortement en accord
Q 9. Les événements de mai 1968 ont eu une influence sur votre vie.	☐	☐	☐	☐	☐

Q 10. Si oui, dans quels domaines.	Fortement en desaccord	En desaccord	Neutre	En accord	Fortement en accord
L'Education	☐	☐	☐	☐	☐
La Politique	☐	☐	☐	☐	☐
Les Relations familiales	☐	☐	☐	☐	☐
Les Conditions de travail	☐	☐	☐	☐	☐
L'Identité régionale	☐	☐	☐	☐	☐
Les Moeurs	☐	☐	☐	☐	☐
Le Féminisme	☐	☐	☐	☐	☐

Q 11. Les phrases suivantes décrivent bien l'attitude de la police pendant les événements de mai 1968.	Fortement en desaccord	En desaccord	Neutre	En accord	Fortement en accord
Scandaleuse	☐	☐	☐	☐	☐
La Police a été provoquée	☐	☐	☐	☐	☐
Opportuniste	☐	☐	☐	☐	☐
Fasciste	☐	☐	☐	☐	☐
Pas assez dure	☐	☐	☐	☐	☐
La police faisait simplement son travail	☐	☐	☐	☐	☐

	Fortement en desaccord	En desaccord	Neutre	En accord	Fortement en accord
Q 12. L'attitude et la conduite de la police pendant les événements de mai 1968 ont changé la façon dont les Francais la perçoivent?	☐	☐	☐	☐	☐

	Fortement en desaccord	En desaccord	Neutre	En accord	Fortement en accord
Q 13. Les événements de mai 1968 étaient exclusivement une révolte parisienne.	☐	☐	☐	☐	☐

	Fortement en desaccord	En desaccord	Neutre	En accord	Fortement en accord
Q 14. Les événements de mai 1968 ont rendu la tâche plus facile pour les étudiants et les lycéens de se manifester dans les rues.	☐	☐	☐	☐	☐

	Fortement en desaccord	En desaccord	Neutre	En accord	Fortement en accord
Q 15. Les personnes/groupes suivants devraient être tenus responsables des événements de mai 1968.					
Les Etudiants	☐	☐	☐	☐	☐
Les Ouvriers	☐	☐	☐	☐	☐
Les Syndicats	☐	☐	☐	☐	☐
Le Gouvernement	☐	☐	☐	☐	☐
De Gaulle	☐	☐	☐	☐	☐
Les Communistes	☐	☐	☐	☐	☐
Les Socialistes	☐	☐	☐	☐	☐
Les Mouvements Etudiants Internationaux	☐	☐	☐	☐	☐

	Fortement en desaccord	En desaccord	Neutre	En accord	Fortement en accord
Q 16. Les personnes/groupes suivants en été les vraies victimes des événements de mai 1968.					
Les Etudiants	☐	☐	☐	☐	☐
Les Ouvriers	☐	☐	☐	☐	☐
Les Syndicats	☐	☐	☐	☐	☐
Le Gouvernement	☐	☐	☐	☐	☐
De Gaulle	☐	☐	☐	☐	☐
Les Communistes	☐	☐	☐	☐	☐
Les Socialistes	☐	☐	☐	☐	☐
La Bourgeoisie	☐	☐	☐	☐	☐

	Fortement en desaccord	En desaccord	Neutre	En accord	Fortement en accord
Q 17. Une situation similaire à celle des événements. de mai 1968 pourrait se produire en France.	☐	☐	☐	☐	☐

Q 18. Les personnes/groupes suivants ont fait le plus pour résoudre la crise de mai 1968.	Fortement en desaccord	En desaccord	Neutre	En accord	Fortement en accord
Les Etudiants	☐	☐	☐	☐	☐
Les Ouvriers	☐	☐	☐	☐	☐
Les Syndicats	☐	☐	☐	☐	☐
Le Gouvernement	☐	☐	☐	☐	☐
De Gaulle	☐	☐	☐	☐	☐
Les Communistes	☐	☐	☐	☐	☐
Les Socialistes	☐	☐	☐	☐	☐
La Bourgeoisie	☐	☐	☐	☐	☐

	Fortement en desaccord	En desaccord	Neutre	En accord	Fortement en accord
Q 19. La crise de mai 1968 a été l'événement le plus important dans l'histoire de France depuis la Deuxième Guerre Mondiale.	☐	☐	☐	☐	☐

Autre commentaires:

Notes

Introduction

1 Jan Assman, 'Collective memory and cultural identity', *New German Critique*, 65 (1995), 125–33.
2 For further discussion on the impact of 1968 in this area see Chris Reynolds, 'May–June 1968: reflector and vector of a nation's diversity – the case of Strasbourg, Alsace', in Murray Pratt, Alistair Rolls and Jo McCormack, *Hexagonal Variations* (Amsterdam/New York: Rodopi, 2011); 'May '68 and the one-dimensional state', *PhaenEx*, 4 (2) (2009), 60–77.

1 The emergence of a convenient consensus

1 Kerwin Lee Klein, 'On the emergence of memory in historical discourse', *Representations*, 69 (2000), 127.
2 Geoffrey Cubitt, *History and Memory* (Manchester: Manchester University Press, 2007), pp. 1–2.
3 Kendall R. Phillips, *Framing Public Memory* (Alabama: University of Alabama Press, 2004), p. 2.
4 James V. Wertsch, *Voices of Collective Remembering* (New York: Cambridge University Press, 2002), p. 30.
5 For example Noa Gedi and Yigal Elam, 'Collective memory – what is it?', *History and Memory*, 8 (1996), 30–50.
6 Much emphasis is placed on Pierre Nora's *Lieux de Mémoire* volumes in sparking the great debate on the relationship between history and memory. Pierre Nora, *Les Lieux de Mémoire*. 1, *La République* (Paris: Gallimard, 1984); 2, *La Nation* (Paris: Gallimard, 1986); 3, *Les France* (Paris: Gallimard, 1992).
7 For example, François Bédarida, 'Le Temps présent et l'historiographie contemporaine', *Vingtième Siècle*, 69 (2001), 153–60.
8 Marie-Claire Lavabre, 'Usages du passé, usages de la mémoire', *Revue Française de science politique*, 3 (1994), 480–93.
9 Gedi and Elam, 'Collective memory – what is it?', 41–2 for a discussion on the circularity of the relationship between history and memory.
10 Klein, 'On the emergence of memory in historical discourse', 127.
11 For example, Yosef Yerushalmi, *Zakhor: Jewish History and Jewish Memory* (London: University of Washington Press, 1982); Pierre Nora, 'Between memory and history: les lieux de mémoire', *Representations*, 26 (1989), 7–24.
12 Michel de Certeau, *La Prise de parole et autres écrits politiques* (Paris: Seuil, 1994), pp. 29–129.
13 '[F]ièvre de témoigner, de raconter, de prophétiser', author's translation from Gilles Bousquet, 'Où en est-on de mai 68?', *Contemporary French Civilisation*, 1 (1992), 70.
14 Keith Reader, 'Joyeux anniversaire! The May 68 industry', *Modern and Contemporary France*, 8(2) (2000), 249–52.
15 Term used by de Gaulle to describe the 1968 events during a televised interview with Michel Droit (7 July 1968).

16 '[L]'un des événements les plus fluctuants [. . .] peut-être l'un des moments les plus mal connus', author's translation from Bousquet, 'Où en est de mai 68?', 69.

17 Jean-Franklin Narot, 'Mai 68 raconté aux enfants. Contribution à la critique de l'inintelligence organisée', *Le Débat*, 51 (1988), 180.

18 Isabelle Sommier, 'Mai 68: sous les pavés d'une page officielle', *Sociétés Contemporaines*, 20 (1994), 63.

19 Bousquet, 'Où en est de mai 68?', 71.

20 Term used to describe the dominant portrayal of the events and their consequences in Sommier, 'Mai 68: sous les pavés d'une page officielle', 74.

21 Jean-Pierre Rioux, 'A propos des célébrations décennales du mai français', *Vingtième Siècle*, 23 (1991), 49; Narot, 'Mai 68 raconté aux enfants', 183.

22 Kristin Ross, *May '68 and its Afterlives* (Chicago: University of Chicago Press, 2002), p. 21.

23 ''68 finit par se décliner en trois mots: mai, Paris, étudiant', author's translation from Sommier, 'Mai 68: Sous les pavés d'une page officielle', 65.

24 Ibid., 67.

25 Patrick Démerin, 'Mai 68 – Mai 88. Choses tues', *Le Débat,* 51 (1988), 174.

26 'Mai 68 [. . .] appauvri, mutilé, biaisé, reconstruit et mythifié avec obstination sans qu'aucune vision historique d'ensemble puisse à temps rectifier ou détourner le cours de ce travail de la mémoire', author's translation from Rioux, 'A propos des célébrations décennales du mai français', 57.

27 Daniel Cohn-Bendit, *Le Gauchisme, remède à la maladie sénile du communisme* (Paris: Seuil, 1968); Philippe Labro, *Les Barricades de mai* (Paris: Seuil, 1968); UNEF/ SNESup, *Le Livre noir des journées de mai* (Paris: Seuil, 1968); J. Sauvageot, A. Geismar. D. Cohn-Bendit and J.-P. Duteuil, *La Révolte étudiante* (Paris: Seuil, 1968).

28 Other notable texts during this period include: André Barjonet, *La CGT, Histoire, Structure, Doctrine* (Paris: Seuil, 1968); André Barjonet, *La révolution trahie de 1968* (Paris: John Didier, 1968); Daniel Bensaid and Henri Weber, *Mai 1968: Une répétition générale* (Paris: Maspéro, 1968); Jean Bertolino, *Les Trublions* (Paris: Stock, 1969); Michel de Certeau, *La prise de parole* (Paris: Desclée de Brouwer, 1968); *Club Jean Moulin, Que faire de la révolution de mai?* (Paris: Seuil, 1968); Adrien Dansette, *Mai 1968* (Paris: Plon, 1971); Alain Geismar, Serge July and Erlyn Moran, *Vers la guerre civile* (Paris: Editions et Publications Premières, 1969); Raymond Marcellin, *L'ordre public et les groupes révolutionnaires* (Paris: Plon, 1969); Edgar Morin, Claude Lefort, Jean-Marc Coudray, *Mai 1968: La Brèche, Premières réflexions sur les événements* (Paris: Fayard, 1968); Mouvement du 22 mars, *Ce n'est qu'un début; continuons le combat* (Paris: Maspéro, 1968); Alain Schnapp and Pierre Vidal-Naquet, *Journal de la commune étudiante – textes et documents: novembre 1967–juin 1968* (Paris: Seuil, 1969).

29 Raymond Aron, *La Révolution introuvable* (Paris: Fayard, 1968); Alain Touraine, *Le Mouvement de mai ou le communisme utopique* (Paris: Seuil, 1968).

30 Jean-Pierre Mocky, *Solo*, 1969.

31 Music by Georges Moustaki.

32 Jacques Doillon, Gébé, Alain Resnais and Jean Rouch, *L'An 01*, 1973.

33 Anonymous, *France mai–juin 1968 pour l'UDR*, 1968.

34 Other significant texts from this period include: Robert Linhart, *L'Etabli* (Paris: Minuit, 1978); Edouard Balladur, *L'Arbre de mai* (Paris: Atelier Marcel Jullian, 1979); Jean-Marc Salmon, *Hôtel de l'avenir* (Paris: Presses d'aujourd'hui, 1978); Maurice Grimaud, *En Mai fais ce qu'il te plait* (Paris: Stock, 1977); André Astoux, *1978. Ondes de choc. Mai 68 à l'ORTF* (Paris: Plon, 1978); Jacques Baynac, *Mai retrouvé. Contribution à l'histoire du mouvement révolutionnaire du 3 mai au 16 juin 1968* (Paris: Seuil, 1978); Jean-Pierre le Dantec, *Les Dangers du soleil* (Paris: Les Presses d'aujourd'hui, 1978); Raymond Marcellin, *L'importune vérité. Dix ans après Mai 68, un ministre de l'intérieur parle* (Paris: Plon, 1978); André Caveau, *De l'autre coté de la barricade* (Paris: Simoen, 1968).

35   Jean-Claude Guillebaud, *Les Années orphelines 1968–1978* (Paris: Seuil, 1978).
36   Ibid., p. 109.
37   Régis Debray, *Modeste contribution aux discours et cérémonies officielles du dixième anniversaire* (Paris: Maspero, 1978), p. 49.
38   Ibid., pp. 26, 45, 87.
39   Gérard Oury, *La Carapate*, 1978.
40   '[C]es petits cons sur leurs barricades', author's translation.
41   '[G]rève de cons', author's translation.
42   Interview accompanying film.
43   Romain Goupil, *Mourir à trente ans*, 1982.
44   *Histoire de mai*, André Frossard, Gérard Guégan and Raphael Boutang, France 3, 7,14, 21 and 28 May 1978.
45   'Ils n'ont pas réclamé l'impossible mais espéré l'improbable', author's translation.
46   William Klein, *Grands soirs et petits matins*, 1978.
47   Cf. for example *Les Dossiers de l'écran, 68 dans le monde*, Antenne 2, 2 May 1968; *Apostrophes*, 24 April 1977.
48   Cf. Rioux, 'A propos des célébrations décennales du mai français', 52.
49   Jo McCormack, *Collective Memory. France and the Algerian War (1954–1962)* (Maryland: Lexington, 2007), p. 57.
50   For example, J. Bouillon, *Le Monde Contemporain. Histoire – Civilisation* (Paris: Bordas, 1979); V. Prévot, *Le Monde depuis 1939. Classes terminales* (Paris: Belin, 1979).
51   For example, Robert Frank, *Le Monde Contemporain. Histoire Terminale G* (Paris: Beline, 1983); Collection GREHG, *Histoire: le Monde de 1939 à nos jours. Terminales ABCD* (Paris: Hachette, 1983), pp. 284–5.
52   Collection Berstein-Milza, *Histoire, Terminale. De 1939 à nos Jours* (Paris: Hatier, 1983), pp. 264–8.
53   J. Bouillon, *Le Temps Présent – Histoire Terminale. Le XXe Siècle depuis 1939* (Paris: Bordas, 1983), pp. 320–4.
54   Denis François, *Histoire de 1939 à nos jours. Classes Terminales* (Paris: Nathan, 1983), pp. 292–4.
55   Philippe Bénéton and Jean Touchard, 'Les interprétations de la crise de mai–juin 1968', *Revue française de science politique*, 10(3) (1970), 503–43.
56   J. Aledebert, *Histoire, Terminales. Aujourd'hui le Monde* (Paris: Delagrave, 1983), pp. 290–3.
57   Collection Berstein-Milza, *Histoire, Terminale*; François, *Histoire de 1939 à nos jours.*
58   Collection Berstein-Milza, *Histoire, Terminale*; François, *Histoire de 1939 à nos jours*; Collection GREHG, *Histoire: le Monde de 1939 à nos jours.*
59   Bouillon, *Le Temps Présent*; Aledebert, *Histoire, Terminales.*
60   Collection Berstein-Milza, *Histoire, Termin*ale; François, *Histoire de 1939 à nos jours*; Collection GREHG, *Histoire: le Monde de 1939 à nos jours*; Aledebert, *Histoire, Terminales.*
61   '[P]eu de traces', author's translation from François, *Histoire de 1939 à nos jours*, p. 294.
62   Rioux, 'A propos des célébrations décennales du mai français', 53.
63   Roger Martelli, *Mai 68* (Paris: Messidor, 1988).
64   Henri Weber, *Que reste-t-il de mai 68? Essai sur les interprétations des «événements»* (Paris: Seuil, 1988); Luc Ferry, Alain Renaut, *La Pensée 68. Essai sur l'anti-humanisme contemporain* (Paris: Gallimard, 1988).
65   Other noteworthy texts from this period include: Nicolas Daum, *Des révolutionnaires dans un village parisien. Mai 68 vingt ans après* (Paris: Londreys, 1988); Jean-Pierre Duteuil, *Nanterre. 1965–66–67–68. Vers le mouvement du 22 mars* (Mauléon: Acratie, 1988); Mavis Gallant, *Chroniques de Mai 68* (Paris: Editions Tièrce, 1988); Pierre Grappin, *L'Ile aux peupliers. De la Résistance à Mai 68. Souvenirs du doyen de Nanterre* (Nancy: PUN, 1988); Daniel Cohn-Bendit, *Nous l'avons tant*

aimé la révolution (Paris: Bernard Barrault, 1988); Alain Krivine and Daniel Bensaid, *Mai si ! 1968–1988, rebelles et repentis* (Paris: La Brèche, 1988).

66 Hervé Hamon and Patrick Rotman, *Génération. 1. Les Années de rêve* (Paris: Seuil, 1987); Hervé Hamon and Patrick Rotman, *Génération. 2. Les Années de poudre* (Paris: Seuil, 1988).

67 Antoine Prost, 'Quoi de neuf sur le Mai français?', *Le Mouvement social*, 143 (1988), 97.

68 Hamon and Rotman, *Génération. 2*, p. 10.

69 Jacques Capdevielle and René Mouriaux, *Mai 68 – L'Entre-deux de la modernité. Histoire de trente ans* (Paris: Presses de la Fondation Nationale des Sciences Politiques, 1988).

70 Ibid., pp. 12, 21.

71 *Génération*, Hervé Hamon, Patrick Rotman and Daniel Edinger, a series of fifteen 30-minute documentaries that went out on TF1 over the period May–July 1988.

72 Louis Malle, *Milou en mai*, 1990.

73 *Le Procès de mai*, Roland Portiche and Henri Weber, TF1, 22 May 1988.

74 *Que sont nos vingt and devenus?: 1968–1988*, France 3, 22 July 1988.

75 *L'Héritage de 68*, Alain Weider, Antenne 2, 19 May 1988.

76 Collection C. Quetel, *Histoire Terminales* (Paris: Bordas, 1989), pp. 400–1.

77 Jean-Louis Humbert, *Histoire, Terminales. ABCD, Analyse de documents* (Paris: Bordas, 1989), pp. 166–70.

78 Collection GREHG, *Histoire de 1945 à nos jours. Classes de Terminales* (Paris: Hachette, 1989), pp. 345–9.

79 '[S]emblent l'avoir [le débat] obscurci advantage', author's translation from ibid., p. 348.

80 M. Humbert-Jean, 'Ce qu'il reste de mai 68', *Le Monde des dossiers et documents*, 155, May 1988.

81 Georges Marchais, 'De faux révolutionnaires à démasquer', *L'Humanité*, 3 May 1968.

82 Georges Pompidou, *Pour rétablir une vérité* (Paris: Flammarion, 1982).

83 Collection P. Wagnet, *Histoire Terminales* (Paris: Istra, 1989), pp. 306–7; Formulo-Bac, *Histoire, Terminales ABCD* (Paris: Gammaprim, 1990).

84 See, in particular, Mavis Gallant, *Chroniques de Mai 68* (Paris: Rivages, 1998); Michel Gomez, *Mai 68 au jour le jour* (Paris: L'Esprit frappeur, 1998).

85 For example, Luc Ferry and Alain Renaut, *La Pensée 68* (Paris: Gallimard, 1998); Weber, *Que reste-t-il de mai 68?*.

86 Christine Fauré, *Mai 68 jour et nuit* (Paris: Gallimard, 1998); M.-C Lavabre and H. Rey, *Les Mouvements de 1968* (Firenze: Casterman, 1998).

87 Other notable texts from this period include: Yair Auron, *Les Juifs d'extrême gauche en mai 68* (Paris: Albin Michel, 1998); Grégory Barrau, *Le Mai 68 des Catholiques* (Paris: Editions de l'Atelier/Editions Ouvrières, 1998); Gérard Filoche, *68–98: histoire sans fin* (Paris: Flammarion, 1998); Danielle Tartakowsky, *Le Pouvoir est dans la rue* (Paris: Aubier, 1998); Jean Sur, *68 Forever* (Paris: Arléa, 1998); Maurice Rajfus, *Mai 1968. Sous les pavés la répression* (Paris: Le cherche midi éditeur, 1998); Alain Corbin and Jean-Marie Mayeur, *La Barricade* (Paris: Publications de la Sorbonne, 1998).

88 Jacques Tarnero, *Mai 68, la Révolution fiction* (Toulouse: Milano, 1998), p. 5.

89 Ibid., pp. 20, 16, 34–5, 55.

90 Jean-Pierre le Goff, *Mai 68, l'héritage impossible* (Paris: La Découverte, 1998), pp. 317–77.

91 Ibid., p. 460.

92 Romain Goupil, *A Mort la Mort*, 1998.

93 Philippe Garrel, *Le Vent de la nuit*, 1999.

94 *Débat Mai 1968. D'Une Génération à l'autre*, France 2, 26 April 1998.

95 *La Preuve par trois. Mai 68 a 30 ans, et alors?* France 3, 7 April 1998.

96 *Dany dans tous ses états*, France 2, 23 April 1998.
97 *10 semaines qui ébranlèrent la France*, Patrick Rotman and Virginie Linhart, France 3, 24 April 1998.
98 Hervé le Roux, *Reprise*, 1997. For a detailed analysis of this film and the broader context for French film of the time, see Martin O'Shaughnessy, 'Post 1995 French cinema: return of the social, return of the political', *Modern and Contemporary France*, 11 (2) (2003), 189–203.
99 'Mai 68 et les archives secrètes de la police', *L'Express*, 19–25 March 1998; *Le Nouvel Observateur*, 23–9 April 1998.
100 J. Le Pellec, *Histoire Terminale* (Paris: Bertrand Lacoste, 1998), pp. 268–9; Collection J. Marseille, *Histoire Terminales – Le Monde de 1939 à nos jours* (Paris: Nathan, 1998), p. 272; pp. 330–1.
101 Jean-Michel Lambin, *Histoire Terminales* (Paris: Hachette, 1998), pp. 312–17; H. Baylac, *Histoire Terminale: Le Monde de 1939 à nos jours* (Paris: Bordas, 1998), pp. 282–3, 300.
102 Serge Berstein and Pierre Milza, *Histoire Terminale (Nouveau Programme)* (Paris: Hatier, 1998), pp. 256–7.
103 Collection G. Donel Ferré, *Histoire, Classes de Terminales, L/S/ES – Le Monde de 1939 à nos jours* (Paris: Bréal, 1998), pp. 274–5, 284–5; Robert Frank, *Histoire Terminale STT* (Paris: Belin, 1998), pp. 19, 24–5.
104 '[A]spirations sont toujours d'actualité', author's translation.
105 '[L]a jeunesse d'aujourd'hui jette un regard étonné', author's translation.
106 Pierre Nora, *Realms of Memory: The Construction of the French Past* (New York: Columbia University Press, 1998), p. 611.
107 John Bodnar, *Remaking America: Public Memory, Commemoration and Patriotism in the Twentieth Century* (Princeton NJ: Princeton University Press, 1992); Robert Gildea, *The Past in French History* (London, New Haven: Yale University Press, 1994), p. 10.
108 Bédarida, 'Le Temps Présent et l'Historiographie Contemporaine', 155–6.
109 Maurice Halbwachs, *Les Cadres Sociaux de la Mémoire* (Paris: Alcan, 1925); Maurice Halbwachs, *La Mémoire Collective* (Paris: Presses universitaire de France, 1950).
110 Maurice Halbwachs and Lewis A. Coser, *On Collective Memory* (Chicago: University of Chicago Press, 1992), p. 25
111 Ibid., p. 40.
112 James E. Young, *Holocaust, Memorials and Meaning* (Yale: Yale University Press, 1994), p. 2.
113 Gildea, *The Past in French History*, p. 10.
114 Barry Schwartz, 'The social context of commemoration: a study in collective memory', *Social Forces*, 61 (2) (1982), 374–402; Jeffrey K. Olick, 'Genre memories and memory genres: a dialogical analysis of May 8, 1945 commemorations in the Federal Republic of Germany', *American Sociological Review*, 64 (3) (1999), 381–402.
115 Olick, 'Genre memories and memory genres', 382.
116 Jan Assman, 'Collective memory and cultural identity', 125–33; Schwartz, 'The social context of commemoration', 374–5; Gildea, *The Past in French History*, p. 342.
117 Robert Gildea, 'Myth, memory and policy in France since 1945', in Jan-Werner Muller, *Memory and Power in Post-War Europe: Studies in the Presence of the Past* (Cambridge: Cambridge University Press, 2002), p. 59.
118 'Autoproclamés et élus par les médias, ils sont désignés comme porte-paroles de la génération', author's translation from Pascale Blanchard and Isabelle Veyrat-Masson, *Les Guerres de Mémoires. La France et son Histoire* (Paris: La Découverte, 2008), p. 131.
119 Wertsch, *Voices of Collective Remembering*, pp. 39–40.
120 Ibid., p. 40.
121 Term used to describe the masses that made up the numbers in 1968 without whom the events would not have taken on the same significance.

122 Cubitt, *History and Memory*, p. 224.
123 Ibid., p. 176.
124 Gedi and Elam, 'Collective memory – what is it?', p. 40.
125 '[L]a quete de recettes publicitaires incite les producteurs à contacter des «stars» plutôt que des anonymes. N'empêche que ces choix traduisaient aussi des conceptions politiques et sociales précises, auxquelles les «commémorés», pour les servir ainsi, paraissent adhérer', author's translation from Patrick Démerin, 'Choses tues', 175.
126 Claude Journès, 'Les interprétations communistes de Mai 68', *Pouvoirs*, 39 (1986), 25–35.
127 Keith A. Reader, *The May 1968 Events in France: Reproductions and Interpretations* (London: Macmillan Press, 1993), pp. 65–70.
128 Schwartz, 'The social context of commemoration', 396.
129 Henry Rousso, *Le Syndrome de Vichy* (Paris: Seuil, 1987), p. 253.
130 'Le mystère 68', *Le Débat*, no. 50/51, May–August 1988/September–October 1988, 153–92.
131 Eric Vigne, 'Des générations 68?', *Le Débat,*' 51 (1988), 157.
132 Prost, 'Quoi de neuf sur le Mai français?', 91–7.
133 Luisa Passerini, 'Peut-on donner de 1968 une histoire à la première personne?', *Le Mouvement social*, 143 (1988), 3–10.
134 Narot, 'Mai 68 raconté aux enfants', 179–92.
135 Daniel Lindenberg, 'Un anniversaire interminable: 1968–1988', *L'Esprit*, 136–137 (1988), 189–97.
136 Demerin, 'Choses tues', 173–8.
137 Rioux, 'A propos des célébrations décennales du mai français', 95–100.
138 Bousquet, 'Où en est-on de mai 68?', 68–89.
139 Sommier, 'Mai 68 : Sous les pavés d'une page officielle', 63–82.
140 This issue sparked a highly mediatized debate concerning the attitude of 'Nouveaux réactionnaires' at the end of 2002 and the beginning of 2003. See Daniel Lindenberg, *Le rappel à l'ordre. Enquête sur les nouveaux réactionnaires* (Paris: Seuil, 2002), and Laurent Joffrin, 'Sommes-nous tous devenus réacs?', *Le Nouvel Observateur*, 21–7 November 2002, 12–36.
141 See Daniel A. Gordon, 'From May to October: reassessing the 1968 generation', *Modern and Contemporary France*, 13 (2) (2005), 229–33.
142 Reader, 'Joyeux anniversaire!', 252.

2 1968: consensus and disagreement

1 Joan Brandt, 'The legacy of May '68 in the era of consensus', *L'Esprit créateur*, 41 (1) (2001), 3.
2 '[L]e débat demeure alors que l'Histoire s'écrit', author's translation from Olivier Lalieu, 'L'Invention du «Devoir de Mémoire»', *Vingtième Siècle*, 69 (2001), 83–94.
3 Ross, *May '68 and its Afterlives*, p. 9.
4 Ibid., p. 9.
5 Such texts include Tarnero, *La Révolution fiction*; Martelli, *Mai 68*; Weber, *Que reste-t-il*; Bernard E. Brown, *Protest in Paris: Anatomy of a Revolt* (Morristown, NJ: General Learning Press, 1974); Daniel Singer, *Prelude to a Revolution* (London: Jonathan Cape, 1970).
6 Maurice Agulhon, André Nouschi and Ralph Schor, *La France de 1940 à nos jours* (Paris: Nathan/HER, 2001), p. 233.
7 Capdevielle and Mouriaux, *L'Entre-deux*, p. 97.
8 Michel Winock, *La Fièvre hexagonale: les grandes crises politiques 1871–1968* (Paris: Seuil, 1995), p. 345.
9 Le Goff, *L'héritage impossible*, p. 33.
10 Henri Lefebvre, *Mai 68 – L'Irruption. . .* (Paris: Syllepse, 1998), p. 91.

11   G. Dreyfus-Armand, R. Frank, M.-F. Lévy and M. Zancarini-Fournel, *Les Années 68: Le temps de la Contestation* (Paris: Complexe, 2000), p. 27.
12   Habia S. Cohen, *Elusive Reform: The French Universities, 1968–1978* (Boulder, CO: Westview Press, 1978), p. 4.
13   A detailed analysis of the plight of the university system in the prelude to the events is provided in chapter four.
14   Touraine, *Le Mouvement de mai*, p. 84.
15   John Gretton, *Students and Workers: An Analytical Account of Dissent in France May–June 1968* (London: Macdonald, 1969), p. 74.
16   François Cusset, *Contre-discours de mai. Ce qu'embaumeurs et fossoyeurs de 68 ne disent pas à ses héritiers* (Paris: Actes Sud, 2008), pp. 115–17.
17   '[L]a version française – hexagonale et pour tout dire «parisienne» – d'un frémissement bizarre qui courait la planète', author's translation from Jean-Claude Guillebaud, *Les Années orphelines*, p. 17.
18   Danielle Tartakowsky, *Le Pouvoir est dans la rue*, p. 166.
19   See Aron, *La Révolution introuvable*; Balladur, *L'Arbre de mai*; Le Goff, *L'héritage impossible*; Epistémon (Didier Anzieu), *Ces idées qui ont ébranlé la France. Nanterre, novembre 1967–juin 1968* (Paris: Fayard, 1969); Hamon and Rotman, *Génération. 1.*; Guillebaud, *Les Années orphelines*; Weber, *Que reste-t-il.*
20   This issue is dealt with in more detail in chapter five.
21   See Capdevielle and Mouriaux, *Mai 68 – L'Entre-deux de la modernité*; Laurent Joffrin, *Mai 68: Histoire des événements* (Paris: Seuil, 1988); Labro, *Les Barricades de mai* and Martelli, *Mai 68.*
22   Martelli, *Mai 68*, pp. 62–5.
23   The majority of texts produced on the events split them into the three phases mentioned. Such texts include: Brown, *Protest in Paris*; Singer, *Prelude to a Revolution*; Alain Griotteray, *Des Barricades ou des réformes* (Paris: Fayard, 1968), Joffrin, *Histoire des événements*, Pierre Sorbon Lepavé, *Le Journal insolite de Mai 68* (Paris: Raymond Castells, 1998); Winock, *La Fièvre hexagonale.*
24   Joffrin, *Histoire des événements*, p. 131.
25   Claude Fohlen, *Mai 1968: Révolution ou psychodrame?* (Paris: Presses Universitaires de France, 1973), p. 12.
26   The Odéon was evacuated on 14 June and the Sorbonne on 16 June.
27   See Rajfus, *Sous les pavés, la répression.*
28   On 12 June the newly appointed Minister of the Interior, Raymond Marcellin, outlawed eleven extreme left-wing organizations, including the JCR, the *Mouvement du 22 mars* and the FER.
29   Fohlen, *Mai 1968: Révolution ou psychodrame?*, p. 46.
30   'Rares sont ceux qui parlent des événements de mai–juin 1968', author's translation from Capdevielle and Mouriaux, *Mai 68 – L'Entre-deux de la modernité*, p 131.
31   'De faux révolutionnaires à démasquer', author's translation.
32   Balladur, *L'Arbre de mai*, p. 135.
33   Sorbon-Lepavé, *Journal insolite*, p. 117.
34   Le Goff, *L'héritage impossible*, p. 47.
35   Ibid., p. 150.
36   Richard Johnson, *The French Communist Party Versus the Students: Revolutionary Politics in May–June 1968* (Yale: Yale University Press, 1972), p. 160.
37   The latest text to deal with this issue is Henri-Christain Giraud, *L'Accord secret de Baden-Baden. Comment de Gaulle et les soviétiques on mis fin à mai 68* (Paris: Rocher, 2008).
38   Epistémon, *Ces idées qui ont ébranlé la France*, p. 37.
39   Brown, *Protest in Paris*, p. 48.
40   Didier Fischer, *L'Histoire des étudiants de 1945 à nos jours* (Saint-Amand-Montrond: Flammarion, 2000), p. 396.
41   Brown, *Protest in Paris*, p. 161.
42   Cohn-Bendit, *Le Gauchisme*, p. 268.

43 Le Goff, *L'héritage impossible,* p. 129.
44 This refusal to get involved in the first week of the events is summed up by the famous anecdote in which, during the extremely violent 'Night of the Barricades', the general was sleeping and, even in the absence of Georges Pompidou, no one felt it necessary to disturb him.
45 Agulhon, Nouschi and Schor, *La France de 1940 à nos jours,* p. 233; Debray, *Modeste contribution,* p. 41.
46 Pompidou was not happy with de Gaulle's disappearance to Baden-Baden and was obviously in disagreement over the need of a referendum: 'My General, the referendum took place yesterday and you were successful. It is now best that I resign to leave your hands free.' Author's translation from 'Mon Général, le référendum a eu lieu hier. Vous l'avez emporté, il faut que je parte pour vous laisser les mains libres' (quoted in Balladur, *L'Arbre,* p. 336).
47 For a detailed analysis of the process leading Pompidou's replacement with Couve de Murville see Jacques Foccart, *Le Général en Mai: Journal de l'Elysée – II. 1968–1969* (Paris: Fayard/Jeune Afrique, 1998), pp. 245–85.
48 D. L. Hanley and A. P. Kerr, *May '68: Coming of Age* (London: Macmillan, 1989), p. 70.
49 Bensaïd and Weber, *Mai 68: une répétition générale.*
50 Aron, *La Révolution introuvable.*
51 Touraine, *Le Communisme utopique;* Morin, Coudray and Lefort, *La Brèche.*
52 Debray, *Modeste contribution.*
53 Ferry and Renaut, *La Pensée 68.*
54 Gilles Lipovetsky, *L'Ere du vide. Essais sur l'individualisme contemporain* (Paris: Gallimard, 1983).
55 Weber, *Que reste-t-il.*
56 François Goetz, *Mai 68, une imposture qui nous a coûté cher* (Paris: Editic, 1993).
57 Bénéton and Touchard, 'Les Interprétations de la crise de mai/juin 1968', 503–44.
58 Fohlen, *Révolution ou psychodrame.* p. 5.
59 The suggestion that the crisis was the result of some sort of premeditated plot against the Gaullist regime orchestrated from abroad.
60 Philippe Ardent and Olivier Duhamel, 'Mai 68', *Pouvoirs,* 39 (1986).
61 'Si ces mois de travail pour le réaliser [the special edition of *Pouvoirs* dedicated to the conference] ont confirmé une chose, c'est l'urgence d'un autre colloque, d'une autre publication sur «les événements des mai 68»', author's translation from ibid., p. 3.
62 Weber, *Que reste-t-il,* p. 27.
63 Ferry and Renaut, *La Pensée 68,* p. 115.
64 'A ma connaissance, aucune nouvelle théorie de la révolution de Mai n'est venue enrichir le corps des interprétations disponibles. C'est pourquoi cet essai n'a, à mon sens, rien perdu de son actualité,' author's translation from Weber, *Que reste-t-il,* p. 9.
65 Ross, *May '68 and its Afterlives,* p. 3.
66 Le Goff, *L'héritage impossible,* p. 59; Capdevielle and Mouriaux, *L'Entre-deux,* p. 10.
67 Grappin, *L'Ile aux peupliers.*
68 '[L]es pires ennuis', author's translation from ibid., p. 245.
69 '[V]a-t-en d'ici en vitesse!', author's translation from ibid., p. 250.
70 Pierre Viansson-Ponté, *Le Monde,* 15 March 1968.
71 Ross, *May '68 and its Afterlives,* p. 26.
72 'tous les mouvements sectoriels et locaux, sparodiques, violents, déclenchés un peu partout' Jacques Kergoat, 'Sous la plage, la grève', author's translation from Antoine Artous (ed.), *Retours sur Mai* (Montreuil: La Brèche-PEC, 1988), p. 53.
73 'On comprend mieux que lorsque l'occasion de frapper arrive, ces hommes pénètrent dans l'univers mystérieux de la violence. Les coups qu'ils vont porter seront le substitut de la mort qu'ils n'ont pas le droit de donner', author's translation from Grimaud, *En Mai fais ce qu'il te plaît,* p. 169.

74 '[S]ang-froid', author's translation from Foccart, *Le Général en mai*, p. 137.
75 For examples of this footage see documentaries such as Claude le Brun, *Mai 68 – 5 Ans après* (1973), Lawaetz Guide, *Mai 68: Il y a 25 ans* (Gaillon, 1993), Pierre-André Boutang, *Histoire de Mai*, France 3, 1978.
76 UNEF/SNESup, *Le Livre noir*, p. 14. This text was produced during the events themselves and is full of first-hand accounts of severe police brutality. It could be claimed that some of the accounts were exaggerated; however, there is a real connection between such accounts and the images filmed during some of the heated battles.
77 David Caute, *Sixty-Eight: The Year of the Barricades* (London: Hamish Hamilton, 1988), p.190; Hamon and Rotman, *Génération 1*, p. 490.
78 A student, Gilles Tautin, drowned trying to escape from the CRS on 10 June. Two workers died in confrontations with the police at the Peugeot factory in Sochaux; Pierre Beylot was gunned down by the CRS and Henri Blanchet died as a result of a CRS grenade bringing down a wall in the factory.
79 Debré was extremely annoyed at not being invited to participate in the Grenelle negotiations; however, Pompidou was quite clear that he did not want the Minister for the Economy to be present as he would only be another obstacle to reaching an agreement with the trade unions.
80 'C'est un accord fécond [. . .] Nous pensons que sur la base des appréciations et des renseignements que nous leur donnerons, les travailleurs pourront prendre leur décision, dans les meilleurs délais', author's translation from Gomez, *Mai 68 au jour le jour*, p. 76.
81 The principal concessions gained included a 35 per cent increase in the SMIG (minimum wage), a 10 per cent rise in salaries, the recognition of trade unions within the workplace and a two-hour reduction in the working week. These concessions were considered as a victory by the unions.
82 Singer, *Prelude to a Revolution*, p. 184; Gretton, *Students and Workers*, p. 190.
83 CGT secretary from 1967 to 1972.
84 Kergoat, 'Sous la plage, la grève', p. 59.
85 Balladur, *L'Arbre de mai*, p. 265.
86 Tarnero, *La Révolution fiction*, p. 44.
87 Général Massu, *Baden 68. Souvenirs d'une fidélité gaulliste* (Paris: Plon, 1983), p. 79–88.
88 Daniel Cohn-Bendit, *Le Grand Bazar* (Paris: Pierre Belfond, 1975), p. 98; Ross, *May '68 and its Afterlives*, p. 58–9.
89 Lefebvre , *Mai 68 – L'Irruption*. . ., p. xiii; Winock, *La Fièvre hexagonale*, p. 355.
90 '[U]ltime énigme', author's translation from Alexandre Duyck, *Le Journal de Dimanche*, 27 October 2002.

3 Current attitudes to the events of 1968

1 Students of different levels and in a range of departments from the following higher education establishments took part in the survey: Université Rennes 2/ Université de Haute Alsace/Université de Poitiers/Université Paris 12/Université de Corse, Pasquale Paoli/Université March Bloch – Strasbourg/Université de Pau et des Pays de L'Adour/ENITIAA – Nantes/Université François Rabelais – Tours/ Université de Bretagne Occidentale – Brest/Université de Reims – Champagne-Ardenne/Université de Provence Aix–Marseille 1/Université Blaise-Pascal – Clermont-Ferrand/Université d'Angers/Université du Sud – Toulon-Var/Université Jean Moulin – Lyon 3.
2 Term used by Benjamin Stora in Blanchard and Veyrat-Masson, *Les Guerres de Mémoires*, p. 7.
3 This question is the focus of chapter five.
4 This is particularly evident when one considers the disastrous June 1968 election results for both the Communists and the Socialists.

5   This will be the focus of chapter five.
6   A study of the impact of 1968 on the system of higher education in general is the focus of chapter four.
7   This assumption is examined in detail in chapter four.
8   For a discussion of the impact of 1968 on regional issues see Reynolds, 'May–June 1968: reflector and vector of a nation's diversity'; Reynolds, 'May '68 and the one-dimensional state'.
9   See chapters four and five.
10 'En répondant à ce questionnaire, je me rends compte que j'ai bien entendu parler de mai 68, les événements, mais qu'il n'y a aucun approfondissement de réalisé. Je connais «mai 68», mais ne sais pas vraiment quels ont été les éléments déclencheurs, les protagonistes essentiels, les conséquences. Dommage! J'essayerai d'y remédier', author's translation.
11 'Je me rends compte que je n'en connais pas assez sur les événements de mai 68', author's translation.
12 'Un cours sur mai 68, please!' Author's translation.
13 'Pour notre génération, les événements de mai 1968 ne sont pas très connus et [sont] peu étudiés en cours. A l'origine, mouvement ouvrier qui se déplace vers les étudiants', author's translation.
14 'Je n'étais pas né en 1968, mais ces événements n'ont a priori rien changé', author's translation.
15 'Pour des jeunes de mon âge cet événement est très peu connu voire non important! Pour les provinciaux, on en parle très peu et en histoire il n'est pas évoqué. On en entend parler de temps en temps aux infos sans explications', author's translation.
16 'Je regrette un manque de renseignements sur mai 1968 dans l'éducation, du moins, au lycée', author's translation.
17 'Ma génération subit peut-être les conséquences de mai 68, mais elle n'en est pas consciente', author's translation.
18 'Les jeunes générations ont quasiment tout oublié de mai 68 ou n'en ont rien su', author's translation.
19 In reference to Jean-Marie Le Pen's shock second place in the first round of the 2002 presidential elections. 'Mai 68 est responsable du malaise français jusqu'au 21 avril y compris', author's translation.
20 'La crise de 68 n'est qu'un caprice de Gauche pour couler le gouvernement de Droite, de la provocation pour rendre de Gaulle moins populaire. Les Français devraient avoir honte de ces événements', author's translation.
21 'Révolution de «gosses» de riches qui ne savaient pas quoi faire de leurs journées', author's translation.
22 'Mai 1968 a surtout été un mouvement de fils à papa en ce qui concerne les étudiants', author's translation.
23 Raymond Marcellin (appointed Ministre de l'Intérieur on 30 May 1968) was one of the most famous proponents of this theory. Raymond Marcellin, *L'Importune Vérité*.
24 'Les événements de 68 sont liés à l'alliance d'étudiants, qui vu leur âge n'avaient plus rien à faire à l'université, à la collusion USA–Chine–Israël pour chasser de Gaulle du pouvoir', author's translation.
25 'Révolution politique manquée, amenée par les étudiants et reprise par les ouvriers de la base, encadré par les syndicats et réprimé par le gouvernement gaulliste et la police, mai 68 est plutôt une révolution des mœurs et un conflit de générations. Malheureusement, cette tradition semble aujourd'hui terminée notamment pour les soixante-huitards eux-mêmes qui sont devenus pour beaucoup des capitalistes', author's translation.
26 'Pour notre génération, les acquis de mai 1968 semblent naturels. Ce sont des mouvements que l'on connaît mal mais il est certain qu'ils ont changé les mœurs générales des Français', author's translation.

27   'Cette situation ne se reverra jamais car nous sommes dans une société pour chacun. On ne s'intéresse plus au général mais seulement à sa personne', author's translation.
28   'Maintenant, ce serait plus difficile de réorganiser un mouvement de cette ampleur. Les mentalités et les motivations sont différentes', author's translation.
29   'Peut-être ne serait-il pas une mauvaise idée d'organiser une deuxième «révolution» pour que les choses bougent un peu plus en France', author's translation.
30   'Mai 68; c'était l'espoir. Aujourd'hui on espère un nouveau mai 68', author's translation.

4   May/June 1968 and the French university system

1   For example, Sauvageot, Geismar, Cohn-Bendit and Duteil, *La Révolte étudiante;* Cohn-Bendit, *Le Gauchisme.*
2   Aron, *La Révolution Intouvable;* Touraine, *Le Communisme utopique.*
3   Epistémon, *Ces idées qui ont ébranlé la France.*
4   Hamon and Rotman, *Génération. 1.*; Hamon and Rotman, *Génération. 2. Les Années de poudre;* Weber, *Que reste-t-il.*
5   Rotman and Hamon, *Génération. 1.*, pp. 424–5.
6   Weber, *Que reste-t-il,* pp. 107–12.
7   Joffrin, *Mai 68: Histoire des événements,* p. 63.
8   Martelli, *Mai 68,* p. 69.
9   Capdeveille and Mouriaux, *L'Entre-deux,* pp. 112–22.
10   Jacques Tarnero, *Mai 68, la Révolution fiction,* p. 54.
11   Fauré, *Mai 68 jour et nuit,* pp. 27–44 ; p. 59.
12   Lavabre and Rey, *Les Mouvements de 1968.*
13   '[U]ne franche rigolade', author's translation from Le Goff, *L'héritage impossible,* p. 44; p. 49; p. 55.
14   Christine Musselin, *La longue marche des universités françaises* (Paris: PUF, 2001), p. 24.
15   Napoleon's Imperial University was effectively the beginning of the Ministry of Education, comprising all sectors of secondary education, of which the 'university' was only one part. 'The Imperial University effectively brought together all secondary and third-level education establishments and bore no relation, whether structurally or in spirit, to what we today call a university.' Author's translation from 'L'Université impériale regroupe en effet l'ensemble des établissements du secondaire et du supérieur et ne correspond en rien, ni dans sa composition, ni dans son esprit, à ce que nous appelons aujourd'hui une université' (Musselin, *La Longue marche,* p. 25).
16   Musselin, *La longue marche,* p. 29.
17   '[D]ispersion et éparpillement', author's translation from Felix Ponteil, *Histoire de l'enseignement en France. Les grandes étapes 1789–1964* (Paris: Sirey, 1966), p. 248.
18   '[B]lanc' dans l'histoire de l'institution universitaire française', author's translation from Alain Renaut, *Que faire des universités?* (Paris: Bayard, 2002), p. 76.
19   Christine Musselin, 'Etat, Université: la fin du modèle centralisé?', *Esprit,* no. 7 (1997), 18–29.
20   Olivier Galland and Marco Oberti, *Les Etudiants* (Paris: La Découverte, 1996), p. 11.
21   Musselin, *La longue marche,* p. 43.
22   Ibid., p. 38.
23   In the absence of university selection, the *propédeutique* was an examination taken at the end of the first year of university in order to determine which students were suited to continue: 'If to obstruct university entry was not amongst the options retained, it was nevertheless necessary – given the exponential failure rates in the first two years of university, notably in humanities, in sciences but also in law – to find a way to allow these new students a new approach to pursue satisfactory

studies. This is how the idea of the *propédeutique* came about.' Author's translation from 'Si faire barrage à l'entrée de l'Université n'était pas dans les options retenues, il fallait bien pour les taux d'échec impressionnants dans les deux premières années universitaires, notamment en lettres, en sciences mais aussi en droit, trouver un moyen qui permette à ces nouveaux étudiants une mise à niveau pour poursuivre des études satisfaisantes. C'est comme cela que naquit l'idée de propédeutique' (Fischer, *L'Histoire des étudiants*, p. 102).

24   Necessary requirement to undertake a teaching career at secondary level.

25   Centre nationale de recherche scientifique. 'La création du CNRS, en 1945, a pour une large part fait sortir la recherche hors des universités' (Renaut, *Que faire des universités?*, p. 85). Ecole nationale d'administration: one of the most important branches of the *Grandes Ecoles* system. Many of its graduates have gone on to have distinguished political careers.

26   François Bourricaud, *Universités à la dérive. France, Etats-Unis, Amérique du Sud* (Paris: Stock, 1971), p. 51.

27   Fischer, *L'Histoire des étudiants*, p. 225.

28   Ibid., p. 300.

29   'The rise in student numbers was unprecedented. Student numbers grew very quickly between 1960–61 and 1967–68. The annual increase was 40,000 or between 10–15 per cent. In seven years, the number of students multiplied by 2.5. This can be talked of as an explosion in numbers.' Author's translation from 'L'effectif des étudiants a progressé très rapidement de 1960–1961 à 1967–1968: le rythme d'augmentation est de 40 000 par an, soit entre 10 et 15 per cent. En sept ans, le nombre d'étudiants a été multiplié par 2,5. On peut parler d'explosion des effectifs' (Antoine Prost, '1968: mort et naissance de l'université française', *Vingtième Siècle*, 23 (1989), 61).

30   Fischer, *L'Histoire des étudiants*, p. 107.

31   Ibid., p. 107.

32   The sole requirement for a university place has always been the *baccalauréat*. This tradition was entrenched in the values attached to the education system and has been a constant focus of debate.

33   The newly founded *Instituts Universitaires de Technologie* awarded the *Diplôme Universitaire de Technologie* (DUT).

34   DEUL – *Diplôme d'études universitaires littéraires*, DEUS – *Diplôme d'études universitaires scientifiques.*

35   Fischer, *L'Histoire des étudiants*, p. 306.

36   For a description of life at Nanterre see Robert Merle, *Derrière la vitre* (Paris: Gallimard, 1970).

37   '[U]n fossé [qui] s'approfondissait chaque année, entre les professeurs, plus âgés, plus attachés aux traditions universitaires, et les assistants, souvent très jeunes, beaucoup plus proches des façons de penser et de sentir des étudiants', author's translation from Prost, *Mort et naissance*, p. 62.

38   'L'université est un lieu où se trouvent des jeunes qui doivent réfléchir et l'université de 68 était encore sclérosée alors que c'était elle qui était soumise, à cette époque-là, à des problèmes avec cet influx massif d'étudiants', author's translation from Edmond Monange, interview with author, Brest, 2 August 2004.

39   'On était dans l'institution la plus conservatrice avec les usagers les plus révolutionnaires', author's translation from Christian Thibon, interview with author, Pau, 19 May 2004.

40   'Parce que c'est là où le déphasage était le plus fort. Ils [les étudiants] avaient le couteau et le pain, donc ils ont fait la tartine', author's translation from Philippe Blanchet, interview with author, Rennes, 16 June 2004.

41   'L'université est un exemple particulièrement révélateur de la mutation que vit la société française et du climat d'insignifiance auquel la jeunesse est particulièrement sensible', author's translation from Le Goff, *L'héritage impossible*, p. 43.

42 Especially a law forbidding visits from members of the opposite sex to halls of residence, which led to large demonstrations around the country and was a significant mobilizing issue at the beginning of the 1968 university protest movement.

43 'Mandarin' was the term used to describe the eminent professors so influential in the decision-making process of universities. Their conservative nature and elusiveness made them a particularly popular target for student frustration: 'This term denounces university professors who are attributed several – negative – traits. . .1) They are regularly absent. . .; 2) Their teaching is outdated. . .; 3) They exploit the prestige of their title.' Author's translation from 'Ce terme dénonce le professeur auquel plusieurs traits, tous négatifs, sont attribués. . .1) Il est absentéiste. . . ; 2) Son enseignement est dépassé. . . ; 3) Il exploite le prestige de son titre. . .' (Bourricaud, *Universités à la dérive*, p. 60).

44 Cohen, *Elusive Reform*, p. 26.

45 Le Goff, *L'héritage impossible*, p. 47.

46 Fischer, *L'Histoire des étudiants*, pp. 329–33.

47 'un enseignement de consommation des connaissances, non de formation humaine', author's translation from Epistémon, *Ces idées*, p. 45.

48 'Dans leur majorité, les étudiants français se montraient réticents, pour ne pas dire hostiles, au modèle gauchiste', author's translation from Fischer, *L'Histoire des étudiants*, p. 396.

49 Le Goff, *L'héritage impossible*, p. 60.

50 'Il y a eu là, pratiquement d'emblée, une collaboration absolument extraordinaire entre étudiants et enseignants', author's translation from Monange, interview.

51 Dreyfus-Armand, Frank, Lévy and Zancarini-Fournel, *Les Années 68*, p. 287.

52 Ibid., p. 288.

53 Epistémon, *Ces idées*, p. 114.

54 Edgar Faure, *Philosophie d'une réforme* (Paris: Plon, 1969), p. 164.

55 Pierre Mendès-France in Jean-Jacques Servan-Schreiber, *Le Réveil de la France* (Paris: Denoël, 1968), p. 45.

56 Aron, *La Révolution introuvable*, p. 181.

57 Dreyfus-Armand, Frank, Lévy and Zancarini-Fournel, *Les Années 68*, p. 285.

58 Le Goff, *L'héritage impossible*, p. 79.

59 Aron, *La Révolution introuvable*, p. 55.

60 Touraine, *Le Mouvement de mai*, p. 236.

61 '[U]ne inadaptation profonde', author's translation from Antoine Prost, *Histoire générale. L'Enseignement et l'éducation en France. L'Ecole et la famille dans une société en mutation, 1930–1980* (Paris: Nouvelle Librairie de France, 1981), p. 289.

62 '[A]ussi insaisissable qu'une vedette', author's translation from Bourricaud, *Universités à la dérive*, p. 59.

63 Ibid. p. 62. The term lottery relates to the fact that in many cases the subjects studied in exams were drawn from a hat.

64 Prost, *1968: Mort et naissance*, p. 62.

65 '[M]enace [qui] planait à l'horizon', author's translation from ibid., p. 63.

66 The Minister for Education when the events began, Alain Peyrefitte, resigned on 28 May. Pompidou took charge of the ministry until the end of the revolt.

67 Faure, *Philosophie d'une réforme*, p. 21.

68 Sidney Tarrow, 'Social protest and policy reform. May 1968 and the *Loi d'Orientation* in France', *Comparative Political Studies*, 25 (4) (1993), 589.

69 Ibid., p. 591.

70 M. Ilari – a student in 1968 at the University of Dijon where he actively participated in the events and current-day lecturer at the ENITIAA in Nantes – described to me how, as a student, he was contacted by Edgar Faure enquiring about how he felt the university system should be reformed in the aftermath of the events: 'For half an hour, he asked me questions on what I thought of it all. That proves that he wanted direct contact'. Authour's translation from 'Il m'a posé des questions pendant une demi-heure par rapport à ce que je pensais de tout ça. C'est la preuve

qu'il a cherché des contacts directs', Jean-Luc Ilari, interview with author, Nantes, 11 May 2004.

71 Musselin, *La longue marche*, p. 57.

72 The law was passed with 441 votes for, 0 against and 39 abstentions. Agulhon, Nouschi and Schor, *La France de 1940 à nos jours*, p. 250.

73 *Loi d'orientation de l'enseignement supérieur*. No. 68–978. 12 November 1968. (*http://guilde.jeunes-chercheurs.org/Textes/Txtfond/L68–978.html*)

74 Cohen, *Elusive Reform*, p. 60.

75 '[U]ne plus grande souplesse, il permet aussi de restructurer l'ensemble de relations universitaires', author's translation from Fischer, *L'Histoire des étudiants*, p. 427.

76 Ibid., p. 427.

77 '[U]ne expérience sérieuse', author's translation from Faure, *Philosophie d'une réforme*, p. 106.

78 Fischer, *L'Histoire des étudiants*, p. 430.

79 Musselin, *La longue marche*, p. 55.

80 Le Goff, *L'héritage impossible*, p. 158.

81 If fewer than 60 per cent of students participated in the elections their share of the vote was reduced accordingly.

82 Cohen, *Elusive Reform*, p. 61.

83 Musselin, *La longue marche*, p. 59.

84 Le Goff, *L'héritage impossible*, p. 157.

85 Ibid., p. 161.

86 Prost, *1968: Mort et naissance*, p. 69.

87 Prost, *Histoire générale*, p. 314.

88 'La loi Faure avait subi avec succès le baptême des urnes', author's translation from Prost, *1968: Mort et naissance*, 69.

89 Tarrow, 'Social protest and policy reform', 595.

90 Ibid.

91 Raymond Boudon, 'The French university since 1968', *Comparative Politics*, 10 (1) (1977), 105.

92 W. D. Halls, *Education, Culture and Politics in Modern France* (Oxford: Pergamon, 1976), p. 212.

93 Tarrow, 'Social protest and policy reform', 595.

94 La Gauche Prolétariate. Created in February 1969 by disillusioned left-wing militants, the GP embarked on a campaign of headline-grabbing actions in a bid to perpetuate the crisis. Upon its dissolution in 1970, the NRP (*Nouvelle Résistance Populaire*) was formed. This clandestine organization was involved in increasingly violent attacks and even high–profile kidnappings. For more details, see Hamon and Rotman, *Génération 2*, or Le Goff, *L'héritage impossible*, pp. 143–237.

95 As Didier Fischer comments: 'Le castrisme et le maoïsme rejoignaient dans le discrédit le communisme soviétique auquel l'écrivain russe Alexandre Soljénitsyne par son *Archipel du Goulag* venait de porter le coup de grâce' (Fischer, *L'Histoire des étudiants*, p. 422).

96 Tarrow, 'Social protest and policy reform', 596.

97 OPEC significantly increased the price of oil. This created great problems for all nations relying on importation of *l'or noir* and was to prove extremely detrimental to their respective economies.

98 '[L]'enjeu social se situe désormais en dehors des universités', author's translation from Yolande Cohen and Claudie Weill, 'Les Mouvements étudiants: une histoire en miettes ?', *Le Mouvement social*, 120 (1982), 8.

99 Tarrow, 'Social protest and policy reform', p. 599.

100 '[N]'allons-nous pas connaître un nouveau mai 68?', author's translation from Le Goff, *L'héritage impossible*, p. 15.

101 'Je crois qu'inconsciemment mai 68 a crée une tradition de manifestation universitaire', author's translation from Monange, interview.

102   This is backed up by the results of question 14 of the survey – see pp. 68–9.

103   'C'est sûr que ça a débridé les choses. Les étudiants savent qu'ils ont leur voix et qu'ils peuvent avoir une influence', author's translation from Alain Collange, Mulhouse, interview with author, 13 May 2004.

104   '[D]ans le rite mais les motivations sont différentes. Dans la forme mais pas dans le fond. Ça a montré la pratique qu'on suit maintenant', author's translation from Jean-Pierre Barraqué, interview with author, Pau, 19 May 2004.

105   'Un ministre de l'éducation ne peut plus se permettre d'aborder une réforme sans tenir compte de la réaction étudiante', author's translation from Jean-Jacques Alcandre, interview with author, Strasbourg, 14 May 2004.

106   '[V]eille tradition de mouvements populaires, de manifestations de rue et du droit à la grève', author's translation from Blanchet, interview.

107   'Il y a une veille tradition de mouvements populaires [. . .] je ne pense pas que 68 a inventé quelque chose là-dessus', author's translation from Blanchet, interview.

108   '[U]ne tradition, et pas seulement étudiante mais plus généralement et ça a existé avant 68', author's translation from Mme O'Dea, interview with author, Lyon, 14 May 2004.

109   The UERs introduced under the Faure law were renamed *Unité de Formation et de Recherche* (UFR) under the 1984 Loi Savary.

110   '[P]our que les étudiants s'investissent plus', author's translation from Collange, interview.

111   '[O]n hurle victoire parce qu'on arrive à avoir 12 per cent de participation', author's translation from Alcandre, interview.

112   '[N]'ont aucun intérêt', author's translation from Francis Favereau, interview with author, Rennes, 11 June 2004. Francis Favereau is a lecturer and researcher at the University of Rennes 2 and is author of a number of publications on Breton culture and society.

113   '[U]ne petite poignée d'étudiants qui participe et pas toujours dans l'intérêt des tous les étudiants, ils sont parfois sectaires', author's translation from O'Dea, interview.

114   '[L]a plupart des étudiants s'en foutent royalement', author's translation from Barraqué, interview.

115   '[R]ichesse folle [. . .] un débridement de toutes les forces actives qu'il y avait à l'intérieur de la société', author's translation from Jacques Gozart, interview with author, Tours, 16 May 2004.

116   'On était dans une logique de plein emploi, donc les conditions pour les jeunes étaient moins dures – ce qui n'est pas le cas aujourd'hui', author's translation from Gérard Binder, interview with author, Mulhouse, 13 May 2004.

117   'En 68 les étudiants ne voulaient pas rentrer dans le système alors qu'actuellement les étudiants disent «moi, je veux rentrer dans le système»', author's translation from Barraqué, interview.

118   '[L]'étudiant a très vite compris qu'il avait intérêt à avoir des diplômes', author's translation from Jean Dewitz, interview with author, Strasbourg, 14 May 2004.

119   '[Q]ui avait une chance extraordinaire. [. . .] Il suffisait de se faire couper les cheveux, mettre un costard et on trouvait du travail', author's translation from Barraqué, interview.

120   'Récemment pendant des grèves les étudiants écrivaient des slogans sur les murs. Cependant ils les écrivaient très proprement à la craie pour qu'on puisse ensuite les effacer. Et ça, ce n'est pas du tout l'esprit de 68', author's translation from M. Blanchet, interview.

121   '[I]ls n'ont pas les mêmes consciences politiques, leurs intuitions de citoyens prennent d'autres formes et véhiculent d'autres objectifs que la génération précédente', author's translation from M. Blanchet, interview.

122   '[P]rocessus de réforme universitaire qui n'est toujours pas terminé', author's translation from M. Le Moigne, interview with author, Brest, 21 May 2004.

123 'On a changé les examens de fin d'année, la fac est devenue plus ouverte, plus transversale, plus professionnelle avec d'autres filières. Il y a eu aussi la massification de l'université, le contrôle continu, etc. 68 a permis tout ça', author's translation from Mme Ducol, interview with author, Tours, 16 May 2004.

124 '[l'université] est mieux. Il fallait ce changement. Elle est mieux même s'il reste des problèmes', author's translation from M. Binder, interview.

125 'Le système pyramidal s'est effondré petit à petit pour donner place à un système plus horizontal de réseau d'échange de savoir', author's translation from Blanchet, interview.

126 'Mai 68 a changé l'organisation des cours [avec] l'introduction du contrôle continu et une démocratisation de l'université', author's translation from Brigitte Dumortier, interview with author, Paris, 17 May 2004.

127 'L'époque du mandarinat est une époque révolue', author's translation from Monange, interview.

128 '[A]près 68, les étudiants et les enseignants se parlaient', author's translation from Favereau, interview.

129 'Mai 68 a permis l'ouverture de l'université', author's translation from Thibon, interview.

130 'Le système universitaire était immergé et mai 68 a vu l'adaptation du système aux besoins de la société', author's translation from Philippe Cadène, interview.

131 '[L]e cloisonnement pluridisciplinaire', author's translation from Monange, interview.

132 '[P]our ceux qui croient que la mission de l'université est beaucoup plus que la formation d'élites, 68 est une nette amélioration', author's translation from Blanchet, interview.

133 'On était vraiment dans un régime de mandarinat et on est passé dans un régime qui parfois est arrivé dans le chienlit', author's translation from Collange, interview with author, 13 May 2004.

134 'Avant 68 la fac était cohérente, elle ne l'est plus aujourd'hui. On est allé trop loin', author's translation from Barraqué, interview with author, 19 May 2004.

135 '[L]a pagaille', author's translation from M. Bastié, interview with author, Paris, 17 May 2004.

136 'Vu la manière dont les choses étaient organisées à l'époque, c'est inconcevable que ça aurait continué encore plus longtemps', author's translation from Collange, interview.

137 Ducol, interview.

138 '[S]e serait fait plus doucement ou autrement', author's translation from Dumortier, interview.

139 '[I]l aurait fallu longtemps pour les avoir', author's translation from Dewitz, interview.

140 '[I]l fallait un événement comme 68 pour changer des choses', author's translation from O'Dea, interview.

141 '[S]i on n'avait pas eu la force de la rue, ça aurait changeait moins et moins vite', author's translation from Blanchet, interview.

142 '[C]'est le résultat direct, c'est sur. Jamais l'administration n'aurait cédé autant, pas à cette époque', author's translation from Ilari, interview.

143 'Ils [les changements] n'ont pas eu lieu sans 68. Je ne pense pas qu'on les aurait eus sans 68 ou quelque chose de similaire', author's translation from Binder, interview.

144 '[O]nt donné à l'université actuelle le visage qu'elle a', author's translation from Binder, interview.

145 '[V]ivre sous ce qui a été fait après 68', author's translation from Dewitz, interview.

146 '[P]our eux c'est un mythe et les médias et des acteurs de 68 sont responsables pour la création de cette image des événements. Il me semble qu'ils n'ont aucune idée de ce qu'il s'est passé', author's translation from Cadène, interview.

5 May/June 1968 in the regions

1 Guillebaud, *Les Années orphélines*, p. 17.
2 Aron, *La révolution introuvable*; Tourraine, *Le Mouvement de mai;* Epistémon, *Ces idées qui ont ébranlé la France. Nanterre.*
3 Debray, *Modeste contribution*; Balladur, *L'Arbre de mai.*
4 Henri Weber, *Que reste-t-il de mai 68?*
5 Hamon and Rotman, *Génération. 1.*
6 Le Goff, *L'héritage impossible*, p. 19.
7 '[U]ne literature de falsification', author's translation.
8 Gérard Guégan, *Mai 68 à l'usage des moins de vingt ans* (Paris: Actes Sud, 1998), p. 9; pp. 29–201.
9 Labro, *Les Barricades de mai*, pp. 107–9.
10 Sauvageot, Geismar, Cohn-Bendit and Duteil, *La Révolte étudiante*, p. 37.
11 Cohn-Bendit, *Le Gauchisme*, pp. 23–8; pp. 98–113.
12 Alain Griotteray, *Des Barricades ou des réformes.*
13 'Mai 68 – Mai 78', *Syndicalisme*, 1704 (11 May 1978), 16–18.
14 'Colloque sur mai 68', *Le Peuple*, 1704 (1–15 July 1978), 19; 46.
15 Alain Delale and Gilles Ragache, *La France de 68* (Paris: Seuil, 1978), pp. 83–95.
16 Martelli, *Mai 68*, pp. 102–25.
17 Joffrin, *Histoire des événements*, pp. 150–66.
18 Capdevielle, Mouriaux, *Mai 68 – L'Entre-deux de la modernité.*
19 Lavabre and Rey, *Les Mouvements de 1968*, p. 19; pp. 86–9.
20 Ibid., pp. 112–15.
21 Tartakowsky, *Le Pouvoir est dans la rue*, p. 166; p. 186; p. 157; p. 205.
22 François le Madec, *L'Aubépine de mai. Chronique d'une usine occupée. Sud-Aviation, Nantes 1968* (Nantes: CDMOT, 1988), p. 45; p. 129.
23 Georges Chaffard, *Les Orages de mai* (Paris: Calmann-Lévy, 1968), p. 56.
24 Ross, *May '68 and its Afterlives*, p. 9.
25 Sommier, 'Mai 68 : Sous les pavés d'une page officielle', p. 65.
26 'Dans les commémorations on n'a toujours pas bougé, c'était mai 68 à Paris. Ça commencé à la rue Gay Lussac et ça a fini au Ministère du Travail', author's translation from Vincent Porhel, interview with the author, Paris, 18 January 2005.
27 'Il n'y aurait pas eu de mai 68 brestois s'il n'y avait pas eu de gauchistes à Nanterre, des échauffourées à la Sorbonne, des barricades sur le boul'Mich', author's translation from Edmond Monange, 'Mai 68 à Brest', *Les Cahiers de l'Iroise*, 176 (1998), 21.
28 'C'est historiquement une erreur. C'est une erreur qui rend fausse l'interprétation de ces événements. On ne prend pas tout en compte et donc forcément on a une idée fausse de la chose. C'est étonnant. C'est choquant au point de vue de la raison', author's translation from Bernard Boudic, interview with author, Rennes, 24 January 2005.
29 For example Le Goff, *L'Héritage impossible*, p. 59; Capdevielle and Mouriaux, *L'Entre-deux*, p. 10.
30 Francis Favereau, *Bretagne contemporaine. Langue, culture, identité* (Morlaix: Embannadurioù Skol Vreizh, 1993), p. 55.
31 For a more detailed overview of this early history see Philippe Meyer, *Histoire de l'Alsace* (Paris: Perrin, 2008).
32 These are described as cultural 'épurations' in Pierre Klein, *L'Alsace inachevée* (Colmar: Jérôme, 2004), p. 19.
33 For discussion of the issue of collaborators see Jean Ritter, *L'Alsace* (Paris: PUF, 1985), p. 62; Bernard Vogler, *Histoire politique de l'Alsace. De la Révolution à nos jours, un panorama des passions alsaciennes* (Strasbourg: La Nuée Bleue, 1995), pp. 264–6.
34 For more details on this question see Michel Phlipponneau, *Debout Bretagne* (St Brieuc: Presses Universitaires de Bretagne, 1970), pp. 29–31.

35   For example, the famous occupation of the sous-préfecture in Morlaix in 1961 see
     Henri Poisson and Jean-Pierre le Matt, *Histoire de la Bretagne* (Nantes: COOP
     Breizh, 2000), pp. 478–9.

36   For an analysis of the escalating violence in Brittany at this time see Claude Brunel,
     'En Bretagne, l'Escalade de la violence', *Lectures pour tous. Je sais tout*, Numéro
     spécial, 'Pourquoi cette révolte? Mensuel', No. 174, July 1968, 84–9.

37   Jean-Luc Poussier, *Bretagne* (Paris: Lec, 1997), p. 53

38   'La défense de l'emploi. La garantie des ressources. L'amélioration du pouvoir
     d'achat', author's translation from a CGT–CFDT tract calling on support for the 8
     May *Ouest Veut Vivre* day of action.

39   '[D]ans le cadre de la Bretagne, on peut dire que l'ampleur de «mai 1968» ne
     devait pas surprendre, les événements de Paris jouent un rôle de résonance mais le
     «mai 68» breton n'arrive pas comme «un coup de tonnerre dans un ciel serein»,
     des mécontentements de tous ordres et dans de nombreux domaines existent',
     author's translation from Jacqueline Sainclivier, *La Bretagne de 1939 à nos jours*
     (Rennes: Editions Ouest France, 1989), p. 430

40   Gireg Aubert and Aurélie Sonocinski, '1945–2004: le regain du régionalisme',
     News d'ill, February 2004, 75, 14–15.

41   '[L]'éffondrement de la vie culturelle régionale', author's translation from
     Bernard Vogler, *Histoire culturelle de l'Alsace. Du Moyen Age à nos jours, les très riches
     heures d'une région frontière* (Strasbourg: La Nuée Bleue, 1993), p. 461.

42   'Le dialecte tend peu à peu à être considéré comme une tare, une maladie
     honteuse, un comportement préjudiciable à la francophonie, l'expression d'un
     sous-développement culturel, tout juste bon pour valet de ferme, rimeur du
     dimanche ou autre amateur de grosses farces', author's translation from Vogler,
     Histoire culturelle de l'Alsace, p. 462.

43   Skol Vreizh, *La Bretagne au XX siècle. Histoire de la Bretagne et des pays celtiques de 1914
     à nos jours*, (Morlaix: Skol Vreizh, 1983), p. 184.

44   For a more in-depth analysis of the demographic situation of the region see
     P. Quintin, 'De l'exode rural à la rurbanisation: les mouvements de population
     active dans l'Ouest entre 1962 et 1990', *INSEE*, octant no. 75, 1998.

45   'Le désenclavement reste toujours imparfait, la décentralisation, vigoureuse au
     début de la décennie, s'essouffle et l'emploi paraît beaucoup plus menacé
     qu'ailleurs, bien des jeunes devant se résoudre à l'exode pour trouver du travail',
     author's translation from Monange, 'Mai 68 à Brest', p. 12.

46   'J'ai toujours été surpris parce que nous étions au courant de rien [. . .] il n'a
     jamais été question de ce qui est arrive, de ce qui se préparait, on faisait le travail
     classique', author's translation from Dewitz, interview.

47   For an overview of the economic situation in region at the time see Léon Strauss
     and Jean-Claude Richiez, 'Le Mouvement social de mai 1968 en Alsace: décalages
     et développements inégaux', *Revue des sciences sociales de la France de l'Est*, 17 (1989–
     90), 117–21; Yvonne Wendling, *Les feuilles de mai 68 à Strasbourg* [Mémoire de
     Maitrise], University of Strasbourg, 1992, p. 14.

48   See Vogler, *Histoire politique de l'Alsace*, pp. 292–8; Wendling, *Les feuilles de mai 68 à
     Strasbourg*, pp. 14–17; Straus and Richiez, 'Le Mouvement social de mai 1968 en
     Alsace', 119.

49   Ritter, *L'Alsace*, p. 69.

50   'Pour eux la fac c'est pour trouver du boulot et pour trouver du boulot vite. On n'a
     pas du tout le même profil que l'étudiant parisien. Ils ne sont pas là pour faire la
     révolution', author's translation from Porhel, interview.

51   For a detailed analysis of the 1968 events in the CLU de Brest see Vincent Porhel,
     Mai 68 au CLU de Brest, [Mémoire de maîtrise], UBO (supervised by Edmond
     Monange), 1988.

52   Monange, 'Mai 68 à Brest', 16.

53   'A Brest comme à Paris, le malaise étudiant existe, mais la poudre et l'étincelle
     n'étant pas de même nature, l'explosion n'a pas les mêmes effets', author's transla-
     tion from Porhel, 'Mai 68 au CLU de Brest', p. 9.

54 For analysis of the problems experienced within the university system nationally see Musselin, *La longue marche*; Fischer, *L'Histoire des étudiants de 1945 à nos jours*; Prost, '1968: Mort et naissance de l'université française.'

55 See Agnès Ackner, 'Révolte de mai 1968' in *Encyclopédie de l'Alsace* (Strasbourg: Publitotal, 1982), p. 6369; Pierre Feuerstein, *Printemps de révolté à Strasbourg, Mai–Juin 1968* (Strasbourg: Saisons d'Alsace, 1968), pp. 16–17.

56 See Feuerstein, *Printemps de révolté à Strasbourg*, p. 20; Georges Livet, *50 années à l'université de Strasbourg* (Strasbourg: Société Savante d'Alsace, 1998), p. 159.

57 For details of the extraordinary coup by which the *Situationnistes* distributed their pamphlet see Livet, *50 années à l'université de Strasbourg*, pp. 155–7; [Anon.], 'De Strasbourg, Lettrisme et Sitautionnisme hier et aujourd'hui', *Cahiers/Chroniques*, 3, Université de Strasbourg, 61–3.

58 Feuerstein, *Printemps de révolté à Strasbourg*, p. 20.

59 Livet, *50 années à l'université de Strasbourg*, pp. 159–60.

60 [Anon.], '10 jours qui ébranlèrent Strasbourg ou l'internationale situationniste se donne en spectacle', *Gros sel*, 8, 1968, 56.

61 Remy Amann, *Le Scandale de Strasbourg ou l'épisode situationniste de la capitale alsacienne*, [Mémoire de Maitrise], Université de Strasbourg, 1990, p. 131.

62 Wendling, *Les feuilles de mai 68 à Strasbourg*, p. 23.

63 'Le situationisme dans le monde étudiant n'était pas tellement connu. On savait que c'était un mouvement extrémiste qui avait des idées assez surréalistes, mais ça n'allait pas plus loin', author's translation from Georges Foessel, interview with author, Strasbourg, 20 June 2008.

64 Fischer, *L'Histoire des étudiants de 1945 à nos jours*, p. 382.

65 Feuerstein, *Printemps de révolté à Strasbourg*, p. 17.

66 Porhel, *Mai 68 au CLU de Brest*, p. 46.

67 'Plus de 100 000 ouvriers, paysans, étudiants [qui] ont manifesté pour la survie de leur région', author's translation from *Ouest France*, 9 May 1968, p. 6.

68 'A 14h, Brest reprend son aspect normal : les embarras de la circulation recommencent, la journée du 8 mai s'est déroulée de bout en bout dans l'ordre', author's translation from Annie Jeffroy, *Chronique des événements de mai 1968 à Brest d'après le «Télégramme» et «Ouest–France»*, [Mémoire de maîtrise], UBO, 1987, p. 57.

69 Monange, 'Mai 68 à Brest', 15.

70 Porhel, *Mai au CLU de Brest*, p. 54.

71 Jeffroy, *Chronique des événements de mai 1968 à Brest*, p. 60; p. 93.

72 Monanage, 'Mai 68 à Brest', 18; 17.

73 Jeffroy, *Chronique des événements de mai 1968 à Brest*, p. 139.

74 Monanage, 'Mai 68 à Brest', p. 20.

75 A range of sources including interviews with participants, consultation of Archives in *Les Archives de la Ville et de la Communaute Urbaine* (which houses an excellent collection on May '68) as well as the following texts were used to put this section together; Françoise Olivier-Utard, 'Les 'événements' de mai 68 en Alsace', *Almémos*, 12 (2008), 2–5; Hervé de Chalendar, 'Mai 68, Un printemps en Alsace, *L'Alsace*, Hors Série, February 2008, 4–11;Wendling, *Les feuilles de mai 68 à Strasbourg*; Straus and Richiez, 'Le Mouvement social de mai 1968 en Alsace', 121–8; Jean-Paul Haas, *La Révolution inutile* (Strasbourg: Oberlin, 1987); Ackner, 'Révolte de mai 1968', pp. 6369–74; Feuerstein, *Printemps de révolté à Strasbourg*, pp. 24–57; [Anon.], 'Le mai de Strasbourg. Chronologie des mouvements étudiants qui se manifestent à Strasbourg en particulier durant le mois de mai et juin 1968', *Bulletin d'information*, Université de Strasbourg, 15, 1968, 118–24.

76 Feurestein, *Printemps de révolté à Strasbourg*, pp. 23–4.

77 'Il y avait des jeunes enseignants, mes collègues, qui la nuit faisaient des textes critiques et on fondait l'université critique. [. . .] On a fait des travaux de commissions et on le faisait la nuit en occupant', author's translation from Lucien Braun, interview with the author, Strasbourg, 27 June 2008

78   '[S]ymbole de l'université', author's translation from Braun, interview. See also
     Haas, *La Révolution inutile*, pp. 2–3.
79   Feurestein, , *Printemps de révolté à Strasbourg*, pp. 30–3; Acker, p. 6371; Haas, *La
     Révolution inutile*, pp. 6–7.
80   '[A] dit qu'on pouvait faire une expérience et puis on en tirera les conclusions
     après', author's translation from Braun, interview.
81   Straus and Richiez, 'Le Mouvement social de mai 1968 en Alsace', 124–8; Ackner,
     'Révolte de mai 1968', p. 6372.
82   This episode had always been one of the mysteries of the events in Strasbourg as
     no one ever accepted responsibility and no one was found guilty. A huge polemic
     broke out in the aftermath as students went as far as to produce a tract with draw-
     ings of the location so as to highlight how it was impossible for them to have
     carried out such an act. In so doing they always implied that it was clearly an act by
     the opposition to cast derision on the student movement. The mystery was eventu-
     ally solved in 2008 when one student from the time eventually explained how she
     was present when two bourgeois students decided to carry out this provocative act
     with no other motive than the thrill of such a serious transgression. See Elisabath
     Schulthess, 'Mai 68: Le Révélation de Bichette sur «l'affaire du Monument aux
     Morts»', *L'Alsace*, 20 May 2008.
83   '[E]rreur à ne pas commettre', author's translation from Foessel, interview.
84   Utard, 'Les "événements" de mai 68 en Alsace', 4.
85   Feurestein, *Printemps de révolté à Strasbourg*, pp. 43–4.
86   For details see Feurestein, *Printemps de révolté à Strasbourg* p. 43; Livet, *50 années à
     l'université de Strasbourg*, pp. 199–200.
87   Feurestein, *Printemps de révolté à Strasbourg*, p. 47. It is also worth noting that a
     national meeting of *Anciens Combattants* had been held in Strasbourg between 23
     and 27 May. This undoubtedly heightened tension and demonstrates the signifi-
     cance of the war in this region. See *Les Dernières Nouvelles d'Alsace*, 17 May 1968,
     p. 23.
88   '[C]ontre-offensive politique', author's translation from Straus and Richiez, 'Le
     Mouvement social de mai 1968 en Alsace', 143.
89   For more detail on this critically important moment see *Les Dernières Nouvelles
     d'Alsace*, 2/3 June 1968, pp. 21–2.
90   Vogler, *Nouvelle Histoire d'Alsace*, p. 273.
91   'Si le mouvement baisse et l'occupation cesse; c'est parce que la vacance des
     grandes valeurs provient de la valeur des grandes vacances', author's translation
     from anonymous tract in 'Les événements de mai 68 à la faculté des lettres de
     Strasbourg', Documents légués aux archives par Marc Schweyer, Archives de la
     Ville, Strasbourg, Box 114Z, No. 5, pièce 3.
92   For example, see Hamon and Rotman *Génération 1.*, pp. 514–15; Singer, *Prelude to a
     revolution*, pp. 152–5.
93   '[U]n volcan sur une banquise', author's translation from Foessel, interview.
94   '[V]écu dans une bulle', author's translation from Dewitz, interview.
95   See interview with Jean Kaspar in De Chalendar, 'Mai 68, Un printemps en Alsace',
     p. 25.
96   'Les grèves en Alsace ont été moins suivies, cela était vu comme du désordre par
     rapport aux ouvriers de la banlieue parisienne qui étaient solidaires, d'accord, qui
     faisaient le mouvement, tandis qu'ici le mouvement ouvrier avait timidement suivi
     le mouvement, qui restait majoritairement étudiant et intellectuel', author's trans-
     lation from Roger Siffer, interview with author, Strasbourg, 26 June 2008.
97   '[L]e syndicat de reference', author's translation from Porhel, interview.
98   'Nos relations étaient plus faciles, on était plus en phase avec des gens de la CFDT',
     author's translation from Jean Le Roux, interview with author, Brest, 22 January
     2005.
99   'Nous, on était ouvert, avec les étudiants de gauche on travaillait bien [...] Il y
     avait une bonne entente et même une bonne coordination [...] Il n'y avait pas

deux mouvements mais un seul', author's translation from Henri Didou, interview with author, Brest, 19 January 2005.

100 'Les revendications des travailleurs, leurs luttes, sont celles des Enseignants, des Etudiants et d'autres catégories de la population laborieuse [. . .] Vive l'union des travailleurs et des étudiants', author's translation from a tract produced by the CGT, the CFDT, the FEN (Fédération de l'Education Nationale) and the AGEB and distributed prior to 13 May demonstration.

101 'Comme les syndicats ouvriers, enseignants et paysans avaient du mal à trouver quelqu'un pour présider les manifestations on a relié ça aux étudiants', author's translation from Boudic, interview.

102 'Avant meme qu'E Descamps ne demande une union dans la lutte entre ouvriers et étudiants, cela s'était réalisé à la CSF. Les travailleurs de la CSF ont discuté tant avec des responsables étudiants de l'AGEB qu'avec des étudiants inorganisés. Après qu'ils aient expliqué les motifs et le sens de leur lutte, ils écoutaient le point de vue ouvrier. Chaque fois, on arrive aux conclusions suivantes: Nous voulons plus être comme les cadres d'aujourd'hui; Il faut se soutenir mutuellement, en permanence; Il faut multiplier les contacts, les conférences, les explications entre nous', author's translation from Syndicat Métaux Brest, 'Mai 1968 – CSF Brest' (summary of the CSF strike and occupation in 1968 compiled in weeks following the events by those involved), 1968, p. 3.

103 '[L]e travailleur demandant le droit à participer (non pas seulement à donner son avis) à l'organisation du travail et à la gestion des entreprises, l'étudiant ayant les mêmes revendications pour ce qui est de l'Université', author's translation from Jean Le Roux, 'Mai 1968 et les étudiants de Brest', *En Avant*, 317 (1968), 36.

104 As Straus and Richiez argue, despite an intensification of the strike movement towards the end of May, the aim on behalf of the trade unions was to strengthen their hand in forthcoming negotiations and the strength of the movement at this stage should be read as a result of this desire and not as fitting the nationwide trend of a complete standstill. Straus and Richiez, 'Le Mouvement social de mai 1968 en Alsace', 129.

105 'Lorsque le mouvement de 68 est allé en diminuant à l'intérieur de la France, l'une des questions posées par les syndicats était: «Comment arrêter une grève, comment en sortir?»; en Alsace l'on se posait la question: «Est–ce que l'on va faire grève?»', author's translation from Jean-Michel Mehl, interview with author, Strasbourg, 24 June 2008.

106 'L'Alsace a une histoire particulière. Les habitants ont quand même souffert, la plupart du temps doublement souffert par rapport aux autres. Et donc la crainte du chaos était encore forte ici qu'ailleurs', author's translation from Hervé de Chalendar, interview with author, Strasbourg, 23 June 2008.

107 'Ils ne leurs manquaient pas de nourriture, ils ne leurs manquaient pas d'essence, d'argent [. . .] et tout ça grâce à la proximité de l'Allemagne', author's translation from Foessel, interview.

108 Foessel, interview.

109 '[O]nt fait que le mouvement finalement paraissait plus agaçant qu'autre chose', author's translation from Foessel, interview.

110 '[T]hèmes proprement universitaires: organisation des enseignements, des examens, formation pédagogique et technologique, débouchés [. . .] problèmes de structures de l'université', author's translation from Le Roux, ' Mai 1968 et les étudiants de Brest', p. 36.

111 For more details see Porhel, *Mai 68 au CLU de Brest*, pp. 63–85.

112 'Il y a un point beaucoup plus concret, je dirais beaucoup plus réaliste, à la limite beaucoup plus matériel qu'à Paris y compris dans le mouvement étudiant', author's translation from Monange, interview.

113 'Du genre, la révolution sexuelle, il est interdit d'interdire, la chasse aux flics, de tout ça on était complètement étranger', author's translation from Boudic, interview.

114 '[A]ttitude plus respectueuse', author's translation from Boudic, interview.
115 The collection of les Archives de la Ville are dominated by the work of the various *commission paritaires* and underline the importance of the reformist sector in the Strasbourg university movement.
116 'Il y avait une frange qui voulait diriger, celle du «Manifeste», que l'on a appelée le gauchisme anarchiste, mais le reste était réformateur beaucoup plus que révolutionnaire', author's translation from Alphonse Irjud, interview with author, Strasbourg, 28 June 2008.
117 '[L]'implication de pas mal d'enseignants [. . .] a donné un aspect presque officiel au movement [. . .] qui a fait que Strasbourg est devenu un pole qu'on a pris au sérieux', author's translation from Jean Dewitz, interview with author, 2 July 2008.
118 François Igersheim in Livet, *50 années à l'université de Strasbourg*, p. 171.
119 For details of how this conversation unfolded see Livet, *50 années à l'université de Strasbourg*, pp. 188–91.
120 '[U]n peu de farine à moudre', author's translation from Foessel, interview.
121 'C'était une façon de se dégager, ça n'avait rien de politique dans la tête de Peyrefitte, c'était pour les satisfaire pour le moment', author's translation from Braun, interview.
122 'Personne à l'époque savait bien comment les choses allaient se passer en Allemagne. Alors ils redoutaient un triomphe du mouvement allemand et l'arrivée des milliers d'étudiants allemands révolutionnaires à Strasbourg. C'était une hantise des autorités', author's translation from Foessel, interview.
123 'Le fait que ce soit Strasbourg qui ait décidé de devenir autonome était extrêmement mal ressenti au niveau hexagonal, l'on faisait un collage rapide entre «autonome» et «autonomisme», donc séparation de l'Alsace de la France, retour dans le giron de la grande Allemagne, le pan-germanisme, la vieille haine héréditaire de l'ennemi allemand est ressortie à Paris', author's translation from Siffer, interview.
124 Livet, *50 années à l'université de Strasbourg*, p. 201.
125 Monange, 'Mai 68 à Brest', 21.
126 'Ce n'était pas l'ambiance, il n'y avait pas besoin de chercher la bagarre', author's translation from Didou, interview.
127 '[P]endant le mouvement de 68, les CRS à Brest il n'y en avait pas', author's translation from Le Roux, interview.
128 'Nous avons montré que nous étions plus mûr, nous avons fait 68 mais plus *soft*, tranquille', author's translation from Mehl, interview.
129 'Strasbourg, toujours à l'avant-garde du retour à l'ordre', author's translation from Archives de la Ville, Box 114Z, No. 2, pièce 11.
130 'Ce n'était pas le but de la manœuvre de casser du flic, c'était de réfléchir à changer les choses', author's translation from Siffer, interview.
131 'J'ai donné l'ordre de charger et de la faire vigoureusement. J'en prends la responsabilité, il y a des limites à ne pas dépasser. Nous ne tolérons pas que Strasbourg devienne une ville de barricades', author's translation from Livet, *50 années à l'université de Strasbourg*, p. 200.
132 'C'est germanique, il y a l'esprit germanique en Alsace [. . .] On aime l'ordre ici [. . .] c'est une tradition germanique', author's translation from Braun, interview.
133 There is a photo showing the CRS at the foot of the steps of the PU with their backs to the students and facing the Gaullist demonstrators in Les Archives de la Ville, Box 114Z, No. 6, Pièce 2.
134 '[I]l est paradoxal de voir les CRS et les gardiens de la paix empêcher les Strasbourgeois d'enlever le drapeau rouge qui flotte sur leur université', author's translation from *Les Dernières Nouvelles d'Alsace*, 2/3 June 1968, p. 22.
135 'C'est un étonnant chassé-croisé où chaque camp prend soin d'éviter l'adversaire, montrant ainsi que, de part et d'autre, la prudence et la sagesse l'emportent sur le

fanatisme et l'exaltation', author's translation from Monange, 'Mai 68 à Brest', 20.

136 'Il y avait des occupations d'usines, moins sans doute que dans d'autres régions, mais il y a eu des occupations particulières comme à Brest à la Thomson-CSF', author's translation from Le Roux, interview.

137 'Il y a même eu une réunion commune entre des étudiants littéraires et des représentants syndicaux de la Thomson (CSF)', author's translation from Monange, interview.

138 'La création des commissions ouvrières n'est qu'une première étape. Elle doit permettre aux travailleurs de vouloir aller plus loin dans la perspective de l'autogestion', author's translation from Centre CSF-Brest, 'Notre Combat' (1968), p. 2.

139 Delale and Ragache, *La France de 68*, p. 94.

140 'Mai 68 – Mai 78,' *Syndicalisme,* no. 1704 – 11 (1978), 16.

141 Vincent Porhel, (2000) 'L'Autogestion à la CSF de Brest', in Dreyfus-Armand, Frank, Lévy and Zancarini-Fournel, *Les Années 68*, pp. 379–97.

142 Dreyfus-Armand, Frank, Lévy and Zancarini-Fournel, *Les Années 68*, pp. 405–7.

143 '[U]n projet de réforme crédible', author's translation from Porhel, *Mai 68 au CLU de Brest*, p. 64.

144 Fanch Broudig, interview with author, Brest, 3 August 2004.

145 'Les représentants des différentes facs à ces assises avaient décidé de retenir comme projet de réflexion pour les assises ultérieures à Grenoble le projet brestois. Donc ça prouve que le travail qui avait été fait à Brest était quand même un travail sérieux', author's translation from Monange, interview.

146 See p. 90 for example.

147 In the vast majority of texts on 1968 that make any mention of Strasbourg it is generally only to highlight the role of the Situationnistes. For example, see Jacques Capdevielle and Henry Rey, *Dictionnaire de Mai 68* (Paris: Larousse, 2008), pp. 392–3.

148 '[V]ouloir attribuer aux Situationnistes Strasbourgeois une participation majeure [est] un jugement abusive, d'ailleurs très favorables aux spéculations les plus fantaisistes', author's translation from Amann, *Le Scandale de Strasbourg*, p. 140

149 '[U]n petit mouvement intellectuel, élitiste, dont l'on ne parlait que dans les salons, qui ne sont à l'origine de quoi que ce soit', author's translation from Philippe Breton, interview with author, Strasbourg, 4 July 2008.

150 For more details see Amann, *Le Scandale de Strasbourg*, pp. 138–50.

151 '[L]'étudiant n'a décidémment rien compris', author's translation from anonymous tract in 'Les événements de mai 68 à la faculté des lettres de Strasbourg', Documents légués aux archives par Marc Schweyer, Archives de la Ville, Strasbourg, Box 114 Z, no. 5, pièce 1.

152 'C'est un peu dommage du point de vue historique que de parler des Situationnistes, en 68 ils ne représentent rien du tout, ils se sont amusés, ils ont fait leur coup et sont passés à autre chose, c'est pratique au point de vue image, mais c'est historiquement faux', author's translation from Daniel Coche, interview with author, Strasbourg, 25 June 2008.

153 'Finalement les Situationnistes ont mis sur le mouvement de mai 68 une voile de folklore et on n'a pas du tout cherché ce qu'il y avait de sérieux et de profond dans le mouvement', author's translation from Foessel, interview.

154 'Des représentants de l'université de Strasbourg ont été reçus par M. Edgar Faure', *Dernières Nouvelles d'Alsace*, 6 September 1968.

155 'A certain égards, la Loi Faure, puis d'autres qui ont suivi, ont repris ces concepts', author's translation from *Les Dernières Nouvelles d'Alsace*, 18 May 2008, p. 10.

156 '[L]es gens ont plus tendance à regarder l'écume de mai 68 plutôt que le fond de ce qui se produisait à cette époque-là, les embruns plus que les vagues', author's translation from Monange, interview.

Conclusion 2008: 'liquidate', consolidate and innovate

1   Nicolas Sarkozy, speech at Bercy, 29 April 2007.

2   For example, Patrick Rotman, *Mai 68 raconté à ceux qui ne l'ont pas vécu* (Paris: Seuil, 2008); André Glucksmann, *Mai 68 expliqué à Nicolas Sarkozy* (Paris: Denoël, 2008); Collectif, *Mai 68, le pavé* (Paris: Fetjaine, 2007); Vasco Gasquet, *Affiches de Mai 68, l'intégrale* (Bruxelles: Aden, 2007); Julien Besançon, *Mai 68. Les murs ont la parole* (Paris: Sand, 2007); Maurice Grimaud, *Je ne suis pas né en mai 68* (Paris: Tallandier, 2007); Gérard Filoche, *Mai 68. Histoire sans fin. Liquider mai 68? Même pas en rêve* (Paris: Jean-Claude Gawswitch, 2007).

3   Daniel A. Gordon, 'Memories of 1968 in France: Reflections on the 40th Anniversary', in Ingo Cornilis and Sarah Waters (eds), *Memories of 1968: International Perspectives* (Bern: Peter Lang, 2010), pp. 49–78; Aude Lancelin, 'Trop de pavés pour les 40 ans: liquider le merchandising ?', *Le Nouvel Observateur*, 8–14 May 2008; 'Une profusion de livres pour les 40 ans de Mai 68,' *Le Monde*, 21 March 2008; Vérane Noël, 'Mai 68 énième' (*http://bibliobs.nouvelobs.com/20071016/1070/mai–68–eniem*).

4   The FNAC even dedicated a specific section of its website to the 68 anniversary (*http://www.fnac.com/magazine/themas_transversaux/68_court_toujours/*).

5   For example, 'Il y a quarante ans dans Le Monde,' *Le Monde*, 3–31 May 2008' (Each day of May 2008, *Le Monde* published their front page from May 1968); 'Dossier spécial: Quarante après. . . Vive 68,' *Libération*, 1 February 2008, pp. 1–10; 'Cahier spécial – 1968–2008, Quel héritage politique? Quarante ans après, que reste-t-il des engagements politiques de 68? Au–delà du mythe révolutionnaire, le rapport au pouvoir a–t–il changé?', *Libération*, 23–4 February 2008; 'Dossier: Mai 68 en héritage', *Le Monde des livres*, 21 March 2008, pp. 6–7; 'Numéro spécial. Quarante ans après, le Libé des étudiants', *Libération*, 21 March 2008 ; Alain Guyot, 'En 1968, il n'y avait pas que les manifs. . .', *Ouest-France* (Magazine), 22 March 2008; 'Mai 68 non, ce n'est pas fini. . .', *L'Humanité hors série*, April 2008; 'Dossier: Les Français et 68', *Le Nouvel Observateur*, 27 March–2 April, pp. 12–26; 'Spécial MAI 68', *Télérama* 3037, 29 March–4 April 2008, pp. 13–30; 'Cahier central Mai. L'héritage culturel', *Libération*, 19–20 April 2008; Eric Conan, 'Mai 68. Commémoration piège à cons!', *Marianne*, 575, 26 April–2 May 2008, pp. 66–71; 'Dossier: 40 ans après 68. La révolution réac*'*, *Le Monde de l'éducation*, 369, May 2008, pp. 24–48; 'Dossier spécial: Mai 68 raconté par nos lecteurs,' *Le Parisien*, 4 May 2008; 'Mai 68 L'Héritage', *Télérama hors série*, 2008. The above are but a small percentage of the number of articles and special editions published in the written press marking the fortieth anniversary. For a more through list see *http://www.mai–68.fr/bibli/index.php*.

6   Some of the television programmes include: *Droit d'Inventaire: MAI 68*, presented by Marie Drucker, France 3, 23 January 2008; *Comment sortir du «blabla» de Mai 68?*, presented by Frédéric Taddeï, France 3, 10 April 2008; *Faut-il interdire d'interdire?*, presented by Daniel Leconte, Arte, 15 April 2008; *Les Enfants de Mai 68*, Fabienne Servan Schreiber and Estelle Mauriac, France 5, 5–16 May 2008. Some of the films shown include: Chris Marker, *Le fond de l'air est rouge* (1977), Arte, 15 April 2008; Bernardo Bertolucci, *Les innocents* (2003), Arte, 17 April 2008; Romain Goupil, *Mourir à trente ans* (1982), Arte, 17 April 2008; Gérard Oury, *La Carapate* (1978), France 3, 1 May 2008. For a more complete list of May '68 coverage on television see *http://www.mai–68.fr/dossiers/dossiers.php?val=18_tv*.

7   Some examples of the coverage can be found at *http://www.mai–68.fr/dossiers/dossiers.php?val=21_radio*.

8   The following are just some examples of the innumerable academic conferences that took place to mark the fortieth anniversary: *Mai 68, le temps de l'histoire*, Bibliothèque publique d'information, Centre Georges Pompidou, 16 February 2008; *Georges Pompidou et Mai 1968*, L'association Georges Pompidou, l'Assemblée nationale, 14 March 2008; *40 ans après, «la pensée 68»: Deleuze et Guattari*, Université Paris 8, 15 March 2008; *Autour de l'ouvrage: Mai–Juin 68*, La Maison des Sciences de

l'Homme de Nantes, 20 March 2008; *La musique en Mai 68/Mai 68 dans la musique*, Conservatoire national de région de Paris, 2–4 April 2008; *Le PSU en mai 68*, L'Association des Amis de Tribune Socialiste, Paris – Mairie du 3ème, 9–10 May 2008; *La CGT de 1966 à 1984. L'empreinte de Mai 1968*, L'Institut d'histoire sociale de la CGT, L'IHS–CGT, 14–15 May 2008; *May '68 Forty Years On/Mai 68 Quarante Ans Après*, University of London in Paris (ULIP), 15–17 May 2008; *Mai 68 à l'épreuve des sciences sociales*, L'Institut de recherches de la FSU, La Sorbonne, 21 May 2008; *Le Mai 68 des historiens: entre identités narratives et histoire orale*, Collège de France, 23–4 October 2008.

9   For example, 'Autour de 68', *Le Mouvement Social*, 223, (April–June 2008), 3–40; 'Autour de 1968: années utopiques, années parasites?', *Esprit*, 344, May 2008; 'Dossier: L'Ombre portée de mai 68', *Vingtième Siècle*, 98 (2008–2); 'Mai 1968, quarante ans après', *Le Débat*, 149, (March–April 2008). Cf. also 'Dans les revues, regards savants et souvenirs', *Le Monde*, 16 May 2008.

10   *http://www.mai–68.fr/welcome/index.php*

11   Jean-Marc Manach, 'Internet; Et si le Web avait existé il y a quarante ans . . . en 1968', *Le Monde*, 11 May 2008.

12   'Internet; Une mémoire collective en ligne nourrie de récits individuels', *Le Monde*, 10 June 2008.

13   For example, he was a guest on the following television shows; *Des Mots*, France 2, 16 April 2008; *Ripostes*, France 3, 2 March 2008; *Droit d'inventaire*, France 2, 23 January 2008; *1968: Un monde en révolte*, France 3, 2 March 2008. His omnipresence on radio was matched by his prolific output on this fortieth anniversary. He wrote prefaces for a number of anniversary texts; for example, Alexandre Franc and Arnaud Bureau, *Mai 68, histoire d'un printemps* (Paris: Berg, 2008); Collectif, *Mai 68* (Paris: Denoël, 2008); Collectif, *Mai 68* (Paris: Lafon, 2008). He also put his name to two other texts: Daniel Cohn-Bendit, *Ah! Les beaux jours* (Paris: Radio France, 2008); Daniel Cohn-Bendit, *Forget 68* (Paris: Editions de l'Aube, 2008).

14   Marie-France Etchegoin and Sylvain Courage, 'Dossier. Un sondage CSA–«le Nouvel Observateur». Les Français votent 68', *Le Nouvel Observateur*, 2264, 27 March – 2 April, pp. 12–16. Another survey released for the 40th anniversary is assessed in Jerome Fourquet, 'L'Héritage de Mai 68', *L'Humanité des débats*, 22 March 2008. The complete survey is available at *http://www.csa-fr.com/dataset/ data2008/opi20080507-l-heritage-social-de-mai-1968.pdf*.

15   For example, one question asks respondents what images come to mind when they think of May '68. The options offered (with percentage results) were as follows: scenes of street battles (49 per cent); the occupied Sorbonne (29 per cent); Daniel Cohn-Bendit face to face with CRS officer (21 per cent); flowers on the barricades (19 per cent); the Renault strike at Boulogne-Billancourt (16 per cent); the counter-demonstration on the Champs-Elysées (15 per cent); Jean-Luc Godard organizing a meeting at Cannes (15 per cent). Other questions focus on the stereo-typical slogans, the clichéd consequences and the limited interpretations. Full details of results can be found at *http://www.csa-fr.com/dataset/data2008/ opi20080320-que-reste-il-de-mai-1968.htm*.

16   Almost three-quarters of respondents declared their opposition to Nicolas Sarkozy's 2007 Bercy speech and there was an overwhelmingly positive response as to the impact of May '68 generally (74 per cent) as well as in areas such as union rights, parent–children relations, social mores and politics.

17   Perhaps most indicative of this were the responses to the question that asked 'When you think of May '68, you think above all of . . .' with the options: a student revolt; modernization of social mores; a general strike. The fact that a student revolt remains the most popular option (40 per cent) and a general strike only received 25 per cent of responses highlights the impact of the narrow portrayal.

18   Glucksmann, *Mai 68 expliqué à Nicolas Sarkozy*, p. 31.

19   Rotman, *Mai 68 raconté*, pp. 9–11.

20   Filoche, *Mai 68. Histoire sans fin*, pp. 462–4.
21   Mathieu Grimpret and Chantal Delsol, *Liquider Mai 68?* (Paris: Presses de la Renaissance, 2008).
22   Alain Griotteray, *Mai 68. Des barricades ou des réformes* (Monaco: Alphée, 2008).
23   Régis Debray, *Mai 68 une contre-révolution réussie* (Paris: Mille et une nuits, 2008).
24   '[P]lutot gagné que perdu en actulaité', author's translation from ibid., p. 9.
25   Edgar Morin, Claude Lefort and Cornelius Castoriadis, *La Brèche: Suivi de vingt ans après* (Paris: Fayard, 2008).
26   Laurent Joffrin, *Mai 68, une histoire du mouvement* (Paris: Points, 2008).
27   Henri Weber, *Faut-il liquider? Essai sur les interprétations de mai 68* (Paris: Seuil, 2008).
28   Collectif, *Mai 68. Le Débat* (Paris: Gallimard, 2008).
29   G. Dreyfus-Armand, R. Frank, M.-F. Lévy and M. Zancarini-Fournel, *Les Années 68. Le temps de la contestation* (Brussels: Editions Complexe, 2008).
30   Christine Fauré, *Mai 68 jour et nuit* (Paris: Découvertes, 2008); Gérard Guégan and Jean-Franklin Narodetzki, *Mai 68 à l'usge des moins de vingt ans* (Paris: Actes Sud, 2008); Jacques Tarnero, *Mai 68, la révolution fiction* (Toulouse: Milan, 2008).
31   For example, Patrick Mahé, *68 nos années de choc* (Paris: Plon, 2008); Anne Dary, Pascale Le Thorel, Didier Semin and Serge July, *Les Affiches de mai 68* (Paris: ENSBA, 2008); Alexandre Franc and Arnaud Bureau, *Mai 68, histoire d'un printemps* (Paris: Berg, 2008); Laurence Godec, Philippe Tamic and Hossein Tengour, *Quiz Mai 68* (Paris: Hors Collection, 2008); Collectif, *Mai 68, le pavé*.
32   Rotman, *Mai 68 raconté*, pp. 111–13.
33   Giraud, *L'Accord secret de Baden-Baden*.
34   Ibid., pp. 489–526.
35   Ibid., pp. 527–38.
36   Benoît d'Aigullhon and José Lenzini, *Mai 68. Baden: La mort du Gaullisme* (Marseilles: Transborders, 2008).
37   Guests included Max Gallo, Daniel Cohn-Bendit, Edouard Balladur and Charles Fiterman.
38   Collectif, 'Mai 68 – Hors série', *Liaisons*, May 2008.
39   Régis Debray, 'Carte blanche; Hommage au préfet Grimaud', *Le Monde*, 9 May 2008.
40   Grimaud, *Je ne suis pas né en 68*.
41   Georges, Séguy, *Résister: De Mauthausen à Mai 68* (Paris: L'Archipel, 2008).
42   Ibid., p. 162.
43   For example Fournel's *Le Moment 68* provides an excellent overview of the challenges faced in trying to impose some interpretative model on 1968. Michelle Zancarini-Fournel, *Le Moment 68* (Paris: Seuil, 2008), pp. 19–97.
44   Olivier Ducastel and Jacques Martineau, *Nés en 68*, 2008.
45   Robert Gildea, 'Forty years on: French writing on 1968 in 2008', *French History*, 23 (1), 109.
46   Gisèle Lougart, *Pays Basque nord: Mai 68 en mémoires* (Bayonne: Elkar, 2008).
47   Pierre Robin, *Mai 68 en Lot-et-Garonne* (Narrosse: Albret, 2008).
48   Some examples include *Mai 68. Un printemps en Alsace*, Hors série, *L'Alsace*, February 2008; Breton newspapers *Ouest France* and *Le Télégramme* provided daily coverage with accompanying online dossiers – *http://www.letelegramme.com/ig/dossiers/mai68/mai–68–la–chronologie-30–12–2008–184906.php* / *http://www.ouest-france.fr/dossiers/Mai-68.php*; *La Provence* provided testimonies from local personalities such as the mayor of Marseilles, a theatre director and a writer of children's books on how they experienced the 1968 events in the region; *Bordeaux 68*, Supplément special, *Sud Ouest*, April 2008.
49   For example, *Les spectacles de 68*, Université Marc Bloch – Strasbourg 2, 24 April 2008; *L'intelligence d'une ville: Mai 68 à Lyon*, Bibliothèque de la Part-Dieu, Lyon, 26 April 2008; *Les quarante ans de Mai–Juin 68 en Seine-Maritime*, l'Institut CGT d'histoire sociale de la Seine-Maritime, Salle du département – Quai Jean Moulin

– Rouen, 20 May 2008; *Mai 68 à Besançon,* les Amis de la Maison du peuple, Faculté de lettres de Besançon, 29 May 2008; *Des salles de classe aux luttes sociales: Mai–juin 1968 dans les Cotes-du-Nord,* l'IUFM de Saint-Brieuc, 28 May 2008; *Mai–juin à Strasbourg et en Alsace,* Almémos, IEP Strasbourg, 21 June 2008. More examples can be found at *http://www.mai-68.fr/agenda/archives.php?val5=220_10.*

50 Some more national events with a focus on regional dimensions include: *Mai 68, ce n'est toujours qu'un début,* May–June 2008, *www.mai–68.org* (this collective organized an array of activities which included involvment in some regional activities); the conference *Le Mai 68 des historiens. Entre identittés narratives et histoire oral,* Collège de France, 23–4 October 2008 included a panel entitled 'Les facultés françaises. Panorama'; the seminar *Autour de Mai 68,* L'Association Café Sciences Humaines, 6 May 2008 included a paper by Serge Der Loughian, 'Mai 68 en Ardèche'; the conference *Mouvements étudiants: crises et mobilisations collectives, 1907–2008,* Université Blaise Pascal, Clermant Ferrand II, 13–14 November 2008 included two papers on May 1968 in Clermont-Ferrand; the conference *May '68 Forty Years On/ Mai 68 Quarante Ans Après,* University of London in Paris (ULIP), 15–17 May 2008, included a panel of four papers entitled 'Decentring May '68/Mai 68 dans les regions'.

51 INA, *Mai 68. Les images de la télévision,* 2008.

52 *Mai 68, esprit es-tu là?,* Karine Bonjour and Philippe Cahn, France 3 Sud, 2008; *Un si joli de mai,* Bertrand Delais, France 3 Normandie, 2008; *Mai 68 en Lorraine, Champagne-Ardenne,* Jean-Luc Marino, France 3 Lorraine, Champagne-Ardenne, 2008; *Mai 68 en Alsace,* Hubert Schilling, France 3 Alsace, 2008; *Mon mai 68,* Michel Marié, France 3 Rhône-Alpes, Auvergne, 2008; *L'autre Mai,* Jacques Vilemont, France 3 Ouest, 2008; *Mai 68. . .tu disais,* Gérard Miller, France 3 Paris Ile de France, Centre, 2008. Each film went out on 26 April 2008 at 4.20pm.

53 Dominique Damamme, Boris Gobille, Frédérique Matonti and Bernard Pudal, *Mai Juin 68* (Paris: Editions de l'Atelier/Editions Ouvrières, 2008). For example see Muriel Damon, 'Les transformations de la discipline dans un lycées de province, 1940–1970', chapter 4, pp. 75–88; Bernard Pudal and Jean-Noël Retière, 'Les grèves ouvrières de 68, un mouvement social sans lendemain mémoriel', chapter 13, pp. 207–21; Ivan Bruneau, 'Quand des paysans deviennent «soixante-huitards»', chapter 23, pp. 344–56.

54 Fournel, *Le Moment 68,* pp. 49–77.

55 Philippe Artières and Michelle Zancarini-Fournel, *68. Une histoire collective [1962– 1981]* (Paris: La Découverte, 2008). For example, see Michelle Zancarini-Fournel, 'Grenoble, un labaratoire d'experimentation sociale', pp. 18–24; Michelle Zancarini-Fournel, 'Sud-Aviation, Nantes: la première occupation de mai', pp. 326–31; Xavier Vigna, 'Lip et Larzac: Conflits locaux et mobilisations nationales', pp. 487–93; Vincent Porhel, 'Creys-Malville contre Plogoff: les nouveaux visages de la lutte antinucléaire', pp. 710–16.

56 Gordon, 'Memories of 1968 in France', p. 51.

57 For example, Ingo Cornilis and Sarah Waters (eds), *Memories of 1968;* Phillipe Gassert and Martin Klimke, '1968. Memories and Legacies of a Global Revolt', *Bulletin of the German Historical Institute,* Supplement 6 (2009); Patrick Dramé and Jean Lamarre, *1968. Des sociétés en crise: une perspective globale/Societies in Crisis: A Global Perspective* (Laval: Les Presses de l'Université de Laval, 2009); Martin Klimke and Joachim Scharloth, *1968 in Europe. A History of Activism, 1956–1977* (Hampshire: Palgrave Macmillan, 2008); Nora Farik, *1968 Revisited. 40 Years of Protest Movements* (Brussels: Heinrich Böll Foundation, 2008); Gerd-Rainer Horn, *The Spirit of '68: Rebellion in Western Europe and North America, 1956–76* (Oxford: OUP, 2007).

58 Geneviève Dreyfus-Armand, *Les Années 68. Un monde en mouvement. Nouveaux regards sur une histoire plurielle* (Paris: Syllepse, 2008).

59 For example, '1968. Revolutions', Hors-série, *Le Monde 2,* March–April 2008; 'Que reste-t-il de 68', *Courrier International,* 894–5, 20 December 2007–1 January 2008;

'Mai 68 dans le monde', Dossier Spéciale, *L'Histoire*, April 2008; '68, l'année qui a changé le monde', Numéro Spécial, *L'Express*, 2968, 1–7 May 2008, pp. 82–141.

60   *Mai 68: une contestation mondialisée*, Bibliothèque de documentation internationale contemporaine, Nanterre, 19–20 May 2008; *68 à travers le monde*, L'Université Paris 8 Vincennes – Saint–Denis, 27 May 2008; *Mai 68 en France et dans le Monde*, Siège du Parti Communiste Français, Paris, 13 May 2008; *1968 dans le monde*, CEDETIM, CERI Sciences-Po, 16 May 2008.

61   For example, *68 année zero*, Ruth Zylberman, Arte, 30 April 2008; *68*, Patrick Rotman, France 2, 8 April 2008; *1968, Un monde en révolte*, Michèle Dominici, France 3, 22 March 2008.

62   Artières and Fournel, *68. Une histoire collective*. See the four 'Ailleurs' sections; pp. 86–124; pp. 291–315; pp. 462– 86; pp. 693–709.

63   Boris Gobille, *Mai 68* (Paris: La Découverte, 2008), pp. 18–19.

64   Damamme, Gobille, Matonti, Pudal, *Mai–Juin 68*. See, for example, Romain Bertrand, 'Mai 68 et l'anticolonialisme', pp. 89–101; Isabelle Sommier, 'Les gauchismes', pp. 295–305.

65   Fournel, *Le moment 68*, pp. 185–223.

66   This broadening national/international perspective is discussed in 'Mai 68: aspects régionaux et internationaux', *Revue Dissidences*, 5 (October 2008).

67   For example, Ahmed Boubecker and Abdellali Hajjat, *Histoire politique des immigrations (post)coloniales. France, 1920–2008* (Paris: Editions Amsterdam, 2008).

68   Jean Raguenes, *De mai 68 à LIP – Un dominicain au cœur des luttes* (Paris: Karthala, 2008); Jean-Pierre Filiu, *Mai 68 à l'ORTF* (Paris: Nouveau Monde, 2008); Etienne Fouilloux, *Les chrétiens français entre guerre d'Algérie et mai 68* (Lyon: Paroles et Silence, 2008); Faouzi Mahjoub, Alain Leiblang, François-René Simon, *Les enragés du football, l'autre mai 68* (Paris: Calmann-Levy, 2008).

69   Nicolas Daum, *Mai 68 raconté par des anonymes* (Paris: Editions Amsterdam, 2008). It is worth noting that this is an updated version of a 1988 text by the same author, Nicolas Daum, *Des révolutionnaires dans un village parisien*.

70   For example, see Gobille, *Mai 68*, pp. 60–80; Catherine Simon, 'Les pied-rouges, hors de l'histoire officielle', in Artières and Fournel, *68. Une histoire collective*, pp. 158–64; Frédéric Bas, 'La «majorité silencieuse» ou la bataille de l'opinion en mai–juin 1968', in Artières and Fournel, *68. Une histoire collective*, pp. 359–65; Laurent Quéro, 'Les prisonniers enfin: de l'indifférence à l' «effet de souffle»', in Artières and Fournel, *68. Une histoire collective*, pp. 566–73; Jean-Louis Violeau, 'L'expérience 68, peinture et architecture entre effacements et disparitions', in Damamme, Gobille, Matonti and Pudal, *Mai–Juin 68*, pp. 222–33; Erik Neveu, 'Trajectoires de «soixante-huitards ordinaires»', in Damamme, Gobille, Matonti, Pudal, *Mai–Juin 68*, pp. 306–18.

71   Xavier Vigna, *L'Insubordination ouvrière dans les années 68* (Rennes: Presses Universitaire de Rennes, 2007).

72   Vincent Porhel, *Ouvriers Bretons. Conflits d'usines, conflits identitaires en Bretagne dans les années 68* (Rennes: Presses Universitaire de Rennes, 2008).

73   Some significant 2008 studies continued in this trend. For example, Jean-François Sirinelli, *Mai 68. L'événement Janus* (Paris: Fayard, 2008).

74   See, for example, Boris Gobille, *Mai 68.*; Artières and Fornel, *68. Une histoire collective*; Damamme, Gobille, Matonti, Pudal, *Mai–Juin 68*; Fournel, *Le Moment 68*; Lutte Ouvrière, *Mai–Juin 68. Histoire et leçons d'une explosion sociale* (Paris: Lutte ouvrière, 2008); François de Massot, *La grève générale. Mai–juin 1968* (Paris: L'Harmattan, 2008); Mouvement Communiste, *Mai juin 1968: une occasion manquée par l'autonomie ouvrière* (Bruxelles: Mouvement Communiste, 2007); Gérard Alezard, 'La CGT et les étudiants à Paris en mai–juin 1968', *L'Humanité*, 11 July 2008; Michel Simon, 'Mai–juin 1968, deux mois de luttes de classes en France', *La Pensée*, 356, October–December 2008.

75 Porhel, *Ouvriers Bretons*; Vigna, *L'Insubordination ouvrière*; Artières and Fournel, *68. Une histoire collective*; Fournel, *Le Moment 68*; Gobille, *Mai 68*; Damamme, Gobille, Matonti and Pudal, *Mai–Juin 68*; Dreyfus-Armand, *Les Années 68*; Dreyfus-Armand, Frank, Lévy and Zancarini-Fournel, *Les Années 68*; Antoine Artous, Didier Epsztajn and Patrick Silberstein, *La France des années 1968* (Paris: Syllepse, 2008); Sébastien Layerle, Sylvie Dreyfus-Alphandéry and Manée Teyssandier, *Les Années 68 au cinema* (Paris: Autour du 1er mai, 2008); Patrick and Charlotte Rotman, *Les années 68* (Paris: Seuil, 2008).

76 As well as his controversial National History Museum remarks, Sarkozy has been heavily criticized for his 2007 intervention on the legacy of colonialism and his 2008 suggestion that every French school child should adopt a Jewish child victim.

77 Ross, *May '68 and its Afterlives*, p. 5.

78 Ibid., p. 157.

79 Ibid., p. 6.

80 Daniel A. Gordon, 'History at last? 1968–2008', *Modern and Contemporary France*, 17(3) (2009), p. 336.

81 Wertsch, *Voices of Collective Remembering*, p. 39.

Bibliography

Books

d'Aigullhon, Benoît and Lenzini, José, *Mai 68. Baden: La mort du Gaullisme* (Marseilles: Transborders, 2008).

Agulhon, Maurice, Nouschi, André and Schor, Ralph, *La France de 1940 à nos jours* (Paris: Nathan/HER, 2001).

Aron, Raymond, *La Révolution introuvable* (Paris: Fayard, 1968).

Artières, Philippe and Zancarini-Fournel, Michelle, *68. Une histoire collective [1962–1981]* (Paris: La Découverte, 2008).

Artous, Antoine (ed.), *Retours sur Mai* (Montreuil: La Brèche-PEC, 1988).

Artous, Antoine, Epsztajn, Didier and Silberstein, Patrick, *La France des années 1968* (Paris : Syllepse, 2008).

Astoux, André, *1978. Ondes de choc. Mai 68 à l'ORTF* (Paris: Plon, 1978).

Auron, Yair, *Les Juifs d'extrême gauche en mai 68* (Paris: Albin Michel, 1998).

Balladur, Edouard, *L'Arbre de mai* (Paris: Atelier Marcel Jullian, 1979).

Barjonet, André, *La CGT, Histoire, Structure, Doctrine* (Paris: Seuil, 1968).

—— *La révolution trahie de 1968* (Paris: John Didier, 1968).

Barrau, Grégory, *Le Mai 68 des Catholiques* (Paris: Editions de l'Atelier/Editions Ouvrières, 1998).

Baynac, Jacques, *Mai retrouvé. Contribution à l'histoire du mouvement révolutionnaire du 3 mai au 16 juin 1968* (Paris: Seuil, 1978).

Bensaid, Daniel and Weber, Henri, *Mai 1968: Une répétition générale* (Paris: Maspéro, 1968).

Bertolino, Jean, *Les Trublions* (Paris: Stock, 1969).

Besançon, Julien, *Mai 68. Les murs ont la parole* (Paris: Sand, 2007).

Blanchard, Pascale and Veyrat-Masson, Isabelle, *Les Guerres de Mémoires. La France et son Histoire* (Paris: La Découverte, 2008).

Bodnar, John, *Remaking America: Public Memory, Commemoration and Patriotism in the Twentieth Century* (Princeton NJ: Princeton University Press, 1992).

Boubecker, Ahmed and Hajjat, Abdellali, *Histoire politique des immigrations (post)coloniales. France, 1920–2008* (Paris: Editions Amsterdam, 2008).

Bourricaud, François, *Universités à la dérive. France, Etats-Unis, Amérique du Sud* (Paris: Stock, 1971).

Brown, Bernard E., *Protest in Paris: Anatomy of a Revolt* (Morristown, NJ: General Learning Press, 1974).

Caveau, André, *De l'autre coté de la barricade* (Paris: Simoen, 1968).

Capdevielle, Jacques and Mouriaux, René, *Mai 68 – L'Entre-deux de la modernité. Histoire de trente ans* (Paris: Presses de la Fondation Nationale des Sciences Politiques, 1988).

Capdevielle, Jacques and Rey, Henry, *Dictionnaire de Mai 68* (Paris: Larousse, 2008).

Caute, David, *Sixty-Eight: The Year of the Barricades* (London: Hamish Hamilton, 1988).

Chaffard, Georges, *Les Orages de mai* (Paris: Calmann-Lévy, 1968).

Club Jean Moulin, *Que faire de la révolution de mai?* (Paris: Seuil, 1968).

Cohen, Habia S., *Elusive Reform: The French Universities, 1968–1978* (Boulder, CO: Westview Press, 1978).

Cohn-Bendit, Daniel, *Le Gauchisme, remède à la maladie sénile du communisme* (Paris: Seuil, 1968).

—— *Nous l'avons tant aimé la révolution* (Paris: Bernard Barrault, 1988).

—— *Le Grand Bazar* (Paris: Pierre Belfond, 1975).

—— *Ah! Les beaux jours* (Paris: Radio France, 2008).

—— *Forget 68* (Paris: Editions de l'Aube, 2008).

Collectif, *Mai 68* (Paris: Denoël, 2008).

Collectif, *Mai 68. Le Débat* (Paris: Gallimard, 2008).

Collectif, *Mai 68* (Paris: Lafon, 2008).

Collectif, *Mai 68, le pavé* (Paris: Fetjaine, 2007).

Cubitt, Geoffrey, *History and Memory* (Manchester: Manchester University Press, 2007).

Corbin, Alain and Mayeur, Jean-Marie *La Barricade* (Paris: Publications de la Sorbonne, 1998).

Cornilis, Ingo and Waters, Sarah (eds), *Memories of 1968: International Perspectives* (Bern: Peter Lang, 2010).

Cusset, François, *Contre-discours de mai. Ce qu'embaumeurs et fossoyeurs de 68 ne disent pas à ses héritiers* (Paris: Actes Sud, 2008).

Damamme, Dominique, Gobille, Boris, Matonti, Frédérique and Pudal, Bernard, *Mai–Juin 68* (Paris: Editions de l'Atelier/Editions Ouvrières, 2008).

Dansette, Adrien, *Mai 1968* (Paris: Plon, 1971).

Dary, Anne, Le Thorel, Pascale, Semin, Didier and July, Serge, *Les Affiches de mai 68* (Paris: ENSBA, 2008).

Daum, Nicolas, *Des révolutionnaires dans un village parisien. Mai 68 vingt ans après* (Paris: Londreys, 1988).

—— *Mai 68 raconté par des anonymes* (Paris: Editions Amsterdam, 2008).

Debray, Régis, *Modeste contribution aux discours et cérémonies officielles du dixième anniversaire* (Paris: Maspero, 1978).

—— *Mai 68 une contre-révolution réussie* (Paris: Mille et une nuits, 2008).

de Certeau, Michel, *La Prise de parole et autres écrits politiques* (Paris: Seuil, 1994).

—— *La prise de parole* (Paris: Desclée de Brouwer, 1968).

Delale, Alain and Ragache, Gilles, *La France de 68* (Paris: Seuil, 1978).

Dramé, Patrick and Lamarre, Jean, *1968. Des sociétés en crise: une perspective globale/ Societies in Crisis: A Global Perspective* (Laval: Les Presses de l'Université de Laval, 2009).

Dreyfus-Armand, Geneviève, *Les Années 68. Un monde en mouvement. Nouveaux regards sur une histoire plurielle* (Paris: Syllepse, 2008).

Dreyfus-Armand, G., Frank, R., Lévy, M.-F. and Zancarini-Fournel M., *Les Années 68: Le temps de la Contestation* (Paris: Complexe, 2000).

—— *Les Années 68. Le temps de la contestation* (Brussels: Editions Complexe, 2008).

Duteuil, Jean-Pierre, *Nanterre. 1965–66–67–68. Vers le mouvement du 22 mars* (Mauléon: Acratie, 1988).

Epistémon (Anzieu, Didier), *Ces idées qui ont ébranlé la France. Nanterre, novembre 1967–juin 1968* (Paris: Fayard, 1969).

Farik, Nora, *1968 Revisited: 40 Years of Protest Movements* (Brussels: Heinrich Böll Foundation, 2008).

Faure, Edgar, *Philosophie d'une réforme* (Paris: Plon, 1969).

Fauré, Christine, *Mai 68 jour et nuit* (Paris: Gallimard, 1998).

—— *Mai 68 jour et nuit* (Paris: Découvertes, 2008).

Favereau, Francis, *Bretagne contemporaine. Langue, culture, identité* (Morlaix: Embannadurioù Skol Vreizh, 1993).

Ferry, Luc and Renaut, Alain, *La Pensée 68. Essai sur l'anti-humanisme contemporain* (Paris: Gallimard, 1988).

—— *La Pensée 68* (Paris, Gallimard, 1998).

Feuerstein, Pierre, *Printemps de révolté à Strasbourg, Mai–Juin 1968* (Strasbourg: Saisons d'Alsace, 1968).

Filiu, Jean-Pierre, *Mai 68 à l'ORTF* (Paris: Nouveau Monde, 2008).

Filoche, Gérard, *68–98: histoire sans fin* (Paris: Flammarion, 1998).

—— *Mai 68. Histoire sans fin. Liquider mai 68? Même pas en rêve* (Paris: Jean-Claude Gawswitch, 2007).

Fischer, Didier, *L'Histoire des étudiants de 1945 à nos jours* (Saint-Amand-Montrond: Flammarion, 2000).

Foccart, Jacques, *Le Général en Mai: Journal de l'Elysée – II. 1968–1969* (Paris: Fayard/ Jeune Afrique, 1998).

Fohlen, Claude, *Mai 1968: Révolution ou psychodrame?* (Paris: Presses Universitaires de France, 1973).

Fouilloux, Etienne, *Les chrétiens français entre guerre d'Algérie et mai 68* (Lyon: Paroles et Silence, 2008).

Franc, Alexandre and Bureau, Arnaud, *Mai 68, histoire d'un printemps* (Paris: Berg, 2008).

Galland, Olivier and Oberti, Marco, *Les Etudiants* (Paris: La Découverte, 1996).

Gallant, Mavis, *Chroniques de Mai 68* (Paris: Editions Tièrce, 1988).

—— *Chroniques de Mai 68* (Paris: Rivages, 1998).

Gasquet, Vasco, *Affiches de Mai 68, l'intégrale* (Bruxelles: Aden, 2007).

Geismar, Alain, July, Serge and Moran, Erlyn, *Vers la guerre civile* (Paris: Editions et Publications Premières, 1969).

Gildea, Robert, *The Past in French History* (London, New Haven: Yale University Press, 1994).

Giraud, Henri-Christain, *L'Accord secret de Baden-Baden. Comment de Gaulle et les soviétiques on mis fin à mai 68* (Paris: Rocher, 2008).

Glucksmann, André, *Mai 68 expliqué à Nicolas Sarkozy* (Paris: Denoël, 2008).

Gobille, Boris, *Mai 68* (Paris: La Découverte, 2008).

Godec, Laurence, Tamic, Philippe and Tengour, Hossein, *Quiz Mai 68* (Paris: Hors Collection, 2008).

Goetz, François, *Mai 68, une imposture qui nous a coûté cher* (Paris: Editic, 1993).

Gomez, Michel, *Mai 68 au jour le jour* (Paris: L'Esprit frappeur, 1998).

Grappin, Pierre, *L'Ile aux peupliers. De la Résistance à Mai 68. Souvenirs du doyen de Nanterre* (Nancy: PUN, 1988).

Gretton, John, *Students and Workers: An Analytical Account of Dissent in France May–June 1968* (London: Macdonald, 1969).

Grimaud, Maurice, *En Mai fais ce qu'il te plait* (Paris: Stock, 1977).

—— *Je ne suis pas né en mai 68* (Paris: Tallandier, 2007).

Grimpret, Mathieu and Delsol, Chantal, *Liquider Mai 68?* (Paris: Presses de la Renaissance, 2008).

Griotteray, Alain, *Des Barricades ou des réformes* (Paris: Fayard, 1968).

—— *Mai 68. Des barricades ou des réformes* (Monaco: Alphée, 2008).

Guégan, Gérard, *Mai 68 à l'usage des moins de vingt ans* (Paris: Actes Sud, 1998).

—— *Mai 68 à l'usage des moins de vingt ans* (Paris: Actes Sud, 2008).

Guillebaud, Jean-Claude, *Les Années orphelines 1968–1978* (Paris: Seuil, 1978).

Haas, Jean-Paul, *La Révolution inutile* (Strasbourg: Oberlin, 1987).

Halbwachs, Maurice, *La Mémoire Collective* (Paris: Presses universitaire de France, 1950).

—— *Les Cadres Sociaux de la Mémoire* (Paris: Alcan, 1925).

Halbwachs, Maurice and Coser, Lewis A., *On Collective Memory* (Chicago: University of Chicago Press, 1992).

Halls, W. D., *Education, Culture and Politics in Modern France* (Oxford: Pergamon, 1976).

Hamon, Hervé and Rotman, Patrick, *Génération. 1. Les Années de rêve* (Paris: Seuil, 1987).

—— *Génération. 2. Les Années de poudre* (Paris: Seuil, 1988).

Hanley, D. L. and Kerr, A. P., *May '68: Coming of Age* (London: Macmillan, 1989).

Horn, Gerd-Rainer, *The Spirit of '68: Rebellion in Western Europe and North America, 1956–76* (Oxford: OUP, 2007).

Joffrin, Laurent, *Mai '68: Histoire des événements* (Paris: Seuil, 1988).

—— *Mai 68, une histoire du mouvement* (Paris: Points, 2008).

Johnson, Richard, *The French Communist Party Versus the Students: Revolutionary Politics in May–June 1968* (Yale: Yale University Press, 1972).

Klein, Pierre, *L'Alsace inachevée* (Colmar: Jérôme, 2004).

Klimke, Martin and Scharloth, Joachim, *1968 in Europe. A History of Activism, 1956–1977* (Hampshire: Palgrave Macmillan, 2008).

Krivine, Alain and Bensaid, Daniel, *Mai si! 1968–1988, rebelles et repentis* (Paris: La Breche, 1988).

Labro, Philippe, *Les Barricades de mai* (Paris: Seuil, 1968).

Lavabre, M.-C. and Rey, H., *Les Mouvements de 1968* (Firenze: Casterman, 1998).

Layerle, Sébastien, Dreyfus-Alphandéry, Sylvie, Teyssandier, Manée, *Les Années 68 au cinema* (Paris: Autour du 1er mai, 2008).

le Dantec, Jean-Pierre, *Les Dangers du soleil* (Paris: Les Presses d'aujourd'hui, 1978).

Lefebvre, Henri, *Mai 68 – L'Irruption. . .* (Paris: Syllepse, 1998).

le Goff, Jean-Pierre, *Mai 68, l'héritage impossible* (Paris: La Découverte, 1998).

le Madec, François, *L'Aubépine de mai. Chronique d'une usine occupée. Sud-Aviation, Nantes 1968* (Nantes: CDMOT, 1988).

Lepavé, Pierre Sorbon, *Le Journal insolite de Mai 68* (Paris: Raymond Castells, 1998).

Lindenberg, Daniel, *Le rappel à l'ordre. Enquête sur les nouveaux réactionnaires* (Paris: Seuil, 2002).

Linhart, Robert, *L'Etabli* (Paris: Minuit, 1978).

Lipovetsky, Gilles, *L'Ere du vide. Essais sur l'individualisme contemporain* (Paris: Gallimard, 1983).

Livet, Georges, *50 années à l'université de Strasbourg* (Strasbourg: Société Savante d'Alsace, 1998).

Lougart, Gisèle, *Pays Basque nord: Mai 68 en mémoires* (Bayonne: Elkar, 2008).

Lutte Ouvrière, *Mai–Juin 68. Histoire et leçons d'une explosion sociale* (Paris: Lutte ouvrière, 2008).

Mahé, Patrick, *68 nos années de choc* (Paris: Plon, 2008).

Mahjoub, Faouzi , Leiblang, Alain and Simon, François-René, *Les enragés du football, l'autre mai 68* (Paris: Calmann-Levy, 2008).

Marcellin, Raymond, *L'ordre public et les groupes révolutionnaires* (Paris: Plon, 1969).

—— *L'importune vérité. Dix ans après Mai 68, un ministre de l'intérieur parle* (Paris: Plon, 1978).

Martelli, Roger, *Mai 68* (Paris: Messidor, 1988).

de Massot, François, *La grève générale. Mai–juin 1968* (Paris: L'Harmattan, 2008).

Massu, Général, *Baden 68. Souvenirs d'une fidélité gaulliste* (Paris: Plon, 1983).

Merle, Robert, *Derrière la vitre* (Paris: Gallimard, 1970).

Meyer, Philippe, *Histoire de l'Alsace* (Paris: Perrin, 2008).

McCormack, Jo, *Collective Memory. France and the Algerian War (1954–1962)* (Maryland: Lexington, 2007).

McCormack, Jo, Pratt, Murray and Rolls, Alistair, *Hexagonal Variations. Diversity, Plurality and Reinvention in Contemporary France* (Amsterdam/New York: Rodopi, 2011).

Morin, Edgar, Lefort, Claude and Coudray, Jean-Marc, *Mai 1968: La Brèche, Premières réflexions sur les événements* (Paris: Fayard, 1968).

—— *La Brèche: Suivi de vingt ans après* (Paris: Fayard, 2008).

Mouvement Communiste, *Mai juin 1968: une occasion manquée par l'autonomie ouvrière* (Brussels: Mouvement Communiste, 2007).

Mouvement du 22 mars, *Ce n'est qu'un début; continuons le combat* (Paris: Maspéro, 1968).

Muller, Jan-Werner, *Memory and Power in Post-War Europe: Studies in the Presence of the Past* (Cambridge: Cambridge University Press, 2002).

Musselin, Christine, *La longue marche des universités françaises* (Paris: PUF, 2001).

Nora, Pierre, *Les Lieux de mémoire. 1, La République* (Paris: Gallimard, 1984).

—— *Les Lieux de mémoire. 2, La Nation* (Paris: Gallimard, 1986).

—— *Les Lieux de mémoire. 3, Les France* (Paris: Gallimard, 1992).

—— *Realms of Memory: The Construction of the French Past* (New York: Columbia University Press, 1998).

Phillips, Kendall R., *Framing Public Memory* (Alabama: University of Alabama Press, 2004).

Phlipponneau, Michel, *Debout Bretagne* (St Brieuc: Presses Universitaires de Bretagne, 1970).

Poisson, Henri and le Matt, Jean-Pierre, *Histoire de la Bretagne* (Nantes: COOP Breizh, 2000).

Pompidou, Georges, *Pour rétablir une vérité* (Paris: Flammarion, 1982).

Ponteil, Felix, *Histoire de l'enseignement en France. Les grandes étapes 1789–1964* (Paris: Sirey, 1966).

Poussier, Jean-Luc, *Bretagne* (Paris: Lec, 1997).

Porhel, Vincent, *Ouvriers Bretons. Conflits d'usines, conflits identitaires en Bretagne dans les années 68* (Rennes: Presses Universitaire de Rennes, 2008).

Prost, Antoine, *Histoire générale. L'Enseignement et l'éducation en France. L'Ecole et la famille dans une société en mutation, 1930–1980* (Paris: Nouvelle Librairie de France, 1981).

Raguenes, Jean, *De mai 68 à LIP – Un dominicain au cœur des luttes* (Paris: Karthala, 2008).

Rajfus, Maurice, *Mai 1968. Sous les pavés la répression* (Paris: Le cherche midi éditeur, 1998).

Reader, Keith A., *The May 1968 Events in France: Reproductions and Interpretations* (London: Macmillan Press, 1993).

Renaut, Alain, *Que faire des universités?* (Paris: Bayard, 2002).

Ritter, Jean, *L'Alsace* (Paris: PUF, 1985).

Robin, Pierre, *Mai 68 en Lot-et-Garonne* (Narrosse: Albret, 2008).

Ross, Kristin, *May '68 and its Afterlives* (Chicago: University of Chicago Press, 2002).

Rotman, Patrick, *Mai 68 raconté à ceux qui ne l'ont pas vécu* (Paris: Seuil, 2008).

Rotman, Patrick and Charlotte, *Les années 68* (Paris: Seuil, 2008).

Rousso, Henry, *Le Syndrome de Vichy* (Paris: Seuil, 1987).

Sainclivier, Jacqueline, *La Bretagne de 1939 à nos jours* (Rennes: Editions Ouest France, 1989).

Salmon, Jean-Marc, *Hôtel de l'avenir* (Paris: Presses d'aujourd'hui, 1978).

Sauvageot, J., Geismar, A., Cohn-Bendit, D., Duteuil, J.-P., *La Révolte étudiante* (Paris: Seuil, 1968).

Schnapp, Alain and Vidal-Naquet, Pierre, *Journal de la commune étudiante – textes et documents: novembre 1967–juin 1968* (Paris: Seuil, 1969).

Séguy, Georges, *Résister: De Mauthausen à Mai 68* (Paris: L'Archipel, 2008).

Servan-Schreiber, Jean-Jacques, *Le Réveil de la France* (Paris: Denoël, 1968).

Singer, Daniel, *Prelude to a Revolution* (London: Jonathan Cape, 1970).

Sirinelli, Jean-François, *Mai 68. L'événement Janus* (Paris: Fayard, 2008).

Skol Vreizh, *La Bretagne au XX siècle. Histoire de la Bretagne et des pays celtiques de 1914 à nos jours,* (Morlaix: Skol Vreizh, 1983).

Sur, Jean, *68 Forever* (Paris: Arléa, 1998).

Syndicat Métaux Brest, 'Mai 1968 – CSF Brest' (Summary of the CSF strike and occupation in 1968 compiled in weeks following the events by those involved), 1968.

Tarnero, Jacques, *Mai 68, la Révolution fiction* (Toulouse: Milano, 1998).

—— *Mai 68, la révolution fiction* (Toulouse: Milan, 2008).

Tartakowsky, Danielle, *Le Pouvoir est dans la rue* (Paris: Aubier, 1998).

Touraine, Alain, *Le Mouvement de mai ou le communisme utopique* (Paris: Seuil, 1968).

UNEF/SNESup, *Le Livre noir des journées de mai* (Paris: Seuil, 1968).

Vigna, Xavier, *L'Insubordination ouvrière dans les années 68* (Rennes: Presses Universitaire de Rennes, 2007).

Vogler, Bernard, *Histoire politique de l'Alsace. De la Révolution à nos jours, un panorama des passions alsaciennes* (Strasbourg: La Nuée Bleue, 1995).

—— *Histoire culturelle de l'Alsace. Du Moyen Age à nos jours, les très riches heures d'une région frontière* (Strasbourg: La Nuée Bleue, 1993).

Weber, Henri, *Que reste-t-il de mai 68? Essai sur les interprétations des «événements»* (Paris: Seuil, 1988).

—— *Que reste-t-il de mai 68? Essai sur les interprétations des «événements»* (Paris: Seuil, 1998).

—— *Faut-il liquider? Essai sur les interprétations de mai 68* (Paris: Seuil, 2008).

Wertsch, James V., *Voices of Collective Remembering* (New York: Cambridge University Press, 2002).
Winock, Michel, *La Fièvre hexagonale: les grandes crises politiques 1871–1968* (Paris: Seuil, 1995).
Yerushalmi, Yosef, *Zakhor: Jewish History and Jewish Memory* (London: University of Washington Press, 1982).
Young, James E., *Holocaust, Memorials and Meaning* (Yale: Yale University Press, 1994).
Zancarini-Fournel, Michelle, *Le Moment 68* (Paris: Seuil, 2008).

Journal articles/book chapters

Ackner, Agnès, 'Révolte de mai 1968', *Encyclopédie de l'Alsace* (Strasbourg: Publitotal, 1982).
Ardent, Philippe and Duhamel, Olivier, 'Mai 68', *Pouvoirs*, 39 (1986).
Assman, Jan, 'Collective memory and cultural identity', *New German Critique*, 65 (1995), 125–33.
Aubert, Gireg and Sonocinski, Aurélie, '1945–2004: le regain du régionalisme', *News d'ill*, 75 (February 2004), 14–15.
Bédarida, François, 'Le Temps présent et l'historiographie contemporaine', *Vingtième Siècle*, 69 (2001), 153–60.
Bénéton, Philippe and Touchard, Jean, 'Les interprétations de la crise de mai–juin 1968', *Revue française de science politique*, 10 (3) (1970), 503–43.
Boudon, Raymond, 'The French university since 1968', *Comparative Politics,* 10 (1) (1977), 89–119.
Bousquet, Gilles, 'Où en est-on de mai 68?', *Contemporary French Civilisation,* 1 (1992), 68–89.
Brandt, Joan, 'The legacy of May '68 in the era of consensus', *L'Esprit créateur*, XLI (1) (2001), 3–7.
Brunel, Claude, 'En Bretagne, l'Escalade de la violence', *Lectures pour tous. Je sais tout*, Numéro spécial, 'Pourquoi cette révolte? Mensuel', 174 (July 1968), 84–9.
Cohen, Yolande and Weill, Claudie, 'Les Mouvements étudiants: une histoire en miettes?', *Le Mouvement social*, 120 (1982), 3–10.
Démerin, Patrick, 'Mai 68–Mai 88. Choses tues', *Le Débat*, 51 (1988), 173–8.
Gassert, Phillipe and Klimke, Martin, '1968. Memories and legacies of a global revolt', *Bulletin of the German Historical Institute*, Supplement 6 (2009).
Gedi, Noa and Elam, Yigal, 'Collective memory – what is it?', *History and Memory*, 8 (1996), 30–50.
Gildea, Robert, 'Forty years on: French writing on 1968 in 2008', *French History*, 23 (1), 108–19.
Gordon, Daniel A., 'From May to October: reassessing the 1968 generation', *Modern and Contemporary France*, 13 (2) (2005), 229–33.
—— 'History at last? 1968–2008', *Modern and Contemporary France*, 17 (3) (2009), 335–42.
Journès, Claude, 'Les interprétations communistes de Mai 68', *Pouvoirs*, 39 (1986), 25–35.
Klein, Kerwin Lee, 'On the emergence of memory in historical discourse', *Representations*, 69 (2000), 127–50.
Lalieu, Olivier, 'L'Invention du «Devoir de Mémoire»', *Vingtième Siècle*, 69 (2001), 83–94.
Lavabre, Marie-Claire, 'Usages du passé, usages de la mémoire', *Revue Française de science politique*, 3 (1994), 480–93.
Le Roux, Jean, 'Mai 1968 et les étudiants de Brest', *En Avant*, 317 (1968), 36.
Lindenberg, Daniel, 'Un anniversaire interminable: 1968–1988', *L'Esprit*, 136–7 (1988), 189–97.
Monange, Edmond, 'Mai 68 à Brest', *Les Cahiers de l'Iroise*, 176 (1998), 11–21.

Musselin, Christine, 'Etat, université: la fin du modèle centralisé?', *Esprit,* 7 (1997), 18–29.

Narot, Jean-Franklin, 'Mai 68 raconté aux enfants. Contribution à la critique de l'inintelligence organisée', *Le Débat,* 51 (1988), 179–92.

Nora, Pierre, 'Between memory and history: les lieux de mémoire', *Representations,* 26 (1989), 7–24.

Olick, Jeffrey K., 'Genre memories and memory genres: a dialogical analysis of May 8, 1945 commemorations in the Federal Republic of Germany', *American Sociological Review,* 64 (3) (1999), 381–402.

Olivier-Utard, Françoise, 'Les «événements» de mai 68 en Alsace', *Almémos,* 12 (2008), 2–5.

O'Shaughnessy, Martin, 'Post 1995 French cinema: return of the social, return of the political', *Modern and Contemporary France,* 11(2) (2003), 189–203.

Passerini, Luisa, 'Peut-on donner de 1968 une histoire à la première personne?', *Le Mouvement social,* 143 (1988), 3–10.

Prost, Antoine, 'Quoi de neuf sur le Mai français?', *Le Mouvement social,* 143 (1988), 91–7.

—— '1968: mort et naissance de l'université française', *Vingtième Siècle,* 23 (1989), 59–70.

Quintin, P., 'De l'exode rural à la rurbanisation: les mouvements de population active dans l'Ouest entre 1962 et 1990', *INSEE,* 75, 1998.

Reader, Keith, 'Joyeux anniversaire! The May 68 industry', *Modern and Contemporary France,* 8 (2) (2000), 249–52.

Reynolds, Chris, 'May–June 1968: reflector and vector of a nation's diversity – the case of Strasbourg, Alsace', in Jo McCormack, Murray Pratt, Alistair Rolls, *Hexagonal Variations: Diversity, Plurality and Reinvention in Contemporary France* (Amsterdam/New York: Rodopi, 2011), pp. 275–97.

—— 'May '68 and the one-dimensional state', *PhaenEx,* 4 (2) (2009), 60–77.

—— May 68: A Contested History, *Sens public, http://www.sens-public.org/spip. php?article472,* 26 October 2007.

Rioux, Jean-Pierre, 'A propos des célébrations décennales du mai français', *Vingtième Siècle,* 23 (1991), 49–58.

Schwartz, Barry, 'The social context of commemoration: a study in collective memory', *Social Forces,* 61 (2) (1982), 374–402.

Simon, Michel, 'Mai–juin 1968, deux mois de luttes de classes en France', *La Pensée,* 356 (October–December 2008), 2–9.

Sommier, Isabelle, 'Mai 68: sous les pavés d'une page officielle', *Sociétés Contemporaines,* 20 (1994), 63–82.

Strauss, Léon and Richiez, Jean-Claude, 'Le Mouvement social de mai 1968 en Alsace: décalages et développements inégaux', *Revue des sciences sociales de la France de l'Est,* 17 (1989–90), 117–53.

Tarrow, Sidney, 'Social protest and policy reform. May 1968 and the *Loi d'Orientation* in France', *Comparative Political Studies,* 25 (4) (1993), 579–607.

Vigne, Eric, 'Des générations 68?', *Le Débat,'* 51 (1988), 157–60.

No author name provided

'Mai 68–Mai 78', *Syndicalisme,* 1704 (11 May 1978).

'Colloque sur mai 68', *Le Peuple,* 1704 (1–15 July 1978).

'De Strasbourg, Lettrisme et Sitautionnisme hier et aujourd'hui', *Cahiers/Chroniques,* 3, Université de Strasbourg, 61–3.

'10 jours qui ébranlèrent Strasbourg ou l'internationale situationniste se donne en spectacle', *Gros sel,* 8 (1968), 56.

'Le mai de Strasbourg. Chronologie des mouvements étudiants qui se manifestent à Strasbourg en particulier durant le mois de mai et juin 1968', *Bulletin d'information,* Université de Strasbourg, 15 (1968), 118–24.

'Mai 68 – Mai 78', *Syndicalisme*, no. 1704–11 (1978).
'Autour de 68', *Le Mouvement Social*, no. 223 (April–June 2008), 3.
'Autour de 1968: années utopiques, années parasites?', *Esprit*, no. 344 (May 2008).
'Dossier: L'Ombre portée de mai 68,' *Vingtième Siècle*, 98 (2008).
'Mai 1968, quarante ans après', *Le Débat*, 149, (March–April 2008).
'Mai 68: aspects régionaux et internationaux', *Revue Dissidences*, 5 (October 2008).

School books

Aledebert, J., *Histoire, Terminales. Aujourd'hui le Monde* (Paris: Delagrave, 1983).
Baylac, H., *Histoire Terminale: Le Monde de 1939 à nos jours* (Paris: Bordas, 1998).
Berstein, Serge and Milza, Pierre, *Histoire Terminal (Nouveau Programme)* (Paris: Hatier, 1998).
Bouillon, J., *Le Monde Contemporain. Histoire – Civilisation* (Paris: Bordas, 1979).
—— *Le Temps Présent – Histoire Terminale. Le XXe Siècle depuis 1939* (Paris: Bordas, 1983).
Collection Berstein-Milza, *Histoire, Terminale. De 1939 à nos Jours* (Paris: Hatier, 1983).
Collection G. Donel Ferré, *Histoire, Classes de Terminales, L/S/ES – Le Monde de 1939 à nos jours* (Paris: Bréal, 1998).
Collection GREHG, *Histoire: le Monde de 1939 à nos jours. Terminales ABCD* (Paris: Hachette, 1983).
Collection GREHG, *Histoire de 1945 à nos jours. Classes de Terminales* (Paris: Hachette, 1989).
Collection J. Marseille, *Histoire Terminales – Le Monde de 1939 à nos jours* (Paris: Nathan, 1998).
Collection C. Quetel, *Histoire Terminales* (Paris: Bordas, 1989).
Collection P. Wagnet, *Histoire Terminales* (Paris: Istra, 1989).
François, Denis, *Histoire de 1939 à nos jours. Classes Terminales* (Paris: Nathan, 1983).
Frank, Robert, *Histoire Terminale STT* (Paris: Belin, 1998).
—— *Le Monde Contemporain. Histoire Terminale G* (Paris: Belin, 1983).
Formulo-Bac, *Histoire, Terminales ABCD* (Paris: Gammaprim, 1990).
Humbert, Jean-Louis, *Histoire, Terminales. ABCD, Analyse de documents* (Paris: Bordas, 1989).
Lambin, Jean-Michel, *Histoire Terminales* (Paris: Hachette, 1998).
Le Pellec, J., *Histoire Terminale* (Paris: Bertrand Lacoste, 1998).
Prévot, V., *Le Monde depuis 1939. Classes terminales* (Paris: Belin, 1979).

Films

Anonymous, *France mai–juin 1968 pour l'UDR*, 1968.
Bertolucci, Bernardo, *Les innocents*, 2003.
Doillon, Jacques, Gébé, Resnais, Alain and Rouch, Jean, *L'An 01*, 1973.
Ducastel, Olivier and Martineau, Jacques, *Nés en 68*, 2008.
Garrel, Philippe, *Le Vent de la nuit*, 1999.
Goupil, Romain, *A Mort la Mort*, 1998.
—— *Mourir à trente ans*, 1982.
Guide, Lawaetz, *Mai 68: Il y a 25 ans*, 1993.
Klein, William, *Grands soirs et petits matins*, 1978.
le Brun, Claude, *Mai 68 – 5 Ans après*, 1973.
le Roux, Hervé, *Reprise*, 1997.
Malle, Louis, *Milou en mai*, 1990.
Marker, Chris, *Le fond de l'air est rouge*, 1977.
Mocky, Jean-Pierre, *Solo*, 1969.
Oury, Gérard, *La Carapate*, 1978.

Television programmes

Les Dossiers de l'écran, 68 dans le monde, Antenne 2, 2 May 1968.
Televised interview with Charles de Gaulle and Michel Droit (7 July 1968).
Apostrophes, 24 April 1977.
Histoire de Mai, Pierre-André Boutang, France 3, 1978.
Histoire de mai, André Frossard, Gérard Guégan and Raphael Boutang, France 3, 7, 14, 21 and 28 May 1978.
L'Héritage de 68, Alain Weider, Antenne 2, 19 May 1988.
Le Procès de mai, Roland Portiche and Henri Weber, TF1, 22 May 1988.
Génération, Hervé Hamon, Patrick Rotman and Daniel Edinger. A series of fifteen 30-minute documentaries that went out on TF1 over the period May–July 1988.
Que sont nos vingt and devenus?: 1968–1988, France 3, 22 July 1988.
La Preuve par trois. Mai 68 a 30 ans, et alors? France 3, 7 April, 1998.
Dany dans tous ses états, France 2, 23 April 1998.
10 semaines qui ébranlèrent la France, Patrick Rotman and Virginie Linhart, France 3, 24 April 1998.
Débat Mai 1968. D'Une Génération à l'autre, France 2, 26 April 1998.
Droit d'Inventaire : MAI 68, presented by Marie Drucker, France 3, 23 January 2008.
Ripostes, France 3, 2 March 2008.
1968: Un monde en révolte, France 3, 2 March 2008.
Comment sortir du «blabla» de Mai 68 ?, presented by Frédéric Taddeï, France 3, 10 April 2008.
Faut-il interdire d'interdire?, presented by Daniel Leconte, Arte, 15 April 2008.
Des Mots, France 2, 16 April 2008.
Les Enfants de Mai 68, Fabienne Servan Schreiber et Estelle Mauriac, France 5, 5–16 May 2008.
Mai 68, esprit es-tu là?, Karine Bonjour and Philippe Cahn, France 3 Sud, 26 April 2008.
Un si joli de mai, Bertrand Delais, France 3 Normandie, 26 April 2008.
Mai 68 en Lorraine, Champagne-Ardenne, Jean-Luc Marino, France 3 Lorraine, Champagne-Ardenne, 26 April 2008.
Mai 68 en Alsace, Hubert Schilling, France 3 Alsace, 26 April 2008.
Mon mai 68, Michel Marié, France 3 Rhône-Alpes, Auvergne, 26 April 2008.
L'autre Mai, Jacques Vilemont, France 3 Ouest, 26 April 2008.
Mai 68. . .tu disais, Gérard Miller, France 3 Paris Ile de France, Centre, 26 April 2008.
68 année zero, Ruth Zylberman, Arte, 30 April 2008.
68, Patrick Rotman, France 2, 8 April 2008.
1968, Un monde en révolte, Michèle Dominici, France 3, 22 March 2008.

Written press

Alezard, Gérard, 'La CGT et les étudiants à Paris en mai–juin 1968', *L'Humanité,* 11 July 2008.
Conan, Eric, 'Mai 68. Commémoration piège à cons!', *Marianne* 575, 26 April–2 May 2008, pp. 66–71.
de Chalendar, Hervé, 'Mai 68, Un printemps en Alsace', *L'Alsace,* Hors Série, February 2008.
Debray, Régis, 'Carte blanche; Hommage au préfet Grimaud', *Le Monde,* 9 May 2008.
Duyck, Alexandre, *Le Journal de Dimanche,* 27 October 2002.
Etchegoin, Marie-France and Courage, Sylvain, 'Dossier. Un sondage CSA–«le Nouvel Observateur». Les Français votent 68', *Le Nouvel Observateur,* 2264, 27 March–2 April, pp. 12–16.
Fourquet, Jerome, 'LHéritage de Mai 68', *L'Humanité des débats,* 22 March 2008.
Guyot, Alain, 'En 1968, il n'y avait pas que les manifs. . .', *Ouest-France* (Magazine), 22 March 2008.
Humbert-Jean, M., 'Ce qu'il reste de mai 68', *Le Monde des dossiers et documents,* 155, May 1988.

Joffrin, Laurent, 'Sommes-nous tous devenus réacs?', *Le Nouvel Observateur*, 21–7 November 2002, 12–36.

Lancelin, Aude, 'Trop de pavés pour les 40 ans: liquider le merchandising?', *Le Nouvel Observateur*, 8–14 May 2008.

Manach, Jean-Marc, 'Internet ; Et si le Web avait existé il y a quarante ans . . . en 1968', *Le Monde*, 11 May 2008.

Marchais, Georges, 'De faux révolutionnaires à démasquer', *L'Humanité*, 3 May 1968.

Schulthess, Elisabeth, 'Mai 68: Le Révélation de Bichette sur «l'affaire du Monument aux Morts»', *L'Alsace*, 20 May 2008.

Viansson-Ponté, Pierre, 'Quand la France s'ennuie,' *Le Monde*, 15 March 1968.

No author provided
Les Dernières Nouvelles d'Alsace, 17 May 1968, 23.
Les Dernières Nouvelles d'Alsace, 18 May 2008, 10.
Les Dernières Nouvelles d'Alsace, 2/3 June 1968, 21–2.
Les Dernières Nouvelles d'Alsace, 6 September 1968.
'Mai 68 et les archives secrètes de la police', *L'Express*, 19–25 March 1998.
Le Nouvel Observateur, 23–9 April 1998.
'Que reste-t-il de 68', *Courrier International*, 894–895, 20 December 2007–1 January 2008.
'Dossier spécial : Quarante après. . . Vive 68', *Libération*, 1 February 2008, 1–10.
'Cahier spécial – 1968–2008, Quel héritage politique? Quarante ans après, que reste-t-il des engagements politiques de 68? Au-delà du mythe révolutionnaire, le rapport au pouvoir a-t-il changé?', *Libération*, 23–4 February 2008.
'Mai 68. Un printemps en Alsace', Hors série, *L'Alsace*, February 2008.
'Une profusion de livres pour les 40 ans de Mai 68', *Le Monde*, 21 March 2008.
'Dans les revues, regards savants et souvenirs', *Le Monde*, 16 May 2008.
'Dossier : Mai 68 en héritage', *Le Monde des livres*, 21 March 2008, 6–7.
'Numéro spécial. Quarante ans après, le Libé des étudiants', *Libération*, 21 March 2008.
'Dossier: Les Français et 68', *Le Nouvel Observateur*, 27 March–2 April, 12–26.
'Spécial MAI 68', *Télérama*, 3037, 29 March–4 April 2008, 13–30.
'Cahier central Mai. L'héritage culturel', *Libération*, 19–20 April 2008.
Bordeaux 68, Supplément spécial, *Sud Ouest*, April 2008.
'Mai 68 dans le monde', Dossier Spéciale, *L'Histoire*, April 2008.
'Dossier spécial: Mai 68 raconté par nos lecteurs', *Le Parisien*, 4 May 2008.
'1968. Révolutions', Hors-série, *Le Monde 2*, March–April 2008.
'68, l'année qui a changé le monde', Numéro Spécial, *L'Express*, 2968, 1–7 May 2008, 82–141.
'Mai 68 non, ce n'est pas fini. . .', *L'Humanité hors série*, April 2008.
'Il y a quarante ans dans Le Monde', *Le Monde*, 3–31 May 2008.
'Dossier: 40 ans après 68. La révolution réac', *Le Monde de l'éducation*, 369, May 2008, 24–48.
Collectif, 'Mai 68 – Hors série', *Liaisons*, May 2008.
'Mai 68 L'Héritage', *Télérama hors série*, 2008.
'Internet; Une mémoire collective en ligne nourrie de récits individuels', *Le Monde*, 10 June 2008.

Internet

Loi d'orientation de l'enseignement supérieur. No. 68–978. 12 November 1968. *http://guilde. jeunes-chercheurs.org/Textes/Txtfond/L68–978.html*
Mai 68 en Bretagne – *Le télégramme http://www.letelegramme.com/ig/dossiers/mai68/mai-68-la-chronologie-30–12–2008–184906.php*
Mai 68, ce n'est toujours qu'un début, mai-juin 2008 *www.mai-68.org*
Il y a quarante ans débutait mai 68 *http://www.ouest-france.fr/dossiers/Mai-68.php*

68 Court toujours, FNAC *http://www.fnac.com/magazine/themas_transversaux/68_court_toujours/*

1968–2008: retour aux sources *http://www.mai-68.fr/welcome/index.php*

Vérane Noël, 'Mai 68 énième,' *http://bibliobs.nouvelobs.com/20071016/1070/mai-68-enieme.*

Unpublished dissertations

Amann, Remy, *Le Scandale de Strasbourg ou l'épisode situationniste de la capitale alsacienne*, [Mémoire de Maitrise], Université de Strasbourg, 1990.

Jeffroy, Annie, *Chronique des événements de mai 1968 à Brest d'après le «Télégramme» et «Ouest-France»*, [Mémoire de maîtrise], UBO, 1987.

Porhel, Vincent, *'Mai 68 au CLU de Brest'*, [Mémoire de maîtrise], UBO, (supervised by Edmond Monange), 1988.

Wendling, Yvonne, *Les feuilles de mai 68 à Strasbourg* [Mémoire de Maitrise], University of Strasbourg, 1992, p. 14.

Miscellaneous

Centre CSF-Brest, 'Notre Combat' (1968).

'Les événements de mai 68 à la faculté des lettres de Strasbourg', Documents légués aux archives par Marc Schweyer, Archives de la Ville, Strasbourg, Box 114Z, No. 5, pièce 3.

Index